D0779970

Divine Hierarchies

Contents

Acknowledgments

I am indebted to many and wish to thank them here. First, I thank Lynn Abbott-McCloud, to whom I have dedicated this book. We have been to many locations together, both physical and social. Some of our travels have been to familiar places, while others have tread territories previously uncharted in our lives. I thank Lynn for guiding me down many fortuitous paths. I also appreciate her patience and compassion when traipsing the muddy trails I have sometimes haphazardly chosen.

Second, I thank Jeff Bulington. I greatly appreciate Jeff's helpful conversations and suggestions about this project, but more generally I have benefited immeasurably from his long-standing friendship. Academia, perhaps like any elite profession, can sometimes be an alien and unwelcoming place for those of us who by some fluke crossed the barriers of social location to enter it. My discussions about such things with Jeff—a fellow interloper—have been indispensable.

In addition to Lynn and Jeff, I thank the other people who have read or listened to, commented on, or otherwise helped shape this work. The two unnamed manuscript readers offered terrific suggestions and encouragement. Katie Lofton read the entire manuscript and provided constructive and bold critique. Judi Fagan closely read and effectively commented on an early version of chapter 2. Bill Mirola, Jeremy Schott, and my editor, Elaine Maisner, were all good conversation partners about this book. Peter Williams, Liz Wilson, and Alan Miller all read and helpfully commented on another version of what is now chapter 6 several years ago. Three graduate students—Ginger Stickney, Chad Day, and Damon Neely—read excerpts of the book-in-progress and/or held valuable discussions with me about some of its subjects. Zeff Bjerken kindly invited me to give a talk on chapter 2 at the College of Charleston. That presentation, in addition to one about chapter 1 at the 2005 Society for the Scientific Study of Religion conference, proved beneficial. Leif Tornquist served as my graduate assistant in spring 2006, freeing me from much of my semester's grading duties and allowing me the time it takes to write. It should, of course, go without saying that none of these individuals are responsible for any problems with the book. But the convention seems to demand it, so here it goes: please don't blame any of these folks for whatever deficiencies you find in the following pages.

My gratitude extends beyond the small circle immediately involved with this project. I thank Mike Bulington, Neil Hoying, Matt Whittaker, Tony Woollard, Alex Cosby, Jake Smith, Paul Sullivan, and Dave Peters. Though they did not have anything directly to do with this book, I owe them all for making the small world from which I came a little bit larger and a lot friendlier. I also thank those former and current colleagues at the College of Charleston, Central Michigan University, and the University of North Carolina at Charlotte who have made the strange world of higher education more welcoming. I thank Sinead for being smarter than I ever was at her age and Joan for being more laid-back than I will ever be at her age. Finally, I thank the Sex Pistols—particularly John Lydon—and the Gang of Four for teaching me at an early age to think critically and not accept anything at face value. The ideas I garnered from their music and lyrics have influenced me as much as any academic text.

Divine Hierarchies

nessed a national trend toward increasing income inequality and a concomitant rise in poverty rates.[5] In other words, the rich were getting richer and the poor were getting poorer and more numerous. But paradoxically, while class became more marked and important in people's lives, it was largely absent from public discussion and debate. Because the influence of class conflicts with an ideology of free will, one that asserts we all have an equal opportunity for success in the United States, to bring it up is to expose oneself to charges of "class warfare." At the very least, it leaves one open to the kind of dismissive comment British social theorist Beverley Skeggs received from an acquaintance: "'I don't know why you talk about class, it's so distasteful.'"[6]

What is class? It is an obvious, yet elusive, concept. At its most basic, class is a combination of variables: income (how much money one makes), occupation (what job one holds), education (how much one has), and wealth (how much one has accumulated or inherited). But class is much more than this. Class is certainly about money and what we consume. But it is also about how we move our bodies, how we use them, and what we put on and into them. Class concerns boundaries, those distinctions we make between ourselves and others. Because of this, class entails relationships, identities, meaning, and power. It foments comfort and discomfort. It can be explicit or hidden, conscious or unconscious. It reveals itself in our most ingrained habits of mind and body. And yet exactly how it concerns and influences these things is not always obvious or consistent. Class may always matter, but sometimes it matters less than other things.

The focus of this book is on what, if anything, class has to do with religion. Class factors into how we vote, what kinds of breads we eat, and even how we worship and live our religion.[7] It partly determines whether we are comfortable with casual or formal dress in church, whether we scowl at plastic flowers placed on the altar next to the Buddha statue, and whether or not we think the faithful will be raptured away to heaven while the sinful are left behind.[8] Some anthropologists studying religion in the North Carolina mountains once suggested that "it is easy to imagine that Baptist tears are different from Pentecostal tears."[9] One may also wonder if Baptists of different classes shed distinctive tears, or if middle-class Pentecostals speak in tongues differently than their lower-class brethren.

Arguments

In this book I examine class in the academic study of religion and in American religious thought and practice. I offer multiple theses. First, and most generally, I argue that despite some contemporary claims to the contrary, class matters in the study of religion, though not in the ways past scholars have asserted. In supporting this point, *Divine Hierarchies* moves in three directions. The initial route, traveled in chapter 1, critiques past scholarship and proposes a new, three-part conception of class for use in the study of religion. The first two components affirm that class has played and still plays an important role in creating and sustaining social, cultural, and religious distinctions. First, class has served as an externally ascribed marker placed upon particular groups by outsiders engaged in boundary demarcation. Second, class has historically been used as an aspect of individual and group identity. With the third component, I move away from issues of representation and offer an account of how class plays a role in determining religious affiliations. Combining and extrapolating theories and concepts from several scholars, I argue that social class relates to religious affiliation in that certain material circumstances enable or constrain individuals and groups in their religious explorations.

The second trajectory, traversed in part 1, entails a selective cultural history of the study of religion, examining how class surfaced in twentieth-century academic explanations of religious affiliation. In this section I argue two things. First, scholarship using class and social location to explain religion changed over time. Eugenics-inflected early twentieth-century studies "biologized" religious practices and beliefs, claiming that the connections between certain classes, races, and religions were the product of genes and evolution. In other words, one was rich, poor, Episcopalian, or Pentecostal because of inherent genetic tendencies and position on the evolutionary ladder. Between the world wars, social science scholarship transitioned away from the "inherent tendencies" understanding of religious affiliation and toward "social sources" explanations. In such models one's historical, social, and material circumstances explicated that person's religious affiliations and activities. This explanatory shift was complete by the 1950s, and deprivation theories dominated social scientific explanations of particular religions through the 1970s.

My second argument in part 1 concerns what remained the same throughout the scholarship under study. I argue that theories using social class to explain beliefs and behaviors consistently replicated existing American class, racial, religious, regional, and gender hierarchies. Religion has often served as a tool of social and cultural distinction. I suggest that the theories set forth to explain religious affiliation often did as well. Whether the explanation they proposed was biological or social, scholars consistently and often explicitly deemed the religions of the "usual suspects"—the poor, minorities, and indigenous peoples—as somehow inferior. Overall, part 1 of this work extends beyond concern with class to argue that theories of religious affiliation and social differentiation—whether proposed by scholars, religious essayists, fiction writers, or journalists—comprise a fruitful field for exploring broader cultural assumptions about class, gender, race, nationalism, and human nature.[10]

Part 2—and the book's third pathway—moves away from the critical analysis of previous scholarship and provides case studies of how religion and class interact. Stressing the need for a truly interdisciplinary study of American religion, the last two chapters offer historical and ethnographic approaches. Whether in the primary text archives or the pews of field research, the second part suggests that class continues to be an important—if neglected—variable in the study of American religion. Together, parts 1 and 2 serve to apply the three-part class conception proposed in chapter 1.

Methods and Caveats

This work offers an interdisciplinary approach that utilizes history, social theory, and ethnography. Part 1 of the work contributes to the emergent field of the cultural history of the study of religion. This growing area of research, represented in several American Academy of Religion units, turns the analytical and historical lens on scholars and their studies of religion. It not only asks what previous scholarship examined and argued but how historical, social, and cultural influences shaped it. The chapters in part 2 contribute to the interdisciplinary study of American religion. Recent decades have witnessed the retreat of the older "church history" model of the discipline that focused on denominational narratives. In its place innovative topics, themes, and methodological approaches have appeared. Today archival research, fieldwork studies, critical theory, and demographic analysis and polling all provide unique methodological sites for the study of American religion.[11] In an era in which monographs have become more focused and field specializations increasingly narrow, this is an intentionally broad and interdisciplinary work of religious studies that strives to put some class back into the study of religion.

I have identified my main arguments and methods. I must also offer a general caveat. My goal in this work is to be broad and suggestive. In turn, this means that the book is not narrowly focused or methodologically uniform. Nor will I claim my arguments to be definitive. Monographic studies attentive to the minutiae of a particular time, place, or group are essential to the study of American religion, but so are comparative and thematic analyses that carefully and reflexively cross temporal, denominational, and spatial boundaries. This book broaches a large and neglected topic (class and religion) from several locations. Because I am convinced that the study of religion and class must be interdisciplinary, my methods are multiple. In religious studies, being "interdisciplinary" often means working with one approach (i.e., history or sociology) while being informed by scholarship from other fields. Here I attempt to put interdisciplinarity into actual practice by including chapters that variously utilize historical, ethnographic, and social theoretical approaches.

Organization

The work consists of six chapters, divided into the three pathways described above and flanked by this introduction and a conclusion. The first chapter, "Class Matters: Resurrecting and Redescribing a Neglected Variable," provides theoretical orientation and justification for the volume. In it I examine studies that argue for and against the salience of class. The most recent scholarship suggests its continuing importance in American religion. At the same time, I agree with critics who note that the past conceptions of class used to study religion were at best simplistic, always insufficient, and often inaccurate. Given this, I propose a tripartite conception of class as an ascribed status, a subcultural identity, and availability and constraint. I provide both religious and nonreligious examples of these three conceptions and discuss both the promises and the problems entailed in returning class to the study of religion.

Part 1, "From Inherent Tendencies to Social Sources in Religion Scholarship," is a selective cultural history of the study of religion. The American religious historian Robert Orsi argues that religious studies "was literally constructed by means of the exclusion—in fact and in theory—of these other ways of living between heaven and earth, which were relegated to the world of sects, cults, fundamentalisms, popular piety, ritualism, magic, primitive religion, millennialism, anything but 'religion.'"[12] The scholars examined in the first section were part of the exclusionary process Orsi describes. One could borrow from the title of Stephen Jay Gould's book on pseudoscientific classifications of humans to declare the subject of part 1 "the mismeasure of religion."[13] The scholarly desire for understanding and order sometimes spurred the writers under study to make tenuous associations between class, religion, and personal dispositions. In trying to understand the relation between certain religions and particular classes of people, scholars made connections that were based on the assumptions they carried with them, attitudes inculcated through the cultural and social locations from whence they came. In doing this, they proposed theories of religious affiliation that served as tools of social, cultural, and religious distinction.

In chapter 2, "The Depraved, the Unevolved, and the Degenerate: Explaining Religious Affiliations in the Age of Eugenics," I examine some American religion scholarship from the first decades of the twentieth century. I argue two things. First, some well-known psychology of religion and rural church sociology works shared themes and idioms with eugenics writings. Second, these writings on religion and eugenics mirrored each other in function: both distinguished, classified, and ordered religious practices, beliefs, and communities in ways that offered a scientific apologetics for existing American class, racial, regional, and religious hierarchies.

I title chapter 3 "The Peyote of the Masses: Cultural Crises and Acculturation between the World Wars." In it I analyze transitional scholarship from the 1920s to the early 1940s and trace the explanatory move from inherent tendencies to social sources. In works ranging from H. Richard Niebuhr's *Social Sources of Denominationalism* to E. T. Krueger's study of "Negro Religious Expression," it was no longer nature but rather the social and economic environment that was seen as the factor driving people toward certain religious beliefs, practices, and communities. In emergent cultural crisis and deprivation theories, humans were no longer seen as slaves to their genetic inheritances. Individual beliefs, values, characteristics, and fates were no longer considered fixed, natural, and inevitable. Like the eugenics-inflected explanations, the theories under examination reflected broader cultural anxieties about order, stability, and national unity. Such concerns particularly emerged in the period's scholarship that pondered which Native new religions could promote the successful acculturation of colonized indigenous Americans.

Chapter 4, "Visions of the Disinherited: The Origins of Religion, Deprivation, and the Usual Suspects after World War II," examines a selection of crisis, revitalization, cargo cult, deprivation, and related studies. In general, all of these models of affiliation suggested that certain religions appealed to those who were disinherited, deprived, and dislocated. Simply put, deprivation theories satisfactorily explained a wide variety of religious groups for many of the period's scholars, popular writers, and journalists. One movement that garnered particular attention during this period—and throughout the twentieth century—was Pentecostalism. Such sustained interest demands at least a brief case study, which this chapter provides. I conclude by examining some critiques of deprivation theories, specifically the work of Virginia Hine, Luther Gerlach, and Joel Martin.

Part 2 of the book, "Putting Some Class in American Religion," provides two case studies—one historical and one ethnographic—that address class in American religion. In chapter 5, "Some Theologies of Class in American Religious History," I name and describe four recurring theologies of class. The first, which I call "divine hierarchies," was closely tied to Calvinist predestinarianism and suggested that socioeconomic differences were divinely ordained.

The second, "economic Arminianism," emerged amidst nineteenth-century Evangelicalism, Republicanism, and the development of industrial class relations. Asserting that all humans have the free will to attain both salvation and wealth, it is the most dominant theology of class today. The third recurring theology, "social harmony," was represented in many Protestant Social Gospel writings as well as a Roman Catholic statement on labor and capital, Pope Leo XIII's *Rerum Novarum*. The fourth theology, "the class-conscious Christ," was espoused by some Gilded Age supporters of the working class and envisioned Jesus as the champion of laborers and the enemy of capitalism. I conclude the chapter by considering the ways in which theologies of class are more than ideas but also disciplinary implements literally inscribed onto human bodies. I do this by comparing Peter Cartwright's and Charles Grandison Finney's interpretations of antebellum ecstatic religious behaviors. In brief, I suggest that their differing conclusions on what constituted "authentic" and "inauthentic" physical manifestations during the Second Great Awakening revivals may be partly attributed to the period's emerging class differences.

In chapter 6, "In the Field: Deprivation, Class, and the Usual Suspects at Two Holiness Pentecostal Assemblies," I report the results of a comparative ethnographic study of two Pentecostal churches. While part 1 and chapter 5 provide numerous examples of class as both ascribed and subcultural identities, this chapter examines it as the enabling and constraining influences on lived religious practice. I critique deprivation explanations of assembly differences and argue that variations in worship styles relate to a variety of factors, including class. This chapter provides descriptions of the two Holiness Pentecostal assemblies, compares them, proposes explanations for their differences, and speculates on the possible existence of diverging class cultures within them.

In the conclusion I discuss the implications of resurrecting the variable of class in religious studies. Influenced by Pierre Bourdieu's notion of "habitus"—but wishing to depart from the ambiguity and intellectual baggage surrounding this concept—I propose and discuss a new term, "socially habituated subjectivities," for use in examining social locations such as class, race, gender, and place and their influence on religious preferences, practices, and affiliations.

tive, historically inaccurate and politically suspect. As part 1 of this book will demonstrate, studies utilizing class tersely connected certain religious groups with everything from biological inferiority to social and economic deprivations. Throughout the twentieth century, religions attracting minorities and the poor garnered special attention from eugenicists, deprivation theorists, and cultural crisis proponents. The idea that the beliefs and practices of sects and new religions attracted society's most disadvantaged was so sweeping that scholars often held this view even when demographics suggested otherwise. As noted in the fourth chapter, Horton Davies's *Challenge of the Sects* (1961) suggested that sects should be conceived of and explained as "churches of the disinherited."[4] But Davies included chapters on Christian Scientists and Theosophists, both of which had mostly middle- and upper-middle-class Cold War memberships.[5]

A second reason that class is often absent in contemporary religious studies is because it lacks a clear, single definition. Class connotes a range of associations, from Marxist analysis to quantitative examinations of education, income, occupation, and wealth. Anyone who samples the growing volume of literature debating the importance or irrelevance of class quickly finds that scholars don't disagree about the data so much as they hold differing conceptions of what class is.[6] In the study of American religion, as in other fields, class has frequently and problematically been tied to the notion of "class consciousness," which assumes that people actively think of and mobilize themselves as members of a group unified by material conditions and attitudes. This concept, grounded as it is in politically oriented Marxist analysis, has contributed to moralistic discussions of the emancipatory and/or oppressive aspects of religion. As discussed in part 1, scholars studying Native new religions, minority spirituality, and the religions of the poor and dispossessed continually returned to questions of whether religion acted as a consciousness-veiling opium or a revolutionary tool of liberation. Their problematic answers often revealed more about their own assumptions, social locations, and historical contexts than it did about the religions under examination. In making such arguments, scholars engaged in a process of classification and distinction that make them subjects for our analysis rather than secondary sources for our research. That's because class is—and always has been—more than a status grounded in material conditions but also an identity rhetorically and symbolically made and unmade through representation. Given the current confusion over what it is and the problematic scholarship that has come before, it is not surprising that class is a neglected variable in the study of religion. But this does not mean that it should be.

Some recent scholarship on religion has—wrongly, I suggest—argued for the relative unimportance of social class. The religious economy and market-place model elaborated by Rodney Stark and coauthor Roger Finke provides a good example.[7] They propose that in a place such as the United States, religion may best be viewed as a good supplied by a variety of sources. In this religious economy, "when faced with choices, humans try to select the most rational or reasonable option."[8] The religious marketplace is governed by subjective, yet rational, choices; and Stark and Finke argue that the connection between religion and social class in such a situation proves weak and inconsistent.[9] "It is past time," they argue, "that we accepted the unanimous results of more than fifty years of quantitative research that show that although class does somewhat influence religious behavior, the effects are very modest, and most religious organizations are remarkably heterogeneous in terms of social status."[10]

Stark and Finke are intentionally iconoclastic, and at times their writings veer away from academic analysis toward ahistorical, vitriolic name-calling directed at liberal Protestants, atheists, and others they view as "losers" in the religious marketplace.[11] At the same time, their criticisms of past sociology of religion scholarship—while seldom discussed in depth—are often accurate and not unlike the arguments set forth in part 1 of this book. Stark and Finke correctly call deprivation theorists to task for their blanket generalizations about the religions of the dispossessed, and they rightly fault scholars for their explicit disdain of high-demand, emotional religions.[12] Yet their squabble against the importance of social class seems overblown and fraught with contradictions. First, their language on the importance of class fluctuates. While they argue that the effects of class on religion are modest, they simultaneously call it a "basis" for religious market "niches," which they define as "market segments of potential adherents sharing particular religious preferences (needs, tastes, and expectations)."[13] While they do suggest that it isn't the only basis, they dub it one nonetheless. Curiously, as an example to prove their point, they correctly note that certain new religions "overrecruit the privileged."[14] Of course, this suggests that social class *does* play a role. Additionally, while critiquing what they refer to as his "crude Marxism," Stark and Finke accept Niebuhr's model of sect-to-church transformation, which relies heavily on sects attracting the dispossessed and churches appealing to the bourgeois.[15]

Second, they argue that social class is less important than "preferences" in accounting for religious behaviors. All people within a culture, they argue, do not act in the exact same way or like the same things because "their choices are guided by their preferences and tastes."[16] Favorably citing the adage "there is no accounting for taste," Stark and Finke suggest that "a great deal of varia-

cation, and wealth) play a large role in one's life trajectory. At the same time, people tend not to consciously identify themselves as members of a distinctive social class, nor do they perceive "how classes are instantiated in people's life histories."[32] Related to discarding class consciousness as a necessary characteristic of class, I suggest severing the naturalized connection between class and collective group action. Finding little empirical evidence in contemporary Britain for strong class consciousness and activism, Savage argues that "class cultures can be usefully viewed as models of differentiation, rather than types of collectivity."[33] In other words, social class in the contemporary United States and Britain may actually more frequently act as a tool of distinction than as a fraternal identity.

Second, class is not just a status grounded in material conditions. As first mentioned above, it is also an identity rhetorically and symbolically made and unmade through representation and discourse. I agree with the suggestion of social theorist Beverley Skeggs that "understanding representation is central to any analysis of class."[34] Representations shape our perceptions of the world, ourselves, and others. As the media scholar Stuart Hall notes, "in part, we give things meaning by how we represent them."[35] So, in addition to being a social location based in material circumstances, class is also about the narratives, motifs, characteristics, and—in Skeggs's words—"amalgam of features of a culture that are read onto bodies as personal dispositions—which themselves have been generated through systems of inscription in the first place."[36] As a discourse, class can be ascribed to others or assigned to oneself as a tool of self-definition. But the playing field is never level. The ability to represent self and others is entwined with social, cultural, economic, and political capital. Simply put, those with more power and access to various mass mediums have the advantage in what Pierre Bourdieu calls the "specifically symbolic struggle to impose the definition of the social world most in conformity with their interests."[37]

Third, class should not be seen as the sole, deterministic basis of everything. Class always matters, but sometimes it matters less than other things. It certainly plays a role in determining religious and other cultural preferences. At the same time, the extent of its role cannot be easily measured because class is a variable that is difficult to separate from related aspects of social location like race, gender, place, age, and access to various mass mediums. Scholars who study class and defend its importance are nearly unanimous on this point. The anthropologist Sherry Ortner, for example, argues that "people are never wholly constructed by their class position, or indeed by any other single aspect of their identity."[38] Savage similarly notes that "people's own class location shapes only some of their views, and even then, in highly mediated and complex ways."[39] The sociologists John Goldthorpe and Gordon Marshall also concur, arguing that "the occupancy of class position is seen as creating only potential interests, such as may also arise from various other structural locations."[40] In the United States, race has historically been a variable that trumped class in many cultural fields, including religion.[41] Such observations do not negate the importance of class, but they do suggest that it is not *the* variable, but one factor among others that must be considered.

Finally, the study of class is not solely the study of the poor, the working class, the dispossessed, and the disinherited. Looking at the history of scholarship on religion and socioeconomic position, one finds that the focus was almost exclusively on the sects, new religions, and fundamentalisms attracting society's most downtrodden. As seen in the earlier discussion of Stark and Finke, this association has been so ingrained and naturalized that even its most vocal critics accept that the study of class and religion is the study of poor and deprived groups. The reasons for such a focus—as discussed in part 1 of this book—historically involved elite concerns with monitoring the marginalized and potentially dangerous masses. They also correlated with the social locations of religion scholars who problematized other people's religions while viewing their own as the status quo. We should not repeat the often unwitting political and symbolic violence enacted in past scholarship by keeping the scope narrowly focused on the disinherited. Scholars debate the number of classes in the United States and set up classificatory categories to map them. Within all of these "classes on paper," as Bourdieu calls them, exist individuals who engage in religious activities, hold certain beliefs, and participate in religious communities.[42] Any contemporary consideration of class and religion must consider the full range of social locations and material conditions in which religious people find themselves.

Detaching class from these associations will hopefully begin a process of resurrecting it for use in the study of religion. At the same time, it still connotes a wide range of things and garners a variety of definitions. Here, I propose a three-part conception of class for use in the study of religion broadly and the study of American religion specifically. The first two parts affirm that class has played an important role in creating and sustaining social, cultural, and religious distinctions. First, class has been an externally ascribed marker placed upon particular groups by outsiders engaged in boundary making. Second, class has been used by individuals and groups as a subcultural identity marker, a tool in a conscious, ongoing process of identity construction. In a third way of conceiving class, I argue that it plays a role in partly determining religious preferences by imposing both availability and constraint. In other words, the material conditions produced by social class and status differentiation make individuals and groups more or less available and constrained when exploring certain religious options.

Class as Distinction 1: Externally Ascribed Status

Class plays an important role in creating and sustaining distinctions. Whether in the religion scholarship examined in part 1 of this work or in popular media, class has been an externally ascribed marker placed upon particular groups by outsiders engaged in social, cultural, and religious boundary demarcation. Recall the basic sociological principle that individuals and groups frequently define themselves by declaring what they are not.[43] Different classes—especially the poor—have historically acted for some as negative reference groups. They serve, in Christian Smith's words, as "categories of people who are unlike them, who actively serve in their minds as models for what they do not believe, what they do not want to become, and how they do not want to act."[44] Through processes of "articulation," certain cultural objects and characteristics—as well as social and psychological dispositions—have been fixed to certain class positions. Skeggs notes that "excess"—in fashion, sexuality, body types, emotions, and popular culture tastes—has historically been linked to the poor and working classes, while the middle class has been identified with restraint and denial.[45]

A good example of such attributions can be found in Paul Fussell's *Class: A Guide through the American Status System*. A mixture of satire and pop sociology, Fussell's work features portraits (literary and penciled) of different social classes based on such things as body types, consumption patterns, and manners. On one page, a drawing features upper-middle-class and "prole" (Fussell's term for working-class) head profiles. The upper-middle-class depiction portrays a small chin, small ears, and a geometrically structured nose. The prole silhouette features a large bent nose, big ears, and a general "excessiveness" of all features.[46] Other pages follow suit with descriptions and drawings that differentiate the dress, furnishings, and drinking glasses of different classes.[47] My informal discussions with students to whom I have assigned Fussell suggest that—regardless of their own self-identified class background—they find the book simultaneously offensive and "true" to their perceptions. Bourdieu and others have long suggested that tastes, ideas, practices, and various habits of mind and body "function as markers of 'class.'"[48] While these connections are often demonstrated statistically (the propensity, for example, for more low-income Americans to be overweight than those with higher incomes), they are also made real, natural, and fixed by discourses such as the one Fussell taps into. Such portrayals do more than just report on and re-

flect some reality that exists; they also contribute to the creation and maintenance of that reality. Marking the boundaries of socioeconomic differences,
discourses on class ascribe and constrict the possible associations and characterizations attributed to particular groups and individuals who are identified
as belonging to a specific class. The image of the poor and/or working-class
individual as fat, loud, and emotional may seem more plausible than imagining the richest Americans the same way. Likewise, envisioning an upper-class
man enjoying a weekend of NASCAR, honky-tonk, and beer is as difficult for
some as picturing a working-class man dining on French cuisine after a day of
polo. The stereotypes have been fixed, the associations concretized.

The external ascription of class onto religion in the United States has followed similar trajectories as Skeggs described above about general working-
class characterizations. Scholars, journalists, and others have identified particular religions with particular classes of people. Predictably, the religions of
the poor and working classes consistently appear emotionally excessive, anti-
intellectual, physically ecstatic, loud, and exotic. Since part 1 of this book focuses on scholars, here some examples from twentieth-century journalism
will illustrate the point.

The historian George Marsden, the anthropologist Susan Harding, and
others have noted that the contemporary image of Protestant Fundamentalism was largely a product of 1920s journalists such as H. L. Mencken.[49]
Despite Fundamentalism's early elite associations with Princeton Theological Seminary and scholars such as J. Gresham Machen, the image of Fundamentalism promoted by journalists during and after the 1925 Scopes evolution trial in Dayton, Tennessee, suggested an ignorant, backwoods peasantry
troubled by complexity. The religiously skeptical and iconoclastic Baltimore
journalist H. L. Mencken argued that "homo boobiens is a fundamentalist for
the precise reason that he is uneducable."[50] Fundamentalism, Mencken asserted, was popular "among the inferior orders of men."[51] "The cosmogonies
that educated men toy with are all inordinately complex," he wrote, "to comprehend their veriest outlines requires an immense stock of knowledge, and a
habit of thought."[52] "It would be as vain to try to teach them to peasants or to
the city proletariat," Mencken suggested, "as it would be to try to teach them
to streptococci."[53]

Such associations were not relegated to the era of the Scopes trial. References to the connections between poor, ignorant, mostly rural folk and Fundamentalists, Pentecostals, and other theologically conservative movements
continued to appear in mid-to-late twentieth-century print journalism. In
Making the American Religious Fringe, I analyzed newsmagazine stories from
the 1950s through the 1980s that connected the working class to religious

emotionalism, exoticism, and anti-intellectualism. In a 1955 *Life* magazine article, for example, *Christian Century* editor Paul Hutchinson suggested that, among people he dubbed "low-brows," "perennial interest is at present showing in so-called ecstatic sects, which specialize in faith-healing, speaking in unknown tongues, spiritualistic séances, or even practices as outlandish as snake-handling."[54] Thirty-two years later, I found that journalists covering televangelist scandals concerning sex and money depicted religious viewers in ways that closely resembled Mencken's and Hutchinson's portrayals. *Newsweek* referred to televangelism viewers as a "species" that was rural, poor, and alienated.[55] While studies by Bobby Alexander and others partially confirm such demographic claims, I found that magazines like *Newsweek* often relied more on class stereotypes than statistics.[56] In general, journalists ranging historically from Mencken in the 1920s to Hutchinson in the 1950s and the writers and editors of *Newsweek* in the 1980s all used the media's power to externally ascribe certain characteristics to theologically conservative forms of Protestantism. In doing this, they welded together lasting associations that continue to constrain our images of such religious groups.

Class as Distinction 2: Subcultural Identity

But class is not just a characterization and status ascribed onto passive, powerless agents by outsiders who have the resources to control representation. Class has also historically been used as a tool of self-definition, an aspect of an individual's or group's subcultural identity. By "subculture" here I first mean a basic definition, found in the *Oxford English Dictionary*, of a group "sharing specific beliefs, interests, or values which may be at variance with those of the general culture of which it forms a part."[57] The term "subculture," Christian Smith notes, "suggests a peculiar group identity, socially constructed by the making of intergroup distinctions through a process of social action."[58] But to this definition and Smith's elaboration I would add that subcultural identification may be highly subjective, individualized, fluid, multiple, and contested. One's proclaimed association with a particular group may entail solidarity and camaraderie with others, but it may also be highly private and individually focused. It is also not necessarily something permanent—one may move in and out of subcultural identifications. In addition, subcultural identity may be multiple. For example, the cultural studies scholar Dick Hebdige has described how white British punks in the 1970s simultaneously referenced their working-class roots while identifying with the black West Indian and Reggae cultures around which many of them grew up.[59] Subcultural identity may also be contested. The debate over who is and who is not a part of any subculture—who was "authentic" and who was a "poseur" in the 1980s American punk or gothic music scenes, for example—reveals the classificatory boundaries that members of the group strive to build and sustain. Whether contested or agreed upon, individualized or group sanctioned, a subcultural identity implies an act of distinction.

Subcultural identification with a particular class may entail expressing an explicit class consciousness. In his autobiography, John Lydon, the singer of the punk band the Sex Pistols and the postpunk Public Image Ltd., continuously references his working-class Irish background. Writing as a successful (and presumably well-off) musician—far removed from the London tenements in which he grew up—Lydon still declares, "I consider myself working class," and laces his book with class-conscious commentary.[60] But identification with a particular class can also be more conflicted, especially when one has crossed class boundaries. For example, the cultural studies scholar bell hooks writes of her experience as a rural, black, and working-class girl coming to class consciousness at an elite private college for women. As a child, she was "still a girl who was unaware of class," yet one who had been raised in a church tradition "that taught us to only identify with the poor."[61] Her first year in college exposed stark class differences between herself and other classmates. "There were not many of us from working class backgrounds," she writes, "we knew who we were."[62] "Slowly," she notes, "I began to understand fully that there was no place in academe for folks from working class backgrounds who did not wish to leave the past behind."[63] While her perception of social differentiation in college drove her to more strongly identify with her working-class background, her academic credentials would statistically move hooks out of her earlier class position and lead to unease. She writes:

> When I finished my doctorate I felt too much uncertainty about who I had become. Uncertain about whether I had managed to make it through without giving up the best of myself, the best of the values I had been raised to believe in—hard work, honesty, and respect for everyone no matter their class—I finished my education with my allegiance to the working class intact. Even so, I had planted my feet on the path leading in the direction of class privilege. There would always be confrontations around the issue of class. I would always have to reexamine where I stand.[64]

Class has been a subcultural identity also used by religious groups and individuals to declare "where they stand." In chapter 5, I examine how late nineteenth-century workers and labor activists used their class positions to claim religious and moral superiority. In that period, Rockefellers and Carne-

Individuals must also negotiate the class-based images placed upon their religious tradition—images that are sometimes so naturalized that believers have little power to contest them. In her study of Evangelicals and mass media, Heather Hendershot notes that the movement continues to be pictured as "low-class." In trying to change this image of being—in *Newsweek*'s phrase, "more K-Mart than Cartier"[75]—Hendershot quotes the Evangelical leader Cal Thomas urging a group of Moral Majority activists in the 1980s to change their clothing styles to dispel stereotypes. His comment revealed reflexive awareness of the connections between consumption patterns, fashion style, and class stereotypes. "'I don't care how much you may love those polyester pantsuits,'" he stated, "'don't wear them.'"[76]

An alternative response from the one promoted by Thomas—which accepts the externally ascribed representations and urges individuals to change according to standards external to the subculture—is to embrace the imposed depictions but reverse their value meanings. Pentecostals and charismatics, long accused of anti-intellectualism and zealous emotionality, tapped into a historical stream of theological apologetics that criticized "religion of the head" and suggested that the most authentic relationship with God was physically experienced through speaking in tongues, dancing in the spirit, and other manifestations of the Baptism of the Holy Ghost. Likewise, as I have elsewhere argued, Nation of Islam theology and rhetoric inverted commonplace American assumptions. Instead of love, Christianity stood for hate and enslavement. Black—not white—was pure and Godly.[77] I call this kind of value reversal "narrative detournement." Popular culture journalist Greil Marcus, a student of the French Situationists, defines "detournement" as "the theft of aesthetic artifacts from their contexts and their diversion into contexts of one's own device."[78] Whether embracing stereotypes of their subculture and distancing themselves from it, or inverting the values of such stereotypes to place their subculture in a religious, moral, or other superior position, individuals and groups must sometimes work with classifications and distinctions of themselves that they do not fully control. To paraphrase Susan Harding's comment about Fundamentalists, individuals and groups create themselves through cultural practices, but the extent of agency is not equal for everyone.[79]

Class as Availability and Constraint

The two conceptions of class discussed above see it as an implement of distinction and involve images and stereotypes that are ascribed to others or embraced as tools of self-identity. But historically, the attention religious studies has given to class has not been about representation. It has been about the possible connections between material conditions relating to income, occupation, education, and wealth and certain religious practices, theologies, and styles. As discussed later in part 1, scholars have long suggested that particular social situations—especially disadvantaged ones—lead people to seek out religions that offer solace for their deprivations. Such arguments proffered that the poor desired theologies that asserted the moral superiority of poverty and rituals that gave them increased—if merely symbolic—status. So the question that remains to be answered is: does one's class lead individuals to be attracted to certain religions? My answer is yes, but with qualification. In a third way of conceiving class, I suggest that it plays a role in religious preferences by imposing availability and constraint. In other words, social class relates to religion in that certain material circumstances make individuals and groups more or less available to explore particular religious options. In proposing this, I combine themes and concepts from the works of Richard Machalek and David Snow, Bonnie Erickson, and Ann Swidler.

Examining conversion to new religious movements, the sociologists Richard Machalek and David Snow have proposed the concept of "structural availability." "The idea of structural availability," they write, "means that either possessing certain social characteristics (e.g., power, wealth, prestige) or not being constrained by role obligations (e.g., duties and responsibilities accompanying occupational, family, civic statuses) increases one's availability for potential affiliation with and conversion to a new religious movement."[80] They argue, for example, that the high percentage of college-age students in new religions of the 1970s and 1980s (the Unification Church and Hare Krishnas would be two examples) can be explained by their relative freedom from role obligations. In other words, they were more available than others to explore communal religions because they were "young, single, and free from occupational and family obligations."[81] Machalek and Snow are careful to suggest that structural availability does not "ordain conversion" but instead is "useful for specifying the social characteristics of populations in which rates of conversion are likely to be higher."[82] They are also assiduous in suggesting—as do other scholars—that one's social networks play an important role in conversion.[83]

Social networks—and the accompanying cultural knowledges and styles that stem from them—are Bonnie Erickson's research focus. She suggests that personal networks are even more important than class as sources of cultural resources. Erickson argues against Pierre Bourdieu's thesis that cultural and class inequality is symbolically promoted and sustained by hierarchies of cultural taste. She writes that "cultural inequality is not so much a hierarchy of tastes (from soap opera to classical opera), as it is a hierarchy of knowledge (from those who know little about soap opera or opera to those who can take part in conversation about both)."[84] "Thus," she suggests, "the most widely useful form of cultural resource is cultural variety, plus the (equally cultural) understanding of the rules of relevance."[85] In other words, it is not the connoisseurs of elite culture who hold an advantage in the social field—as Bourdieu suggests—but instead those "cultural omnivores" who are comfortable and adept in a diverse variety of idioms, styles, and subjects. For Erickson, "the strongest source of cultural variety is social network variety."[86] The more contact with people from diverse social locations, the broader one's cultural competencies. In turn, the broader one's cultural competencies, the more likely an individual is to be able to sustain diverse social networks. This leads her to argue that "network variety is more important than class as a source of cultural variety."[87]

Erickson's assertion that the effect of class is weak and secondary to network variety is problematic in that it ignores the certainty that personal networks and the cultural knowledges they offer are encouraged or inhibited by social class. In other words, the material conditions of socioeconomic position can increase or decrease one's network diversity and accompanying cultural knowledge. Consider one simple example: those families with disposable income and wealth have much greater opportunity to vacation and send their children to college than those with no wealth and no disposable income. Travel and the college experience make more cultural knowledge and social networks available. Erickson acknowledges such when she notes that "cultural variety is related to class: higher-class people know as much or more than others do about all the genres examined here."[88] While Erickson attempts to explain this away by positing that "much of what seems to be individual class effects may be network effects in disguise, since class level and network variety are correlated," her argument connecting higher class with "larger, richer networks" contradicts this.[89] In addition—and despite her assertions otherwise—Erickson's own statistics suggest that early family life and upbringing are very influential, accounting for anywhere from 41 percent to as much as 80 percent of respondents' adult cultural knowledge.[90] While class could not be said to "predispose" the amount of social network variety and cultural knowledge one has, it certainly encourages or constrains such things.

Erickson's focus on cultural "knowledge" relates to the sociologist Ann Swidler's work on cultural "repertoires." Swidler argues that "culture" should not be conceived as a unified and coherent system but is better thought of as either a toolkit or repertoire of symbols, styles, habits, and strategies of action more or less available to individuals. For Swidler, "one advantage of thinking of culture as a repertoire is that it emphasizes the ways culture is like a set of skills, one which one can learn more or less thoroughly, enact with more or less grace and conviction."[91] While not directly addressed by Swidler, one can read into her work the likelihood that individuals in the same culture, because of differing social locations, will have variant cultural repertoires. For example, Swidler favorably cites Basil Bernstein's research on the language differences between middle-class and working-class schoolchildren. Bernstein found that working-class children tended to use a restricted language of concrete terms that assumed "a small, known world of others who share the same references and assumptions."[92] The middle-class youth he studied spoke in more elaborated codes that allowed them, in Swidler's terms, "to communicate in a public sphere with diverse others who do not necessarily share their particular experiences and points of reference."[93] Annette Lareau's 2003 ethnography of parenting styles and educational attitudes concurs by showing how class-specific parenting styles inculcated senses of either entitlement or constraint into the fourth-graders she studied.[94] Though not directly addressed by Swidler, social locations such as class, gender, place, and race—it would seem—make certain "tools" in one's cultural toolkit more or less available to use—if not partly determining what implements the box contains.

"The cultural repertoire a person has available," Swidler argues, "constrains the strategies she or he can pursue, so that people tend to construct strategies of action around things they are good at."[95] Because of this, Swidler posits that changing one's repertoire by "adding a cultural style, mood, or justification of action" may be quite difficult.[96] But she also suggests that when societies become unstable and when individual lives become unsettled, "culture becomes more visible" and people may be forced to actively develop and try new strategies of action.[97] On the individual level, she proposes that "major life transformations—the shift from adolescence to adulthood or the readjustment after a divorce—inspire some cultural rethinking, although people also continue to rely on their existing repertoire of personal and social capacity."[98] Similarly, on the societal level and during periods of cultural transformation, "ideologies—explicit, articulated, highly organized meaning systems (both political and religious)—establish new languages and styles for new strategies of action."[99]

Revising, combining, and extrapolating from the contributions of these scholars, one can argue that class relates to religion in terms of availability and constraint. By this I mean that the material circumstances of social class make one more or less available to affiliate with certain religious groups and try out particular religious ideas and practices. It does this in at least two ways. First, class works to increase or decrease one's social network diversity, which in turn helps determine the size and contents of one's cultural repertoire. Studies show that religious affiliation is closely tied to social networks.[100] One is most likely to affiliate with a religious movement to which friends and family belong. Simply put, a large and diverse social network is likely to provide potential contact with a more diverse collection of religious movements, styles, and beliefs than a restricted, narrow network. In this respect, a larger cultural repertoire garnered from diverse social networks may also encourage a larger religious repertoire.

In the present period, one could test the influence of class on religion by looking for differences between the percentages of "religious omnivores" in different classes. In using the term "religious omnivore," I most closely reference the religion scholar Bradford Verter's concept of "spiritual omnivorosity," but also Erickson's "cultural omnivorosity" conception and the growing literature that both of these scholars utilize on cultural "omnivores" and "univores."[101] By it—and concurring with Verter—I mean the propensity for some to pick, mix, and combine a variety of religious beliefs and practices from various traditions. Robert Wuthnow, Wade Clark Roof, and others have described such combinative religious activities as part of a culturewide trend in late-modern American religion.[102] Polls seem to concur. For example, a 2003 Harris poll showed that 27 percent of all Americans believed in reincarnation, including 40 percent of all twenty-five- to twenty-nine-year-olds.[103] This is a much higher figure than the number of Americans belonging to religions that feature reincarnation doctrines, such as Buddhism and Hinduism. In the United States it's not just Neopagans but also Roman Catholics and a wide swath of Protestants who have added reincarnation to their religious worldview.[104] But does class play a role? Is the propensity to pick, mix, and combine religious beliefs and practices more possible for those who come from social locations that allow more network diversity and accompanying cultural knowledge? Or is combinative spirituality common across all class locations, but more elaborated among higher classes and more restricted among lower ones?

My initial guess on all of these questions is yes, and some research concurs. In their study of the religious lives of American teenagers, for example, the sociologists Christian Smith and Melinda Lundquist Denton found that "those teens most likely to experiment with or practice the spiritualities of other religions also appear socially located in ways that make them more likely to be exposed to and have the resources to appropriate culturally different practices: they tend to live in cities, their parents are more highly educated, and they tend to come from families with higher incomes."[105] In his work on elite occult movements, Verter argues that "conspicuous displays of familiarity with multiple religions further serve the dual function of maximizing one's social network while minimizing the appearance of investment."[106] He adds that "polymorphous spiritual consumption" also reflects a "process of 'aesthetic distancing,' a performative strategy of emotional detachment that is another defining element of an elite disposition."[107] At the same time, studies by folklorists and historians reveal that less elite forms of combinative occultism have existed throughout American religious history, types that were more restricted, or "univorous," in that they picked and mixed from a smaller set of mostly European and African (versus worldwide) traditions.[108] In other words, those of lower classes similarly picked, mixed, and combined, but they did it using a more restricted field of materials.

A second way class makes one more or less available to pursue certain religious options involves Swidler's discussion of settled and unsettled lives and Machalek and Snow's concept of structural availability. Lower class position often entails instability. Social changes such as an economic recession may affect a working-class family with the same amount of stress that a major depression would strike at someone from the upper-middle-class. On an individual level, personal illnesses, automobile breakdowns, and rent increases can literally drive a lower-class, uninsured family into homelessness—an experience rare for those in more economically stable situations. Classic deprivation and cultural crisis theories psychologize the membership of the poor and dispossessed in twentieth-century upstart movements such as Pentecostalism and the Jehovah's Witnesses. The disadvantaged, the argument proceeds, attach themselves to religions that offer theologies and practices that give them succor and status—at least in symbolic form—that they are deprived of. Yet seeing class as availability and constraint, one could instead suggest that people in more unstable situations—whether due to individualized events or societal changes—are more likely to seek out new "strategies of action," sometimes in the form of religion. Recall, as Machalek and Snow noted, that those most likely to join communal new religions in the 1970s and 1980s were a relatively elite group of college students who were not constrained by institutional and family role obligations. In the case of the poor and dislocated, in a time of social transformation or cultural crisis they may become more "available"—if not compelled—to seek out new religious options because their relationships and role obligations radically change or disintegrate. Or conversely, being dislocated from former social networks may move people out of religious affiliations for an indefinite time period. Such scenarios require no psychologizing and place the material conditions of social class as one factor in encouraging or discouraging religious affiliations and activities.

The conception of class as availability and constraint closely mirrors Pierre

Bourdieu's concept of "habitus," which he defines as "a system of lasting, transposable dispositions which, integrating past experiences, functions at every moment as a matrix of perceptions, appreciations, and actions."[109] He calls the habitus a product of history, one formed by "structures constitutive of a particular type of environment (e.g. the material conditions of existence characteristic of a class condition)."[110] Consisting of unconscious presuppositions and other habits of mind and body, the habitus might best be (re)described as a "socially habituated subjectivity" (a term I will return to and elaborate on in the conclusion) that enables certain activities and ways of thinking, yet also constrains the range of possibilities.

Such socially habituated subjectivities entail not just what people think and do, but *how* people go about thinking and doing. Recall that Savage, Bourdieu, and others have suggested that it is best to think of a "class unconscious" rather than a class conscious. The old idea that members of a socioeconomic class believe the same things and share identical political views of the world is less useful than looking at implicitly shared assumptions and—to use Swidler's term—strategies of action. Those searching for connections between class and religion, then, should not exclusively focus on differing denominational affiliations and theologies. They must also consider the possibility of different religious languages, divergent strategies of ritual and practice, and deviating forms of organization and social relations.

These subjects require a truly interdisciplinary examination of religion and class. Such a study needs more than national polls, surveys, and generic classifications. It demands fieldwork attuned to differences *within* denominations and *between* individuals inside single congregations. It also leads to new kinds of questions. Do middle-class Pentecostals speak in tongues and dance in the spirit differently than working-class Pentecostals? Do upper-middle-class Methodists utilize more elaborated codes of religious language than lower-class ones? The sociologist Fred Rose argues that working-class social movements tend to have more clearly marked insider/outsider boundaries than middle-class groups.[111] The sociologist Thad Coreno has found correlations between the lower classes and Fundamentalists that seem to concur with Rose's argument.[112] Likewise, Smith and Faris's 2005 study found that one of the most theologically open and boundary-free denominations, Unitarian Universalism, ranks first or second in the United States in terms of the class variables of income, occupation, and education.[113] But what, one may ask, about boundary demarcation and maintenance within a single denomination? Are working-class Lutherans starker in their divisions between religious insiders and outsiders than their middle- and upper-class brethren? And what are the multiple ways one can demonstrate the differences in boundary construction among different classes of religious people? While one might immediately look to creeds, codes, and theology, we also need to examine the ways that social, family, and individual relations and processes provide clues.

Concluding Caveats

I hope here to have begun an interdisciplinary conversation on putting some class back into religion. Studies show its continuing importance, but our language and assumptions about the concept—and about how it interacts with religion—need to be reviewed and revised. Class is important, but it should not be seen as always being the primary determinant, as entailing class consciousness, or as being in need of psychologizing theories to explain its connection to religion. Sometimes the associations between religion and class may include these things, but making them fixed to the concept narrows its usefulness. Class is about classification, representation, and the availability and constraint particular material conditions promote. Class matters in the study of religion. But other things do too. Class is part of what constitutes our socially habituated subjectivities, but so are other aspects of social location such as gender, race, place, and age. In returning the variable of class to religious studies, we need to avoid two problems of the past. First, we must not underestimate the importance of class. Second, we shouldn't overestimate it either.

A slate of recent studies show the complications of how various social locations relate to what people believe and do. Sometimes physical location matters. In a study of white Evangelical Protestants and their perceptions of race relations in the United States, Michael Emerson and Christian Smith suggest that such Christians utilize a religio-cultural toolkit that contains three things. This "white Evangelical toolkit" includes accountable freewill individualism, which stresses the freedom individuals have to choose the directions of their lives and faith. It also contains relationalism, an implement that places importance on interpersonal relationships. The third tool is antistructuralism, which Emerson and Smith suggest makes individuals unable to perceive and accept the influence of historical social structures on their own or others' lives.[114] Given these implements with which to understand the world, Emerson and Smith show that individual sinfulness and defective personal relationships were "constants in evangelicals' assessments of the race problem."[115] But they also found that the statistically few white Evangelicals who had close contacts with African Americans tended to be less individualistic and more structural in their explanations of racial inequalities and conflicts.[116] In other words, the day-to-day contact and companionship of these whites with African Americans resulted in some different explanatory tools in their cultural repertoire. In a historical study, Kathryn Oberdeck similarly shows how Alexander Irvine's American labor and missionary experiences changed his explanation of class inequalities. "In Irvine's case," she writes of the late-nineteenth-century figure, "evangelical understandings that explained the plight of homeless men in terms of individual moral failing gradually gave way to questions about how material inequalities produced the impoverished lives to which he ministered."[117] In both of these examples, social location literally places you somewhere, and it is in that particular spot that your cultural repertoire and knowledge develop.

To separate class from other variables like location or region is not easy to do. Social class, race, gender, age, and place all intertwine. For example, Coreno's examination of Fundamentalism as a class culture suggests that region—in this case, the American South—is a very important variable.[118] Likewise, historical regional variation partly helps Dwight Billings account for the different reactions of the religious working class toward unions in North Carolina mill towns and West Virginia coal-mining villages.[119] Textile workers in places like 1920s and 1930s Gastonia were embedded in a long tradition of southern Protestantism that eschewed social activism, while the West Virginia coal miners of the same period had a different regional religious history.

While deprivation and cultural crisis studies have long depended upon the poverty and instability of people's lives to explain their religious preferences, a resurrected study of class and religion must understand that a host of other variables matter. This is especially seen in cases where the majority of the population is poor, yet only a percentage of it joins the religious movement under study. In their examination of religious affiliation in El Salvador, José Soltero and Romeo Saravia found that "access to medical care, international migration, age, presence of community organizations, and unemployment" were the strongest factors predicting which Salvadorans joined Protestant churches.[120] Soltero and Saravia conclude that "the implications for future research on religious affiliation point to the importance of avoiding superficial reference to the economic strain and anomic theories."[121]

I concur with Soltero and Saravia's caution. Class does matter in American religion, whether one examines it historically through analysis of events and documents, sociologically through polls and interviews, or ethnographically through participant observation in a single congregation. But how class is relevant is not a simple matter. A resurrected study of class and religion must necessarily also be a transformed study, one that sheds some past assumptions and offers new conceptions and directions.

Part I

From Inherent Tendencies
to Social Sources
in Religion Scholarship

2 | *The Depraved, the Unevolved, and the Degenerate*

Explaining Religious Affiliations in the Age of Eugenics

In 1908, Lester Ward published "Social Classes in the Light of Modern Sociological Theory" in the *American Journal of Sociology*. The argument that the Civil War veteran and former lower-class Illinois son put forth was that social class differences were not the result of inherent biological inferiority. Rather, he asserted, "the existence of lower classes was the result of early subjugation in the struggle of the races which took place in the savage state of man."[1] As evidence, Ward noted that "as a matter of fact, every time that the lower classes have been brought under conditions where they could manifest their natural and inherent equality with the upper classes they have done so in such a manner as to leave no doubt with regard to that equality."[2]

What strikes the contemporary reader about Ward's article is not his argument that there are no inherent natural biological differences between the social classes, but that such a seemingly self-evident thesis would be published in an academic journal. But what seems self-evident today was not so at the turn of the twentieth century. The debate over nature versus nurture raged, and those who promoted biological determinism were in many arenas winning the battle.

In the last several years, a number of works have appeared that examine the attitudes of various early twentieth-century figures and communities toward eugenics. These works show that religious leaders of various stripes responded to, sometimes contested, and more frequently embraced eugenicist goals and terminology.[3] In this chapter I shift the focus from clergy to scholars by examining some American scholarship on religious affiliations during the age of eugenics. Specifically, I argue two things. First, some well-known psychology of religion and rural church sociology scholarship shared themes and idioms with eugenics writings. Second, these writings on religion and eugenics mirrored each other in function: both distinguished, classified, and ordered religious practices, beliefs, and communities in ways that offered a scientific apologetics for existing American class, racial, and religious hierarchies.

Now seen as a discredited pseudoscience, eugenics held much more appeal in the early twentieth century among elites, academics, religious leaders, and the masses than previously thought.[4] Involving things as varied as rural family studies, state fair "fitter family" contests, and forced sterilization laws for those considered "unfit," the movement proved a pervasive current in American culture from the 1880s up to the beginning of World War II. Eugenics was intertwined with and influenced by evolutionary anthropology, nativism, racism, progressivism, and the professionalization of fields such as sociology. As a malleable and inconsistent form of biological determinism, the eugenics movement may be seen as part of a larger early twentieth-century discourse concerned with explaining differences and inequalities among humans. Through the use of photographs, Mendelian genetics, and social Darwinism, eugenicists claimed to offer scientific proof that some individuals, families, and entire races of people were more or less advanced than others.

The American religious historian Ann Taves notes that during the early years of the American and European academic study of religion (though, of course, not restricted to then), "scholars of religion were not the only ones who advanced theories of religion."[5] Those who studied, classified, and attempted to explain religion did not do so in a vacuum. They were historical actors consciously—and unconsciously—influenced by various cultural understandings and idioms. While historians and others have in recent years broadened our definition and view of eugenics and the prominent role it played in early twentieth-century American culture, I here open a related conversation about how eugenics and the American academic study of religion shared significant assumptions and idioms in the first thirty years of the twentieth century. As such, this chapter analyzes theories of religious affiliation before the plethora of socioeconomic explanations in later decades. Social class plays a role in this narrative in that it was frequently explained—like religion—through the trope of inherent biology. But more, social class was often an essential part of the eugenically inflected discourse on religious affiliation.

In the first decades of the twentieth century, during the height of the eugenics movement, a number of prominent psychologists and sociologists suggested that religious differences—like class, racial, and cultural differences—could be partially (and sometimes entirely) explained by inherent human character traits. In other words, certain religious beliefs and practices naturally attracted certain races and classes of people. This line of argumentation mirrored eugenicists' occasional references to religion. For example, in the 1933 revised edition of their popular college textbook *Applied Eugenics*, Paul Popenoe and Roswell Hill Johnson suggested that "the religion of a people corresponds to some extent to the inherent nature of the mind of that people, as well as to its national or racial traditions and economic organization."[6] Eugenicists like Popenoe and Johnson, Ellsworth Huntington, Leon Whitney, and William McDougall saw religious practices and beliefs—like the physical features of human bodies—as providing evidence that some people were more or less evolved or genetically endowed than others. Some psychologists and sociologists who studied religion concurred.

In what follows, I point to shared themes and language that consistently appeared in a selection of popular eugenics, psychology of religion, and rural church sociology writings from 1905 to 1934.[7] First, the eugenic and social scientific writings under study similarly assumed that there were depraved religions that created depraved people. Conversely, some also suggested that depraved people were naturally attracted to depraved religions. Second, eugenicists, sociologists, and psychologists reached nearly identical conclusions about which religious communities were the most depraved, degenerate, or unevolved: Roman Catholic, sectarian, Fundamentalist, ecstatic, minority, and new religious ones. Third, these writings frequently asserted that some modern religious practices and beliefs were inherently "primitive" but persisted among unevolved races and classes of people. Rural whites who participated in ecstatic religious revivals and the burgeoning Pentecostal movement garnered special attention from eugenicists and scholars who held this view. Their participation in supposedly "primitive" religious practices ostensibly contradicted early twentieth-century racist assumptions that white Anglo-Saxons were the most advanced race of humans. Yet the period's popular science easily helped resolve this quandary, as seen in Frederick Morgan Davenport's 1905 work, *Primitive Traits in Religious Revivals: A Study in Mental and Social Evolution*. In this published dissertation, the future New York state representative and Hamilton College law and politics professor used a Lamarckian version of environmental degeneracy theory, a popular idea in much of the nineteenth century, but one that slowly lost favor in the early twentieth. In the three decades after Davenport, both eugenicists and sociologists who studied rural America—Warren Wilson, Edmund Brunner, and others—offered theories of rural white population degeneracy. In brief, they suggested that the best racial "stock" had left the country for the city, leaving "morons" and other "inadequate" and "less favored" individuals who were attracted to emotional, ecstatic religious practices.

Caveats and Considerations

Having identified my subject and main arguments, I must also offer two caveats and a few preliminary considerations. First, my method here is to examine shared themes and language in a selection of texts, not to investigate the
personal connections between particular scholars and eugenicists. This first
caveat relates to my second: I do not suggest that the various writings under
analysis all say the same thing, nor do I argue for any direct historical relations between them. Quite the contrary, these eugenicists, psychologists, and
sociologists had different interests, methods, approaches, and conclusions.
At the same time, the writers were embedded in and shared a larger cultural
discourse concerning difference and distinction within human societies. The
Harlem Renaissance scholar Daylanne English notes that the first decades of
the twentieth century saw the infiltration of eugenics ideology throughout
American literature, scholarship, and popular culture. "Eugenic thinking,"
she writes, "was so pervasive in the modern era that it attained the status of
common sense in its most unnerving Gramscian sense."[8] The doxic status of
eugenics ideas meant that, among other things, the writers under study participated in what the religious historian Anne Rose calls a "common speech
community." Rose defines this as a group of "people sharing a language who
nonetheless differ in other ways" and notes that "elements of verbal consensus
may coexist with dissimilar values."[9] Eugenicists like Ellsworth Huntington
certainly had different concerns than psychologists like Simon Stone, who in
turn had different methods and approaches than rural sociologists like Warren Wilson. These facts make the shared language and theoretical frames of
their works all the more striking.

In arguing that writings on religion and eugenics mirrored each other in
distinguishing and ordering religious phenomena in ways that offered a scientific apologetics for existing American inequalities, I do not suggest any
sort of conscious, conspiratorial motivations. Instead, I am influenced by the
social theorist Pierre Bourdieu's model of society as a collection of groups
with varying interests who, through their frequently unwitting activities, promote their own images of the world as the most natural and acceptable for
all. Bourdieu argues that the different categories and classifications used by
groups and individuals wielding the most power in a society tend to symbolically reproduce—in his term, "homologize"—that society's existing power relations. In terms of the eugenics and religion scholarship under discussion,
these works offered symbolic and cultural capital (in the form of scientific
explanations and classifications) that supported existing social hierarchies.[10]
Here I argue, as does the historian of science George Stocking in his work on

the persistence of Lamarckianism until the 1910s, that "it may be quite illuminating to suggest that the thinking of social scientists was conditioned by assumptions which rarely came fully to their consciousness."[11]

Finally, it is important to note that scholars less influenced by eugenics idioms and still cited favorably in religious studies circles today—for example, William James and Max Weber—were writing during the period in which the works under examination appeared. In addition, the anthropologist Franz Boas actively contested the eugenic, evolutionary, and racist theories represented in some of these texts. So while the ideas in the works discussed here were certainly not the only ones espoused between 1905 and 1934, it would be just as inaccurate to suggest that they were peripheral in their fields. Boas's antiracialist views got him censured in the 1919 American Anthropological Association annual meeting.[12] And, as Ann Taves notes, even though many psychologists were critical of him because his conception of "the subliminal mind somehow ran contrary to accepted ideas of evolution," William James himself was committed to Darwinian theories of social evolution.[13] Though most of the works and authors discussed here may not be "household names" in current religious studies, some were either influential in or reflected the popular ideas of their fields in the early decades of the twentieth century.[14]

Cacogenic People and Their Cacogenic Religions

Sir Francis Galton, Charles Darwin's cousin, first coined the term "eugenics" in 1883.[15] Stemming from his study of prominent British elites, Galton concluded that human mental and physical abilities were a product of heredity uninhibited by environment and education. Eugenics, then, became the study and practice of producing "well-born" humans. It was initially a form of biological determinism, which in the words of the historian of science Stephen Jay Gould, "holds that shared behavioral norms, and the social and economic differences between human groups—primarily races, classes, and sexes—arise from inherited, inborn distinctions and that society, in this sense, is an accurate reflection of biology."[16] While later nineteenth-century currents in the movement offered a "soft eugenics" that accepted the influence of environment, by the turn of the century, eugenics had returned to its biologically deterministic roots. "Ancestry, rather than social life," writes the historian Nancy Leys Stepan, "was taken to determine character; heredity was now all."[17]

Eugenics took several forms that garnered support not just from self-identified white Anglo-Saxon males but also women and African Americans. The movement attracted progressives of every political bent, from conservatives and liberals, to right- and left-wing radicals. The historian of eugenics

Daniel Kevles notes that the activities in which eugenicists engaged "could be divided into two at times overlapping approaches: 'positive eugenics,' which aimed to foster more prolific breeding among the socially meritorious, and 'negative eugenics,' which intended to encourage the socially disadvantaged to breed less—or, better yet, not at all."[18] In the United States, what Kevles identifies as the dominant "mainline" eugenics was frequently not just about creating "well-born" babies, but also (1) preventing conception between those considered eugenically unfit and (2) halting the immigration of supposedly inferior races. Starting in 1907 with Indiana, more than thirty states eventually passed compulsory sterilization laws for those people considered inherently criminal, mentally inferior, or otherwise unfit.[19] This form of negative eugenics partly reflected fears of cultural, social, and national degeneration. Stepan argues that these concerns were related to "the alterations brought about by industrialization, urbanization, migration, immigration, about changing sexual mores and women's work."[20] Nativist anti-immigration sentiments played a large role in mainline American eugenics writings. These eugenicists labeled many European immigrants—in addition to African Americans and poor whites—"cacogenic," a term coined in 1912, meaning "bad-gened."[21] Eugenicists who considered themselves to be of good Anglo-Saxon stock sounded jeremiads that warned of America's demise due to the fecundity of cacogenic races and classes of people. Similar to late nineteenth-century nativists such as Josiah Strong, early twentieth-century eugenicists such as William McDougall asserted that the United States would only remain powerful, moral, and free if dominated by white, Nordic, Teutonic, and Anglo-Saxon Protestants.[22]

Given these concerns, religion was seldom the primary focus of eugenics writings. At the same time, it was a subject that occasionally played an important secondary role. After all, it wasn't just white Anglo-Saxons, but white Anglo-Saxon *Protestants* who usually received marks for genetic superiority. Eugenicists, like the American nativists who came before them, were often virulent anti-Catholics.[23] But they went further than their historical predecessors to suggest that Roman Catholicism was a cacogenic religion that created cacogenic people. In their 1928 work, *The Builders of America*, the eugenicists Ellsworth Huntington and Leon Whitney asserted that they had determined what the most and least intellectual denominations were by counting the religious affiliations of those listed in a *Who's Who* volume of prominent Americans. Assuming the *Who's Who* depicted the country's undisputed leaders and that they were in esteemed positions due to their inherent genetic makeup, Huntington and Whitney concluded that Unitarians were the most advanced, "the product of a prolonged process of selection which has been preeminently intellectual."[24] This should be no surprise, they noted, since "only a thoughtful person in whom intellect dominates the emotions is likely to be attracted to that rather coldly self-contained denomination by reason of its creed."[25] In comparison, Huntington and Whitney found Roman Catholicism seriously wanting. Unitarians, they noted, "appear to furnish 100 times as many leaders as the Roman Catholics in proportion to their total members."[26] This, they argued, was because Catholics had historically been subject to an opposite set of factors than the Unitarians. In what followed, the authors laid out the conditions making Roman Catholicism a breeding ground for genetically inferior, cacogenic stock.

First, they suggested that Roman Catholicism attracted people less moved by reason than by emotion, writing that "in the more advanced countries its converts are likely to be impelled mainly by emotion, or by the desire to solve their intellectual doubts once and for all by a great act of faith."[27] Second, Huntington and Whitney argued that Catholics failed to produce leaders because the Church kept all its members, even the "poorest and weakest," while "other denominations, especially those that are intellectual rather than emotional, let the weaker brothers and sisters drift away, and are thereby purged as it were."[28] Third, they posited that the practice of priest celibacy guaranteed that the best and brightest Catholics failed to reproduce. "In the Roman Catholic church," they asserted, "the great majority of men who burn with zeal for education and science, as well as for religion, have for ages found little chance to follow their deepest inclinations except by way of celibacy and the church. Thus not only the religious temperament, but the intellectual and scientific temperaments, have been weeded out remorselessly."[29] These factors, in addition to Huntington and Whitney's claim that only the most unintelligent Catholics adhere to the Church's ban on birth control, assured that "the prospect for future improvement is slight because the germ plasm has been so terribly depleted."[30]

Huntington and Whitney were not the only eugenicists to declare the genetic inferiority of Roman Catholics. In his 1921 book, *Is America Safe for Democracy?*, the nativist William McDougall used a familiar tripartite division in suggesting that there were inherent genetic traits and resulting character differences in three European races: Nordics, Mediterraneans, and Alpines.[31] Each of these races was, because of biology, attracted to certain kinds of religion. Mediterraneans and Alpines were naturally sociable, passive, and thus predominantly Roman Catholic or Eastern Orthodox.[32] Nordics, being independent and curious, were "by nature Protestants, essentially protestors and resistors against every form of domination and organization, whether by despot, church, or state."[33] "Is it, then," McDougall asked, "mere coincidence that the peoples in which predominate the blood of the curious, inquiring,

high percentage of "morons and inferior humans" found in the countryside.[44] Bemoaning what he described as the "domination of the subnormal" in country churches, Wilson rhetorically tied ecstatic rural Protestant movements to Catholic superstitions and practices.[45] Asserting that the "Jewish-Christian religion has been a progressive application of the critical mind for more than two thousand years to the irrational practices of religious people," Wilson suggested that "probably if there were no Christianity, and certainly if there were no Protestant churches, there would be more religious exercises: more sighing and groaning, more shouting and more kneeling would be ours if it were not for Isaiah, and Augustine, and Luther, and Wesley."[46]

In analyzing Brunner and Wilson, the sociologists Roger Finke and Rodney Stark have appropriately noted that both were mainline Protestants who saw their ecumenical desires challenged in rural areas by "upstart" sects like Pentecostalism.[47] Finke and Stark argue that these rural church sociologists adhered to what they call the "ignorance and poor reasoning theory of religious belief" that was "especially popular among social scientists with liberal religious views."[48] While these observations may be accurate, Brunner's and Wilson's assertions need to be understood within the broader context of their time period. Debates about emotional versus rational religion and the contested boundaries of "normal" versus "excessive" levels of piety are long-standing in American religious history. That these concerns appeared in Brunner's and Wilson's writings on rural churches should surprise no one. What is notable is how the language and ideas they used parallel writings in eugenics and the psychology of religion. When William McDougall asserted that mental defectives and idiots fared best in rural communities, and when Louis Binder suggested that "backward communities and sluggish races . . . always find themselves mirrored in their religious practices," they mined from the same grotto of assumptions as Brunner and Wilson.[49]

The Religions of the Unevolved

Binder's quote about "backward communities and sluggish races" referenced his evolutionary theory of religious preferences, one seen in both eugenic and academic analyses of religion. Just like Huntington and Whitney, religion scholars in the age of eugenics frequently held the view that some modern religious practices and beliefs were inherently "primitive" but persisted among unevolved races and classes of people. Evolutionary theory and the study of religion had, of course, been partners for decades. James Frazier, E. B. Tylor, and others sought to develop evolutionary views of culture and religion.[50] In the late nineteenth century, the religion scholar John Burris notes, "presumptions about the relative degree of people's religious evolution followed assumptions about the extent of their cultural evolution almost verbatim."[51] For some such as Binder, these ideas continued to hold explanatory value well into the twentieth century. "The higher the stage of culture," Binder asserted in 1933, "the nobler has been the type of religion which permeated it and reflected its social life and intellectual progress."[52] He even borrowed directly from Tylor's *Primitive Culture* in suggesting a three-stage hierarchy of human cultural development: savagery, barbarism, and civilization.[53] His conceptions followed Tylor's in conceiving not only some people but also certain religious practices and beliefs as more, or less, evolutionarily advanced. Binder saw modern Spiritualism, for example, as founded on primitive hallucinations and superstitions about communication with the dead.[54]

Ecstatic and experientially based religious activities like revivals, physically demonstrative prayer, and speaking in tongues were consistently picked out as the most primitive and unevolved forms of religious expression being practiced by the most primitive, unevolved people. In his 1927 study, *Speaking with Tongues*, Colgate University president George Barton Cutten asserted that the Pentecostal practice "could be traced to primitive times, for it is a primitive experience, a reverberation of the very early days of the race."[55] To explain how a twentieth-century American could practice such a primitive activity, Cutten referenced a psychology of the subconscious, arguing that "for modern man to permit himself to indulge in this form of expression means that he must put himself in a psychological state where the controlling apparatus of his mind is not functioning, and where the primitive reactions, which usually sleep in the subconscious, find their way to the surface and represent the individual."[56] While this seemed to explain how developmentally advanced people could speak in tongues, he was quick to claim that those who spoke in tongues also possessed naturally low mentality, suffered from illiteracy, and were filled with nervous energy.[57] Cutten decried speaking in tongues, suggesting that "it would be difficult, if not impossible, to find a more useless gift" in Christian history.[58] In fact, he asserted, it "has probably been a detriment to pure religion," and its current manifestations would "probably decrease as knowledge accumulates, and as natural inhibition and control develop."[59]

One of the scholarly sources Cutten cited and favorably used was Frederick Morgan Davenport's *Primitive Traits*. One biographer described Davenport as the "quintessential progressive," and his social location mirrored Cutten's and Warren Wilson's in several ways.[60] He was a white, middle-class, liberal Protestant who espoused Social Gospel ideals.[61] Though perhaps better known as a Republican politician and college professor, for a time he pastored a Methodist church in Yonkers, New York.[62] *Primitive Traits* was a revision of Davenport's Columbia University doctoral dissertation in sociology. Ann Taves notes that the effects of his influential 1905 book "can be seen in virtually all the later synoptic works in the psychology of religion."[63]

Davenport's blending of eugenics, religion, evolutionary theory, and the recurring themes under discussion here calls for extended analysis. In *Primitive Traits*, he offered an evolutionary view of human and religious development. "Religious experience is an evolution," he claimed, "we go on from the rudimentary and the primitive to the rational and the spiritual."[64] Davenport not only asserted that "there is a vast difference between the primitive and the most highly developed modern type of mind" but also found marked differences between evolved and primitive religious activities and beliefs.[65] Mature, evolutionarily advanced religion, he asserted, "is not the subliminal uprush, the ecstatic inflow of emotion, the rhapsody, the lapse of inhibition, but rational love, joy, peace, long-suffering, kindness, goodness, faithfulness, meekness—self-control."[66]

Davenport's focus was the religious revival, in which he found primitive aspects persisting up to his own time. To explain why "primitive" religious traits persisted in an advanced, civilized society, Davenport—like Cutten—posited the presence and persistence of less-evolved humans. He suggested that there was "a marked difference between types of mind in the same modern population at the same moment."[67] While he revealed a common social evolutionary perspective in reporting that a growing number of Americans were driven by "common sense and reason," Davenport also noted that there were still many individuals of the "emotional type" who were "characterized by certain prominent mental traits of primitive man."[68] It was among these sorts with "primitive and instinctive nervous tendencies" that less-evolved revival activities first ensued. "There is a law of origin," Davenport explained, "that impulsive social action originates among people who have least inhibitory control."[69] But in the religious revival such social action became contagious. Influenced by Gustave Le Bon's *The Crowd*, Davenport asserted that the primitive emotionalism exhibited by the least evolved spread in revival contexts, moving to the more "rational" and "intelligent" at a gathering through imitation and suggestibility.[70] The resulting combination of unevolved people and crowd psychology brought forth primitive instincts and activities even in modern American revivals.

Like a number of other scholars, and like some eugenicists, Davenport presumed that the most primitive styles of religious worship were physically demonstrative, ecstatic, and highly emotional. In language somewhat similar and likely influential to Cutten twenty-two years later, Davenport interpreted speaking in tongues. He argued that it was caused by "the loss of rational control on the part of primitive, ignorant, highly excited individuals in a crowd which has been stirred religiously to its depths."[71] He also likely influenced Cutten in favorably citing an 1857 account suggesting that Mormons who spoke in tongues were illiterate.[72] Davenport even preceded Cutten in using the biblical figure of Paul to criticize the spiritual authenticity of the practice, asserting that it was "one of the many marks of the splendid sanity of the Apostle Paul that he regarded the gift of tongues as a low order of spiritual endowment."[73]

In addition to reaching similar conclusions about what the most primitive religious practices were, Davenport mirrored the racist and classist assumptions found in concurrent eugenicist and scholarly writings and anticipated those that came later. He suggested that "by taking account of the indefinite series of gradations from lowest mental faculty to highest, it is possible to discriminate with clearness a number of psychological classes in any population."[74] Dedicating a whole chapter to "the religion of the American Negro," Davenport asserted that primitive religious traits persisted among African Americans because they were less advanced on the evolutionary ladder.[75] "No one doubts, I suppose," he wrote, "that in the negro people, whether in Africa or America, we have another child race."[76] Slavery, he continued, had "snatched the ancestors of this race from savagery only one or two hundred years ago," much too short a time for what Davenport apparently saw as the civilizing process of slavery to have much effect.[77] "Dense ignorance and superstition, a vivid imagination, volatile emotion, a weak will to power, small sense of morality, are universally regarded as the most prominent traits of the negro in those sections of the country, notably some parts of the black belt, where he appears in his primitive simplicity."[78] While Davenport granted that blacks who had been allotted education might not exactly fit his description, he supported his generalizations by taking the excuses of the white supremacist lynch mob at face value, asserting that "the wide prevalence of the crime of lynching among the whites of the South testifies eloquently to the reign of lust among the blacks."[79]

"The most prominent activity of the negro race in America," Davenport suggested, "is religion."[80] He was quick to follow this comment with a qualifier, noting that of course he meant "religion of a certain type, which can only be understood when viewed historically in light of the mental development which this people has attained."[81] Their religious practices and beliefs, Davenport claimed, were childlike, highly emotional, and filled with superstitions concerning signs, charms, spells, and dreams.[82] The African American was not just prone to revivalism, but due to his high suggestibility, was by nature unable "to withstand the almost constant tide of revival that sweeps over his community."[83]

But African Americans were not the only unevolved group of people susceptible to revivals and primitive religions. According to Davenport, Indians and "peasants" tended to have hallucinations and visions that "are not now common within areas of higher development."[84] Discussing the nineteenth-century Ghost Dance among Native Americans, Davenport identified two separable elements: one primitive, and one evolutionarily advanced. "There is the barbaric dance and the cataleptic vision," he wrote, "but there is also the hope of immortality, the ethical uplift, the attempt at righteousness."[85] He also suggested that primitive worship styles "are very common among the peasantry of all nations."[86] In such cases of unevolved religious manifestations, Davenport asserted, "they are evidently the product of a plastic and undeveloped mental and nervous organization."[87]

Overall, Davenport's work contained themes and assumptions similar to those found in works by his contemporaries and those who came after him. Like eugenicists and some other religion scholars, he declared white Anglo-Saxon Protestants the most advanced race and ecstatic religious practices the most unevolved. Davenport's belief that peasant classes were less evolved also mirrored eugenicist ideas that the elite enjoyed some inherent superiority. His distaste for religious emotionalism and his promotion of "reasonable" and "rational" religion sounded like many Protestant progressives of his time period and later. Finally, his evolutionary view of human and religious development was common among both academics and eugenicists during and after his time.

Given these assumptions, one of the subjects in *Primitive Traits* seemed to require special attention. In particular, how was one to account for the fact that many of the most emotional revivals of the past—like the 1800 Kentucky revivals—and some of the most physically demonstrative forms of religion in Davenport's present were frequented and even initiated by white Protestants? While his eugenic and class-based arguments could presumably have found a way to account for this, Davenport made use of another explanatory tool, a once-popular idea that was just beginning to fall out of favor among some academics of his time: a Lamarckian-based form of environmental degeneracy. Decades before Darwin's theory of evolution, Jean-Baptiste Lamarck suggested that the environment could lead organisms to acquire certain traits that would then be inherited by their offspring. The idea that the environment could help—or hinder—evolutionary progress was a popular nineteenth-century idea in biology and social thought. In his examination of social science scholarship from 1890 to 1915, George Stocking argues that "the idea that acquired characteristics might be inherited was stated or implied in the work of so many writers that it is impossible to avoid the conclusion that they were primarily reflecting a widespread popular scientific attitude whose roots lay deep in the Western European cultural tradition."[88] Specifically, Davenport used a mixture of environmental degeneracy theory, biological determinism, and class-based explanations to account for Appalachians and rural whites involved in ecstatic religious practices and demonstrative, revivalist forms of Protestantism. In this move, he paralleled both eugenicists and later rural church sociologists in connecting the American countryside, the unfit, and primitive religion.

The Quandary of Anglo-Saxon Superiority, Primitive Religions, and the Rural Degeneracy Thesis

One of the arguments Davenport used to explain the involvement of whites in primitive religions was race-based, suggesting that not all white ethnics were equally evolved. While he had argued that the psychology of the crowd fomented primitive activities among even the intelligent and evolutionarily advanced, he added that one factor modifying such effects was the "differing temperament of the population."[89] "The Anglo-Saxon crowd is one thing, the Latin or Celtic crowd quite another," he wrote, adding that "the extent, intensity and character of the sympathetic outbreak will vary considerably with populations of different races and different degrees of development within the same race."[90] Davenport noted that the Scots-Irish were the primary participants in the Kentucky revivals of 1800. Being both Teutonic and Celtic, they combined in their character "the shrewd, practical common sense and intelligent purpose of the Teuton with the strong emotionalism of the Celt."[91] While he was quick to assert that the Protestant Scots-Irish who came from Northern Ireland were more intelligent and less superstitious than their Roman Catholic countrymen in the south, he simultaneously implied that the non-Teutonic part of their ancestry put them lower on the developmental scale.[92] Their Celtic blood made them more susceptible to the fits of sympathetic emotion that spread through the frontier revivals.

In addition to having the mark of Celtic ancestry, Davenport asserted, the Scots-Irish stock participating in the Kentucky revivals was a lower-class one. The Scots-Irish settlers, he surmised, were a selected population whose "forceful motor traits" made them well-bred for border life.[93] Apparently, Davenport believed that the wealthiest and most genetically refined of the race had stayed in a more civilized, northeastern, environment. "The professional classes," he wrote, "who at home were great centres of self-control, were comparatively few in this pioneer community."[94] While the more advanced elites were underrepresented, Davenport suggested that criminal and degenerate types were overrepresented.[95] Combining these lower-class and criminal elements with the presence of hotly emotional Celtic blood, Scots-Irish participation in primitive revival activities could be easily explained.

The arguments that an inferior race and an inferior class of white settler spurred the Kentucky revivals logically followed from other arguments in the book. So did Davenport's third explanation. One assumption running through *Primitive Traits* was that the physical environment partially shaped the mental characteristics of human races, hindering or helping evolution. In his first chapter, for example, Davenport posited that we "must notice that there appear to be certain physical and mental conditions which predispose to emotionalism," and he proposed that "sudden changes of climate from summer to winter, combined with monotony of topography, seem to be a factor in fixing the type of mind in the inhabitant of the Russian steppe."[96] In his chapter titled "The Religion of the American Negro," Davenport asserted that "a century or two is not long for the evolution of any people, especially one whose early abode was in the African jungle beneath a tropical sun."[97] When appraising the Kentucky revivals, he suggested that the physical environment had deteriorated the mental attributes of the Scots-Irish. Davenport deduced that the landscape in which the revivals took place—the wild and hilly Kentucky frontier—had "put its stamp upon" the settlers and led to "some disintegration of intellectual elements."[98] Indeed, Davenport argued, "the primitive surroundings once more fanned into flame the primitive traits" and fomented physically demonstrative and ecstatic religious activities.[99]

Davenport's belief that the physical environment in which one resided could cause evolved intellect and reason to degenerate proved equally useful in resolving any quandary over why modern white Appalachian southerners would be drawn to ecstatic and revivalistic religions. In addition to environmental degeneracy, Davenport added poverty and lack of education to explain the "religious excitability" of contemporary southern white mountaineers. He noted that the "three millions of white people in the southern mountains from Virginia to northern Alabama are known chiefly for their moonshine stills, their feuds, their murders, their excitable religious temperament and their illiteracy."[100] It was not that they lacked the inherent capacity, he suggested, "for their Scotch-Irish ancestors have been a great element of national strength. But they have been shut in by poverty and the mountains, their horizon has been limited by ignorance, and they have been at the mercy of primitive passion and primitive superstition."[101] Elsewhere in the book, Davenport added to this assessment, writing at one point that he needed to "pause for a word of appreciation of this magnificent strain in the nation's blood." "The descendents of these people," he continued, "have done much for America, and will do more when the millions of their belated kin in the Southern mountains are brought under the influence of twentieth century enlightenment and culture."[102]

Upon first look, one might see Davenport's theory of environmental degeneracy as being at odds with his social evolutionism. A common history of science narrative views evolutionary theory as neatly supplanting ideas that humans degenerated from some pristine state. How, after all, could an advanced race of people move backward, devolve? In answering this, one finds Davenport's theory firmly embedded in two trends of late nineteenth- and early twentieth-century academic thought. The first, already noted, was the Lamarckian idea that the environment fomented characteristics that could be inherited. This suggested that the physical landscape could inhibit evolutionary development as much as it might advance it. The second, as noted by the religion scholar Hans Kippenberg and others, was the idea of irrationality, which some late nineteenth-century evolutionists had incorporated into their view of human nature and history.[103] Irrationality meant that there could be lags, stops, and reversions along the human evolutionary path. Recalling Davenport's idea that the primitive mind had not entirely disappeared in modern humanity, one sees that his Lamarckian, sociopsychological evolutionism could easily incorporate occurrences of degeneration. Indeed, Davenport believed that the largest churches of his time period were dominated by "feeling, belief, and authority," and he saw this as evidence that "the mental mode of our population is still emotional."[104] Given these considerations, the idea that the physical environment could lead to mental degeneration among even the most advanced races should be unsurprising.

But as a believer in social evolution, Davenport envisioned humankind walking the path of progressive development. While the climate and locality in which one resided could hinder evolution, they could also quicken it. For Davenport, the cosmopolitanism of the city worked to dissipate the primitive emotionalism encouraged by the countryside. He asserted that revivals had declined in large areas of the United States, "particularly in the centres of the population where social organization is highly perfected, where the environment is complex, the interests many, communication easy and education within the reach of all people."[105] Even more, he claimed that "any attempt to maintain the extravagant emotional methods of other days breaks down utterly and inevitably in the midst of the city."[106] Cityscapes, it seemed, could push evolution forward. Rural environments, by contrast, encouraged regressive, primitive emotionalism.

Davenport's explicitly positive view of cities and negative assessment of rural areas seems to contradict what many scholars have noted about how nineteenth- and early twentieth-century Americans imagined these spaces. The religion scholar Robert Orsi, for example, accurately notes that "for two hundred years, despite (or perhaps because of) the ceaseless urbanizing of the population, the city was cast as the necessary mirror of American civilization, and fundamental categories of American reality—whiteness, heterosexuality, domestic virtue, feminine purity, middle-class respectability—were constituted in opposition to what was said to exist in cities."[107] This negative portrayal of the city was often accompanied by positive assessments of town, village, and country life.[108] As the mirror opposite of the city, the pastoral countryside in these depictions appeared to be America's saving grace. This idea was certainly present in Davenport's time, but his comments tapped into another prevalent discourse on cities, towns, and the countryside. While few would join him in arguing that the city offered the best environment for human evolution, many expressed dismay at the presumed prevalence of the unevolved in rural America. Starting with the eugenic family studies of the 1870s and persisting into post–World War I rural sociology, the idea that the most intelligent and eugenically fit had left the countryside and small villages and moved into towns and cities found many avenues of dissemination. Rural areas, in these depictions, became the havens of the cacogenic and undesirable. While the city certainly served for many as the imagined space of moral and religious decay, the rural countryside played a similar role for some progressives, eugenicists, psychologists, sociologists, and scholars of religion.

The idea that the most eugenically fit Americans were leaving the countryside for more urban spaces was common in many of the writings under analysis. In these works, the migration of the fittest was often asserted to be from isolated rural areas and villages to larger towns. In 1883 the "father of eugenics," Francis Galton, asserted in *Inquiries into the Human Faculty and Its Development* that "the more energetic members of our race, whose breed is the most valuable to our nation, are attracted from the country to our towns."[109] Later writers such as William McDougall continued to suggest that villages and rural areas were being "drained more completely of their best elements."[110] Non-eugenicists sounded a similar tone. Recall that in 1933 the sociologist Louis Binder charged "backward communities" and "sluggish races" with displaying emotionally primitive religious styles.[111] Even as late as 1945, the psychologist Anton Boisen asserted that "the American country village has today become a haven of refuge for many inadequate persons."[112]

With these writings we circularly return to a recurrent theme throughout the three decades under study: the idea that some religions created cacogenic or otherwise unfit people and, in turn, cacogenic or otherwise unfit people were attracted to certain kinds of religions. In an additional articulation of that association, cacogenic people became connected to rural areas, spaces that in turn were conjoined to unevolved religious beliefs, practices, and communities. Davenport's connection between the rural environment and revivals and Boisen's assertion that village religion is "static" and uncreative are examples of this. But the connections can perhaps be most clearly seen in the rural church sociology writings of Warren Wilson and Edmund Brunner discussed above. Interestingly, Wilson's 1925 assertion that the countryside was filled with many morons and inferior minds—and the resultant rural spiritual decline—was the reverse of a view found in one of his earlier writings. In 1911 he had suggested that the "degenerate stock in the country has been drawn off into the cities."[113] By 1925, however, Wilson's ideas that the most degenerate sorts could be found in rural America closely mirrored eugenicist and other contemporary writings. "The very persons and families whose genius would have brought God near have been constrained to go elsewhere,—to the West, to Canada, to the city,—and without them there is distorted vision, loss of faith, and no humanity," he asserted.[114] "The evidences of this spiritual decline press upon every one who spends a week or a month in a country place," the former rural minister self-referentially noted.[115] Though less focused on religion, later works in rural sociology explored related subjects, including the number of leaders in villages and the decay of "rural stock."[116] In 1938 Noel Gist and Carroll Clark even used intelligence tests to demonstrate that the "less able and less favored" remained in the countryside, while the more intelligent were moving to urban environments.[117] While Gist and Clark were careful to suggest the possibility that "the progeny of the rural population may be quite as adequately endowed by nature as the children of the urban migrants," they also postulated that "it is entirely possible that the traditional conservatism of the country, the lack of effective rural organization in many areas, and the shortage of qualified leaders may be in part the consequence of selective migrations."[118] Though not as certain in their language as the eugenicists and the rural sociologists such as Wilson who came before them, the influence of heredity still loomed large, though unmarked, for some scholars at the dawn of World War II.

Conclusion

While examples of sterilization laws and biologically deterministic thinking could be found in the United States into the 1960s and even later, World War II and in particular the genocidal horrors of Nazism dampened the strength of the eugenics movement within much of American academics. The religious historian Anne Rose accurately notes that the 1920s also witnessed the beginning of a "transition from natural to social science models."[119] This was mirrored in American religion scholarship after the war by the virtual disappearance of biological explanations of religious preferences.[120] In its place appeared cultural crisis and deprivation theories, which argued that social, economic, and other variables could account for people's participation in certain types of religion.[121] Such explanations, of course, had been present in examinations of religion before World War II, as seen in the writings of H. Richard Niebuhr, Max Weber, Ernst Troeltsch, and Karl Marx.[122] Recall that even Davenport suggested that lack of education and poverty—in addition to genes and evolutionary development—were contributing factors in some primitive religious survivals. But after the war, deprivation theories became the predominant social scientific trope in explaining certain religious preferences. The next chapter traces this shift from "inherent tendencies" to "social sources" in the study of religion.

3 | *The Peyote of the Masses*

Cultural Crises and Acculturation between the World Wars

In the early 1880s the founder of the Carlisle Indian School, Captain Richard Henry Pratt, began using before and after photographs to show his success in assimilating Native Americans, a process he described as "killing the Indian to save the man."[1] The before pictures invariably portrayed an individual or group of long-haired Native Americans—frequently dusty and unkempt—wearing blankets, beads, moccasins, and jewelry. The after shots showed the same individuals sporting trimmed hair and pressed military uniforms. In an era when many Americans believed Natives to be hopelessly primitive and inassimilable, it should not be surprising that some viewed the photographs with great skepticism. "The swine will return to his wallow," suggested one critic, "the savage to his barbarism."[2] Yet, others saw the pictures as evidence of profound character changes in the subjects. "The difference is striking," noted one observer of the photographs, "not in the mere change of clothing and approved carriage, but the development of intelligence shown by the faces."[3]

The previous chapter examined scholarship that, like the people who rejected Pratt's photographic evidence and thought Native Americans' assimilation impossible, suggested that biology and evolution determined religious affiliations more than any environmental factors. This chapter looks at scholarship from the 1920s to the early 1940s, works that thematically resemble the sentiments of the letter writers who believed the photographs showed evidence of profound cultural, intellectual, and personality changes. In these works it was no longer nature, but rather the social and economic environment, that was seen as the factor driving people toward certain religious beliefs, practices, and communities. In many ways this was a radical shift—particularly compared to the eugenicist writings. In cultural crisis and deprivation theories, humans were no longer depicted as slaves to their genetic inheritances. People's beliefs, values, characteristics, and fates were no longer considered

fixed, natural, and inevitable. They could be changed, and their religious propensities could change as well. The Horatio Alger myth, it seemed, could now
apply to religion.

But in some ways, this scholarship served a similar function as the theories
appearing in the first decades of the twentieth century. Though they wielded
different explanatory tools, scholars still felt the need to use them on many
of the same religious groups that occupied the attention of eugenicists, psychologists, and rural church sociologists. After World War II, Roman Catholics were eventually and unevenly "mainstreamed" in some academic work
through tropes such as Will Herberg's "triple melting pot." But scholars still
applied cultural crisis and deprivation theories to the "usual suspects": Pentecostals, Fundamentalists, sectarians, new religions, and movements attracting
poor whites, Native Americans, and African Americans.[4] Like the eugenics-
inflected explanations, the theories under examination in this chapter reflected broader cultural concerns for order, stability, and national unity. They
also unwittingly functioned to distinguish and classify religions in ways that
supported existing racial, class, and regional hierarchies.

In chapter 1, the scholarship under examination viewed religion and class
as a secondary series of correspondences tied together by biological and
evolutionary explanations. One's social class and religion could both be explained by genetics or the stage of one's race on the evolutionary ladder. In
other words, people were not Pentecostal because they were poor; they were
poor and Pentecostal because they were eugenically unfit and/or evolutionarily backward. In this chapter, class—one's socioeconomic and status positions within society—becomes the primary explanation of religious preferences. In the scholarship analyzed here, researchers connected certain classes
and religions not because of biology or evolution but because of the social and
material circumstances of class location itself.

I title this chapter "The Peyote of the Masses" and begin with the story
from the Carlisle Indian School because studies of Native American new religions—those fomented through cultural contact, conflict, and combination
such as the Peyote Way and the Ghost Dance—played a prominent role in the
development of early cultural crisis and deprivation theories. But such theories quickly broadened beyond Native and indigenous groups to explain a variety of religions. After World War II—as seen in the next chapter—scholars
such as Weston La Barre, Anthony F. C. Wallace, and Charles Glock used cultural crisis and deprivation theories to explain not just specific religions but
religion in general.[5]

The shift I trace here, from what might be termed biological toward environmental explanations of religious affiliation, must be placed within the

context of several intellectual, social, and cultural currents and changes, particularly in the 1920s and 1930s. First, the decline of biological explanations of religious preferences in religion scholarship was not unique. Rather, it was part of a larger trend. Several scholars have noted that the decades prior to World War II saw the decline of biological determinism in the social sciences and the rise of the "culture" concept, introduced by scholars such as anthropologist Franz Boas and his students.[6] The religious historian Anne Rose accurately notes that the period witnessed the beginning of a "transition from natural to social science models."[7] The historian of science George Stocking argues that "the working out of all the antibiological tendencies in behavioral science and the complete dissemination of Boasian thinking were not accomplished until after 1930."[8] Roscoe Hinkle's historiographical study concurs, noting an increasing rejection of what he terms "instinctivism" and "linear directionality as a most central and basic feature of social evolutionism" in late 1930s social science textbooks.[9]

Second, the rise of socioeconomic explanations of religious preferences occurred during a time in which a new progressivism emerged, one that eschewed social Darwinism and eugenics and touted the ability of education and science to change society and individuals. The historians Frank Friedel and Alan Brinkley link this progressivism to an emergent professional middle class. "Unlike the older middle-class, whose status often derived from family background and stature within the community," they argue, "the new middle-class placed a far higher value upon education and accomplishment."[10] Represented by such figures as Thorsten Veblen, William James, and John Dewey, the new middle-class progressives, in the words of Friedel and Brinkley, "were no longer content with merely justifying the existing industrial system" but "spoke instead of the creation of a new civilization, one in which the expertise of scientists and engineers could be brought to bear upon the problems of economy and society."[11] The influence of such ideas could be seen in popular culture, such as the *Century Magazine*'s 1925 article "The Decline of the Self-Made Man," which focused on the contemporary need for professional education for success.[12] It could also be seen in historical scholarship, such as Vernon Parrington's *Main Currents of American Thought* (1927) and Charles and Mary Beard's *The Rise of American Civilization* (1927). Friedel and Brinkley note that Parrington "explained the evolution of American culture in largely social and economic terms, implying, like the Beards, that positive social programs could have wide-ranging effects."[13] The new middle-class progressivism's main idea—that society and its individuals could be bettered through science, education, bureaucratization, and professional expertise—depended upon a conception of human beings as malleable and able to quickly change and develop. This was something for which biological determinism and social Darwinism offered little support.

Concomitant with the new middle-class progressivism was a rise in what the historian T. Jackson Lears calls a "therapeutic ethos" that focused on the ability of individuals to improve themselves, regardless of class and family background.[14] This growing trend, which could be seen as early as the 1880s and continued through the twentieth century, was visible in advertising and the development of consumer culture. It was present in the period's emergent New Thought religious movements that touted the spiritual and physical power of positive thinking. It also appeared in self-help literature, such as Dale Carnegie's 1936 bestseller *How to Win Friends and Influence People*. Referencing the behaviorism of B. F. Skinner, Carnegie suggested that people could—with the proper knowledge and sufficient effort—make others like them and listen to them and at the same time gain power and control of their own increasingly complex, interpersonal lives.

All of these developments must also be placed within the national crises and conflicts of the period. The decades between the world wars witnessed a rise in political, racial, class, and religious factionalism. It was during these years that the white Protestant supremacist Ku Klux Klan reached its numerical high point, race riots tore up industrial cities, and labor strikes were violently curbed. It was a period when American and European anti-Semites received verbal and financial support from famous figures such as Henry Ford, and when American communist, socialist, and fascist political parties attracted the largest interest they would garner in the twentieth century. The year 1929 marked the beginning of the Great Depression, and the next decade's dust bowl drought and economic crisis vividly demonstrated the effects of social dislocation and poverty.[15] It was within the context of all these trends, changes, and events that cultural crisis and deprivation theories emerged as dominant ways for American scholars to explain religious affiliations.[16]

In this chapter I examine a selection of works from 1929 through the early 1940s. These academic writings illustrate the transition from biological to social explanations of religion. After World War II, such theories became the dominant explanatory tropes in the American social scientific study of religion.

Shock, Disorganization, and Religion

In October 1940 John Holt, sociologist and employee of the U.S. Department of Agriculture, published "Holiness Religion: Cultural Shock and Social Reorganization." Appearing in the *American Sociological Review*, he had first presented it at the April 1940 Southern Sociology Society Meeting. "The purpose of this paper," he wrote, "is to suggest further research in the field of social organization and cultural conflict."[17] Holt's focus was white southern Holiness and Pentecostal churches, which he noted had seen "phenomenal growth" from the 1910s to 1940. Following a brief and general—yet accurate—description of the theologies of the two movements, Holt offered a series of hypotheses and elaborations that foreshadowed the cultural crisis and deprivation theories that would dominate the post–World War II social scientific study of religion. Beginning in the late 1920s and 1930s, such theories slowly supplanted those that suggested biological and evolutionary explanations for religion.

Despite initially distinguishing the Holiness and Pentecostal movements in terms of theology, in listing his hypotheses Holt referred to them as a single entity. First, he argued that the movement was "largely the natural product of the social disorganization and cultural conflict which have attended the over-rapid urbanward migration and concomitant urbanization of an intensely rural, and among other things, religiously fundamentalist population."[18] Second, he continued, the movement should not be seen foremost as a religious but as a "social" entity, "an attempt on the part of certain groups experiencing acute social maladjustment to recapture their sense of security through religious revival and reform."[19] Third, Holt suggested that Holiness and Pentecostal religion was a "reactionary and reformist" attempt at social adjustment and reintegration, one whose "beliefs and ethics are drawn from a disintegrating rural agricultural tradition."[20] In opposition to movements that were "revolutionary or constructive in character," Holiness and Pentecostal religion did not "promise to help eradicate the maladjustment which brought it forth."[21] Despite this failure, he suggested, "they are successful in inspiring hope and a type of behavior in individuals which may raise their individual or group status above that of their class."[22] Finally, and despite evidence to the contrary in places as diverse as small towns in Indiana, rural parts of Colorado, inner-city Los Angeles, and urban industrial cities throughout the North, Holt argued that Holiness and Pentecostal religion was "regional and primarily southern in character."[23]

Elaborating on these hypotheses, Holt used statistics showing dramatic population shifts throughout the Depression-era South from rural to urban areas. Such migration patterns, Holt asserted, were inevitably accompanied by social dislocation, cultural shock, and psychological distress. He supported this by citing a number of studies, which he summed up colorfully by favorably quoting one Kentucky farm program administrator, who reportedly said that "the physical 'bends' of deep sea divers exposed too rapidly to lighter atmospheric pressure is nothing compared to the psychological or spiritual bends produced in our mountain communities when subjected too rapidly to urban standards and ways of doing things."[24]

Though he did not specifically use the terms "crisis" and "deprivation," Holt proposed that participation in Holiness and Pentecostal religion was a response to cultural dislocation and the economic, status, and psychological stresses accompanying the urbanization of rural white southerners. Holt described the migrants attracted to the religions as poor, uprooted newcomers who had low status among their more established low-income neighbors. "Disturbed emotionally by the necessity to adjust to a changed situation and subjected perhaps also to economic insecurity and want," Holt suggested, "this group of in-migrants would find the situation psychologically distressing."[25] In explaining why some would turn to emotionally ecstatic forms of religion in response to these stresses, Holt argued that "the urgent demand of the migrant's personality for stable and secure social status in the midst of a feeling of isolation, social and economic insecurity, and lack of social adequacy would probably tend to cause the migrant to exploit emotionally any escape-activity or reorganization which presented itself, particularly one in his cultural tradition."[26]

Holt's interpretations of Holiness and Pentecostal movements sound typical to contemporary readers familiar with American social scientific studies of religion. First, as seen in the next chapter, Pentecostalism in particular was singled out in many mid-to-late twentieth-century studies as a religion of the disinherited, a movement that symbolically gave hope to socially and economically dislocated people. Second, in implying that Holiness and Pentecostal religions should be seen as one movement, Holt's article also resembles the genre, which typically asserted that "sects," "cults," and some other types of religion might be different in theology but are similar in their demographics and function. In a related third way, his work illustrates the genre's tendency to downplay liturgy and theology by positing that social and political interests were the fuels fomenting religious fire. This can be seen in the way that Holt tells readers that Holiness religion and Pentecostalism should together be considered foremost a social, rather than a religious, movement. Finally, the piece resembles later cultural crisis and deprivation theories in its attempt to assess the adaptive or maladaptive nature of the religious movement. Does the religion aid or hinder assimilation to the new sociocultural situation? Does it offer demonstrable material, social, and political benefits, or does it only provide psychological solace and theological justification of one's status? Holt's conclusions on this matter are typical in seeing certain religious movements as the ineffective last breaths of dying cultures. While one of his initial hypotheses suggested that Holiness and Pentecostal religion could positively inspire hope and class-climbing behavior among its adherents, his concluding pages asserted otherwise. He argued that "the adjustment of the Holiness and Pentecostal groups represents the defense of the old standards and modes of behavior rather than a reconstruction of attitudes and behavior to fit the altered situation or a revolution against both the old and the new, which would merely postpone the necessary reconstruction."[27]

While all these assertions and interpretations sound familiar today, in the 1940s United States they had only been developing for about a decade. Though modern explanations connecting religion and material conditions had been around since at least Karl Marx, it was not until H. Richard Niebuhr's *The Social Sources of Denominationalism*, published in 1929, that an extended American consideration of socioeconomics and religion appeared. In the next section of this chapter, I examine several works that point to a transition in American social scientific studies of religion in the 1930s, studies that moved explanations of religious preferences from inherent tendencies to social sources.

From Inherent Tendencies to Social Sources

While Holt's article is notable for its clear synthesis of what would become cultural crisis and deprivation theories, ideas connecting religion and material circumstances had been around for awhile. Nearly one hundred years earlier, Karl Marx famously declared that "it is not consciousness that determines life, but life that determines consciousness."[28] "The production of men's ideas, thinking, their spiritual intercourse," he suggested, "here appear as the direct efflux of their material condition."[29] Marx's conviction that the entirety of a person's perceptions and ideas—including religious ones—stemmed from material circumstances led him to see religion as a placebolike opium for the masses who could not afford actual narcotics to dampen their pains.[30] This led Marx and later coauthor Friedrich Engels to see religion as a tool of social control for those in power, as well as a false promise to the poor of justice and rewards, to be collected after death, for their suffering and assent to the exploitative status quo on earth.

In the early twentieth century, one of the European parents of sociology, Max Weber, developed an elaborate sociology of religion that examined the affinities between religion, class, and status. Weber suggested that there were important connections between the social locations of individuals, groups, and their religious beliefs and practices. He asserted that the social group within which a religion first developed left a lasting impression on it, and some of Weber's work set forth to determine the connections between certain occupational groups and the theologies of various world religions. In his 1913 essay "Social Psychology of the World Religions," for example, Weber suggested correspondences between different societal castes (intellectual, political, warrior, peasant) and certain types of religious beliefs. In his 1922 work, *Sociology of Religion*, Weber looked for correspondences between theologies of suffering (theodicies), salvation (soteriologies), and class.[31] Among other things, Weber suggested that emotional, salvific religion was often, though not exclusively, a focus of "disprivileged" classes, while the more privileged groups were attracted to religions that theologically justified their good fortunes and status.[32] Unlike Marx, however, Weber did not see religion as simply a reflection or function of material conditions. He suggested that religion was both influenced by and influenced social and economic conditions. "Not ideas, but material and ideal interests, directly govern men's conduct," Weber wrote, "yet very frequently the 'world images' that have been created by 'ideas' have, like switchmen, determined the tracks along which action has been pushed by the dynamic of interest."[33] In *The Protestant Ethic and the Spirit of Capitalism* (1930), for example, Weber carefully avoided any direct causal argument concerning the concomitant growth of capitalism and Protestantism, instead preferring to suggest elective affinities between this-worldly Protestant asceticism and capitalist accumulation and investment.

In the United States, even during the height of biological determinism in the 1910s and 1920s, scholars such as Lester Ward argued against genetic inheritance and for the importance of material conditions imposed by social class and status.[34] In terms of religion, one of the first and most influential considerations—and one that illustrates the transition from biological and evolutionary explanations to socioeconomic ones—was H. Richard Niebuhr's *The Social Sources of Denominationalism* (1929). Niebuhr wrote as a theologian troubled by what he saw as the lack of unity in Christianity. He declared the prime culprit of disharmony to be denominationalism. "It represents," he asserted, "the accommodation of Christianity to the caste-system of human society."[35] Furthermore, denominations were divided along lines of class, race, and ethnicity: "For if religion supplies the energy, the goal, and the motive of sectarian movements, social factors no less decidedly supply the occasion, and determine the form the religious dynamic will take."[36]

In *Social Sources*, Niebuhr applied the sociology of Max Weber and Ernst Troeltsch, the author of *The Social Teaching of the Christian Churches* and developer of the church-sect classification.[37] Niebuhr saw denominationalism as the sacrifice of universal Christian ideals to the parochial class, political, and ethnic interests of specific groups. Yet the same theories he used to critique denominationalism as a moral fault-line in Christendom also led him to suggest the possibility of periodic renewals of the Christian faith. Favorably citing Troeltsch's comment that "'the really creative, church forming religious movements are the work of the lower strata,'" Niebuhr viewed "sects of the disinherited" as prime movers in a repeating cycle of what a reader of *Social Sources* might call "faith revitalization."[38] "So regarded," he suggested, "one phase of the history of denominationalism reveals itself as the story of the religiously neglected poor, who fashion a new type of Christianity which corresponds to their distinctive needs, who rise in the economic scale under the influence of religious discipline, and who, in the midst of a freshly acquired cultural respectability, neglect the new poor succeeding them on the lower plane."[39] Thus, the cycle recurs. For Niebuhr, the "rise of new sects to champion the uncompromising ethics of Jesus and to 'preach the gospel to the poor' has again and again been the effective means of recalling Christendom to its mission."[40] The religion of the poor, he believed, "by its fruits in conduct often demonstrates its moral and religious superiority."[41]

For Niebuhr, periodic revitalizations of Christianity occurred when society's disinherited, finding that the churches of the privileged did not address their needs, formed their own sects. He saw these sects more closely following the tenets of Christianity than those middle-class churches from which the dispossessed withdrew. If the new sects survived, they eventually became established churches that lost their ethical rigor, pushed out the lower-class parishioners among them, and thus sowed the seeds of another sect. In examples ranging from the first Christians to the Waldensians and Methodists, Niebuhr posited this eternal cycle. Yet in 1929 he lamented that he saw no sect of the disinherited on the American landscape, and "without the spontaneous movement from below, all efforts to repristinate the ethical enthusiasm of the early church and to reawaken the Messianic hope are unavailing."[42] Desiring Christian unity, yet seeing sectarianism as the revitalization of authentic faith, Niebuhr was caught in a bind. He declared that "even sectarianism is preferable to the absence of conviction."[43] But Niebuhr also concluded with a chapter titled "Ways to Unity" in which he suggested that "the history of schism has been a history of Christianity's defeat."[44]

Written by a concerned theologian, *The Social Sources of Denominationalism* may be viewed foremost as a jeremiad, a prophetic call to Christian unity and what Niebuhr believed to be early Christianity's ethical ideals. But the work also became an influential—if not "classic"—study for sociologists of religion.[45] *Social Sources* continues to be cited in textbooks and articles today.[46] Written in 1929, it is also a transitional piece of scholarship lodged between biological and evolutionary explanations of religious affiliations and socioeconomic/materialist ones. First, like Weber and Troeltsch, Niebuhr suggested there were significant differences between the religious practices and beliefs of middle-class and lower-class groups. He asserted that the religion of the middle class was personal in character and, among other things, focused more on happy heavenly rewards than on millennial hopes.[47] The characteristics Niebuhr attributed to the religion of the lower classes in many ways replicated those asserted by the biologically deterministic scholarship seen in the last chapter. For Niebuhr, "the religion of the untutored and economically disfranchised classes has distinct ethical and psychological characteristics."[48] These included a focus on salvation and apocalypticism, as well as "intellectual naivete." The religion of the disinherited was also characterized by emotional fervor, because "where the power of abstract thought has not been highly developed and where inhibitions on emotional expression have not been set up by a system of polite conventions, religion must and will express itself in emotional terms."[49]

Second, Niebuhr showed that he was not completely removed from—nor against all—previous deterministic scholarship when he favorably quoted Werner Sombart's remark that not just cultural and socioeconomic but also biological and ethnological factors played a role in religious preferences.[50] The work Niebuhr cited, *The Quintessence of Capitalism: A Study of the History and Psychology of the Modern Business Man*, was Sombart's 1915 book that sought to trace the origin and growth of modern capitalism. "Either you are born a bourgeois or you are not," Sombart asserted. "It must be in the blood; it is a natural inclination."[51] A biological determinist, Sombart was also an anticapitalist and an anti-Semite who by the 1930s had affiliated with and published for the German Nazi Party. He claimed that some people, by genetic inheritance, made good capitalists. While he suggested that all Europeans had a "germ-capacity for capitalism," he also thought that it was unequally distributed.[52] Certain peoples, such as the Celts, were "under-inclined" to it.[53]

Religion, in addition to race and genes, featured in Sombart's theories. In contrast to Weber's later thesis connecting Protestantism and capitalism, Sombart argued that Protestantism "has been all along the line a foe to capitalism, and more explicitly to the capitalist economic outlook."[54] At the same time, he asserted that movements like Puritanism "unconsciously facilitated its growth."[55] Roman Catholicism offered some teachings that indirectly supported the growth of capitalism, but it was Judaism that provided all the "ethical regulations that were favorable to the development of the capitalist spirit."[56] In making this argument, Sombart managed to conveniently connect the two things—a group of people and an economic system—he disliked the most. In both *The Quintessence of Capitalism* and his earlier 1911 work, *The Jew*

and Modern Capitalism, he suggested that Jews were integral to the development of capitalism, being traders "due to blood inheritance" and having a religious ethic toward strangers that allowed for "unrestricted and unscrupulous
competition."[57] "While Christianity was yet held in bond by the Essene ideal
of poverty," he asserted, "Judaism did not reject riches; while the former was
filled with Pauline and Augustinian spirit of love, the latter preached a rabid
and extremist nationalism."[58]

Niebuhr cited Sombart twice in *Social Sources*, and both times he referred
to the same two pages from *The Quintessence of Capitalism*. But he also wrote
favorably of Weber's and others' works on the connections between capitalism and Puritanism, which casts some doubt on his assent to Sombart's capitalist thesis that downplays Protestantism.[59] At the same time, one section of
Social Sources suggests that Niebuhr may have agreed with Sombart about the
Jewish influence on capitalism. In discussing what he sees as John Calvin's
pro-bourgeois theology, Niebuhr suggests that the "Calvinist could build his
social ethics on the foundation first used by that other great entrepreneur, the
Jew; both were free from the inconvenient counsel of Jesus on wealth and the
devotion to mammon."[60] This comment resembles Sombart's argument and
is typical of distorting Christian apologetic attacks on Jewish ethics and belief. But Niebuhr does not suggest, as Sombart does, that Jews were capitalists
by blood. Instead, Niebuhr focuses exclusively on Jewish teachings lacking
Christ's proclamations. And whereas he does use Sombart to say that biology
is a factor in religious beliefs and practices, he never elaborates. What is clear
throughout the work is that Niebuhr fronts the importance of social and material conditions.

A final way that Niebuhr's *Social Sources* may be interpreted as a transitional piece between the biological and evolutionary theories of religion, on
the one hand, and cultural crisis and deprivation theories, on the other, lies in
its use of climate. As seen in the last chapter, writers such as Frederick Morgan
Davenport asserted that certain environments—hot, hilly, and so on—could
hinder human evolution and even lead to degeneration. While this argument
appears nonbiological, it was often accompanied by arguments of Lamarckian inherited characteristics. In other words, harsh climates could alter humans genetically over time, actually reversing or promoting evolutionary advancement. The explanation became less common as the twentieth century
progressed. Like the question of biological influence, Niebuhr was carefully
indeterminate in his discussion of climatic impact on religion. "Climate," he
noted, "is one of the factors which tend to reduce the religious attitudes and
the cultural heritage of immigrants to a common American pattern, but it is
difficult to determine the extent and character of its influence."[61] "The vari-

ability of North American weather conditions," Niebuhr suggested, "the extremes of heat and cold which succeed each other in the great plains of the West, the consequent stimulation of energy and nervous tension foster an activity which may not be without effect on an activist conception of religious life."[62] But at the same time, he argued, "the tendency toward activism has other, probably more important, sources."[63]

In addition to Niebuhr, two other examples from the 1930s well illustrate the transition from inherent tendencies to social sources. First, E. T. Krueger's 1932 *American Journal of Sociology* article, "Negro Religious Expression," can be compared to a work he cites, Frederick Morgan Davenport's *Primitive Traits in Religious Revivals* (1905), to show the move away from racial and evolutionary-based explanations of religion. As noted in the last chapter, Davenport argued that revivals were primitive manifestations of religion, usually enacted by evolutionarily backward races and classes of people. He referred to African Americans as a "child race" susceptible to revivals and given to "dense ignorance and superstition, a vivid imagination, volatile emotion, a weak will to power, small sense of morality," and other unevolved traits.[64] Davenport asserted that the civilizing slave system had "snatched" Africans out of savagery only a couple of centuries ago, which was little time "in the social evolution of any people, especially one whose early abode was in the African jungle beneath a tropic sun."[65] To Davenport, African Americans were, by nature and biology, a primitive race given to amoral—if not immoral—primitive religion.

Krueger's article in many ways replicated assertions made by Davenport. He wrote that African American religion featured "spontaneity, expressiveness, excitement, rhythm, interest in the dramatic, and love of magic."[66] Like Davenport, he observed that "the Negro is not greatly concerned with his own moral life nor in the intellectual aspects of dogma and the tenets of faith."[67] Instead, Krueger suggested, he preferred "in religious expression to submerge himself in the engulfing waves of ecstatic feeling produced in the religious crowd."[68] Also like Davenport, who argued that education had influenced the character of some southern blacks, Krueger asserted that changes had occurred in some African American religious communities, noting that "the Negro church today seems to be dropping many of these forms and making some of them less expressive and more formal."[69] At the same time, and also like Davenport, Krueger argued that "it is in the churches that are isolated or which include the lower and submerged classes that the traditional forms are chiefly retained."[70]

If one stopped after reading the first several pages of "Negro Religious Expression," one might see Krueger's work as merely a continuation of themes

and arguments from Davenport. But after describing some of the same characteristics of "Negro religion" as Davenport, Krueger proceeded to critique
biologically deterministic and evolutionary theories. First, "it is a mistake
to assume that Negro religious expression is wild and uncontrolled," he asserted.[71] "Such commonly used terms as emotional instability, hypnotic suggestion, emotional fury, and religious frenzy," he argued, "indicate that observers have failed to see that Negro religious expression follows well-defined
patterns and is heavily ritualized."[72]

After suggesting the failure of ethnographers to see structured patterns of
worship amid ecstatic activities, Krueger countered how the "peculiar quali-
ties of Negro religious expression have been variously explained."[73] Referring
directly to Davenport's thesis without naming him, Krueger noted that it was
common to view African American religious expression as a "primitive survival," implying "that the Negro is still in a primitive cultural state or that he
represents a lower or more primitive human biological order."[74] This view, he
asserted, had no corroborating evidence. Krueger argued that elements such
as the Negro spiritual were historically related to English and American revival spirituals, not African survivals. He dubbed the argument of racial inferiority suspect, noting that it relied on intelligence testing that was "open to
criticism in method, content, and interpretation."[75]

Another hypothesis Krueger considered was a variation of biological explanations concerning racial temperaments, one that claimed "that the Negro
possesses a racial temperament, innate in character, unlike that of any other
race."[76] This theory suggested that African Americans readapted white religion to suit their inherent temperaments. Krueger stated that the view had
"some advantage, especially if we assume that temperament is more cultural
than biological in origin."[77] In fact, he continued, "it can be argued that the
Negro's volatile disposition, his lightheartedness, spontaneous mirth, and
sensuous enjoyment are human-nature results of adjustment to social conditions and social role and do not represent anything essentially inherent except as they apply to the human, regardless of race."[78] In other words, while
assertions about "temperament" might partly be correct, they were only so if
temperament was seen not as "inherent" but as culturally and materially conditioned.

Krueger attacked biologically deterministic and evolutionary theories of
religious preferences. He also promoted a theory based on historically determined material circumstances. African American religious activities,
he argued, came directly out of the enslaved peoples' participation in white
religious revivals from the 1730s to the 1850s. "One cannot read first-hand
descriptions of these revival meetings," Krueger wrote, "without sensing im-

mediately that they possessed the same general character as Negro religious expression."[79] Negro religious expression came not from inherent biological tendencies but from historical interaction with white revivalists.

Krueger offered what would later be termed a deprivationist view when he suggested that "the Negro in slavery, uneducated and illiterate, with limited opportunities for social participation, almost hopelessly bound to an inferior status, found in the revival pattern a type of religious expression which met his need for escape and release from a constraint and an authority which was not so much harsh as it was mentally confining and constraining."[80] Furthermore, he continued, any lack of moral tradition in Negro religion came not from racial temperament but from the status inferiority brought on by the system of slavery. The revivals provided a "catharsis for repression," and the "traditional Christian picture" of the earth as a place for tribulation and heaven as a place where "all sorrow and suffering ceased" was one that "found ready acceptance by the Negro."[81] Religion was the African American's "form of escape, a way of securing relief and catharsis."[82] "We may even suggest," he concluded, "that the Negro's religion has aided in preserving his race from the decay and annihilation to which subject and minority alien races seem prone."[83]

In contemporary religious studies, arguing that religion is something that allows oppressed, exploited, and otherwise disprivileged people some consolation is somewhat out of favor—and for good reasons. Such functionalist explanations have historically tended to downplay the views of believers, suggesting that they are not conscious of the *real* reasons for their religious preferences.[84] They also have often suggested that the solace religion offers is a false one, failing to rectify problems with material solutions. But one must place Krueger's article both outside of these criticisms as well as within the context of its period. Krueger's suggestion that the material circumstances of slavery and the historical interactions in revivals fomented African American religious styles seems astute when set against the view that such religious preferences were fixed by inherited tendencies of biology and social evolution. In addition, Krueger's perspective that religion helped protect and preserve African Americans from their harsh material circumstances provided a far more positive picture of religion than more Marxian "opium of the masses" views seen in other contemporaneous studies.

A final example that illustrates the move from inherent tendencies to social sources is Anton T. Boisen's 1939 *Psychology* article, "Economic Distress and Religious Experience: A Study of Holy Rollers." Boisen was a well-known figure in pastoral care and counseling, whose lifework included being a rural church pastor, rural religion researcher for Warren Wilson, and a "mental" hospital chaplain. In the 1920s, he hospitalized himself twice in psychiatric wards. "Mental disorder it was, of the most profound and unmistakable variety," Boisen wrote, "and yet at the same time problem-solving experience."[85] Like the work of Niebuhr and Krueger, Boisen's can be usefully compared to previous scholarship. As someone trained in psychology and writing about Holiness and Pentecostal believers, Boisen traveled similar territory as Colgate University president George Barton Cutten and his 1927 *Speaking with Tongues, Historically and Psychologically Considered*. As seen in the last chapter, Cutten attacked glossolalia psychologically and theologically. Cutten asserted that persons of low mental ability and illiteracy were those most likely to speak in tongues, while "many cultivated persons have longed and sought earnestly for the gift, but without avail."[86] Like Davenport and his view of religious revivals, Cutten saw speaking in tongues as a "primitive experience, a reverberation of the very early days of the race."[87] Theologically, he saw it as "a detriment to pure religion, because it has furnished as a test for religious worth abnormal psychological experiences rather than a changed or an improved life."[88]

Just as Cutten had concerns with glossolalia, Boisen expressed reservations about Holiness and Pentecostal "Holy Rollers," whose faith he dubbed an "extreme form of mystical religion" that attracted the "underprivileged."[89] Boisen compared Holy Rollers to early Christians, asserting that both were from lower-class groups.[90] He also noted that both were given to emotional excesses, but the favorable comparison ended there when he added that, "along with these emotional excesses, the early Christians had insights that went far in advance of their time" as well as "wise leadership."[91] In addition, Boisen argued that Pentecostals were even possibly degenerate, writing that "Pentecostal churches undoubtedly belong in the group of the eccentric and even the regressive."[92] "Their fundamental assumption is highly dangerous," he continued. "They believe that the divine manifests itself in the unusual and that the prompting which seems to come from without is authoritative."[93] Even though such a belief might not cause "personality disorganization" or "commitment to a mental hospital," Boisen asserted, "that assumption is a false premise which is likely to produce all sorts of difficulties in groups as well as in individuals."[94]

In addition to lacking insights, wise leadership, and regressive tendencies, Boisen theologically faulted Holy Rollers for attributing ecstatic motor movements to the Holy Spirit and liturgically accused them of using "questionable devices" to induce religious experiences. Additionally, he criticized them for what might be described as a lack of theological cosmopolitanism. In a statement that recalls the rural church pastor/sociologist complaints about rural congregations seen in the last chapter, Boisen, the former rural church pastor and researcher, wrote that "one is impressed with the diminutive size of the universe which their message depicts."[95] Claiming that "it is only a little larger than that of the private world in which the psychotic lives," Boisen asserted that "it has no room in it for all that we have been finding out about stars and atoms and plants and men. It is merely a tiny world into which they may withdraw and feel themselves secure."[96]

A final criticism Boisen leveled on Holy Roller religion—one he listed next to last in his ordering of defects—was one that recurred in cultural crisis and deprivation theories about Pentecostals and others. He noted that "even though the Pentecostal sects arise among the underprivileged, their religion does not concern itself with improving the social and economic conditions."[97] Nothing in the Holy Roller message, he argued, "goes to the heart of problems of this sick and suffering world."[98] Instead, "they are content to let it get worse" and "have no social vision, no promise of social salvation except that which is to come miraculously when the Lord returns in his glory."[99]

Criticisms such as these resemble not only the scholarship that would follow Boisen but also that which preceded him. Much of his concern repeated the complaints that theologically and socially liberal and progressive Protestants had long voiced against theologically and socially conservative Protestants. Early twentieth-century social scientists, whether rural church sociologists such as Warren Wilson or the eugenicists Ellsworth Huntington and Leon Whitney, frequently connected "backward" people to backward, regressive religions. For such writers, these religions were invariably conservative in theology, yet ecstatic in liturgy and worship. Reading the list of Boisen's criticisms, one would be hard-pressed to see much difference between his views and those of someone such as Cutten.

Yet, despite his reservations about Holy Rollers, Boisen did depart from Cutten in significant ways. After elaborating his concerns, Boisen suggested that he still saw "constructive elements" in the movement. "With all their regressive features," he wrote, "these sects are none the less manifestations of nature's power to heal."[100] In general, he argued, "the rapid growth of eccentric religious cults in recent years may be regarded as a direct result of the shared strain due to economic depression."[101] Specifically, Boisen posited that Holiness and Pentecostal religion represented "spontaneous attempts of the common people to deal constructively with the stresses and trials which fall with peculiar severity upon them."[102] Furthermore, "their unconcern with economic and social conditions which they are powerless to change," which Boisen had previously criticized, "and their turning to problems for which they are directly responsible is not entirely an unwholesome reaction."[103]

For Boisen, like Krueger, religion offered a disadvantaged group "hope and courage and strength to keep going in the face of difficulties."[104] He suggested that the social and economic status of church members might even be raised due to their religion. Boisen's argument in "Economic Distress and Religious Experience" corresponds to his larger corpus of work, which asserted that dramatic religious experiences—even those replicating signs of mental illness—could be productive in an individual's life. But Boisen's argument was also representative of the growing propensity to see material conditions, like those produced by the Great Depression, as explanations for religious preferences. As seen in Holt, Niebuhr, Krueger, and Boisen, the idea that cultural crises and deprivations correlated to the popularity of certain religious beliefs and practices was applied broadly in the Depression-era 1930s and 1940s. African American religions, Methodism, early Christians, and particularly Pentecostal and Holiness churches were explained through tropes of culture shock and the stress accompanying lower-class status. But if there was one focus that "cultural crisis" theories had between the world wars, it was Native American new religious movements.

Deprivations, Autistic Religions, and Assimilation

On 28 November 1890, Alice Fletcher gave a talk at the annual meeting of the American Folk-lore Society titled "The Indian Messiah." Fletcher related the story of a young Cheyenne whose dream visions of replenished lost game, returned dead relatives, and the second coming of Jesus had spurred a pan-Native movement known as the "Ghost Dance." Prophets in the spreading movement suggested that Native Americans who took up the ritualized dance and followed the messiah would survive the approaching Second Coming, while whites and those shunning the Ghost Dance would perish. Fletcher noted that the belief in a "deliverer" was a "fundamental myth" of aboriginal Americans. "In the identification of the mythical deliverer with the Christ of the white race," she asserted, "we see the unconscious attempt of the Indian to reinforce the ancient hero of his myth with all the power of the God of the triumphing white man."[105]

Fletcher argued that the Ghost Dance "craze is confined almost exclusively to the uneducated."[106] Their idea of future happiness, she asserted, "would naturally imply the restoration of past conditions of life, and this would necessitate the absence of the white race."[107] For Fletcher, the "Messiah craze" presented a picture of folk suffering "in a rudely dramatic but pathetic manner."[108] "It is not likely that the 'craze' would have died out without any serious trouble," Fletcher suggested, "having been overcome by the quiet, persistent influence of the progressive and educated part of the people; but the non-progressive and turbulent elements have sought to use this religious movement for their own ends, while conjurers, dreamers, and other dangerous persons have multiplied stories and marvels, growing greater with each recital."[109] "Thus," she continued, "a distrust has grown up around the infected tribes, and a situation of difficulty and delicacy has come about."[110]

Thirty-one days after Fletcher's presentation, over two hundred Lakota Sioux Ghost Dancers were murdered by federal troops at the Massacre of Wounded Knee. The Ghost Dance movement had spread rapidly and had taken on a variety of distinctive forms and practices within different tribes. The Lakota had been the most resistant to the U.S. government's attempts to place them on reservations and had defeated General Custer at the Battle of Little Big Horn in 1876. They adopted the use of "ghost shirts" that they donned during dance rituals. The ghost shirt wearers had thought themselves invulnerable to the bullets of white soldiers. The "situation of difficulty and delicacy" Fletcher had spoken of a month earlier had become a tragedy.

Joel Martin, a historian of Native American religions, argues that "in the discourse of the contemporary study of religion, the Sioux Ghost Dance inevitably stands for a long series of revolts that emerged in other cultural contexts, times, and places."[111] In concurring with Martin, I would suggest that it has frequently been used as an example of a type of religious movement that resists change and ultimately fails, either in colonial or modernizing contexts. It is a representative example, in some scholarship, of the last breath of a dying and outdated religion and/or culture. In articles and textbooks on American religion, Martin notes, the Sioux version of the Ghost Dance is singled out from the larger movement and "all too often described in pejorative language that does not grapple with the movement's internal dynamics and motivations."[112] Furthermore, he argues that the Sioux movement is often placed in such texts next to the Handsome Lake movement, an earlier Native new religion that sanctified European and Christian values. "By juxtaposing a successful Handsome Lake movement and a tragic Sioux Ghost Dance," he writes, "the discourse implicitly celebrates accommodation and condemns resistance."[113]

While Martin's comments are directed at scholarship from the last several decades, the 1930s and 1940s studies under examination below also—and much more explicitly—showed concern with the acculturative and nonassimilationist elements of Native new religions. While the Sioux Ghost Dance did represent the "unsuccessful acculturation" to white colonialism in these studies, the Peyote Way stood in for Handsome Lake as the example of an acculturative movement. This new religion combines Christian and Native elements and was formally recognized by the federal government as "the Native American Church" in 1944. One notable ritual is the consumption of peyote as a sacrament. Peyote is a cactus containing nine different alkaloids, including mescaline. This makes it a class-A narcotic in the United States and led to the 1990 *Oregon Employment Division v. Smith* decision, in which the U.S. Supreme Court ruled that states are not required, but are permitted, to give exemptions to religious groups when their practices violate existing law.[114] The State of Oregon, the court ruled, could ban peyote use, even though it was the Native American Church's sacrament.

In addition to demonstrating a concern with assimilation and acculturation, the studies examined below followed the trend of other works discussed in this chapter by focusing on the influence of social and cultural change versus any inherent biological or evolutionary explanations. Here, the colonial relationship between whites and Native Americans—and the resulting loss of power and resources impacting Native cultures—were seen as primary factors in the development of the Ghost Dance and Peyote Way movements. This was believed to be so much the case that writers tied together religious beliefs and practices to cultural change in an almost mechanistic way. Messianic and nativistic movements appeared as inevitable responses to cultural crisis and deprivation. In addition, these studies followed the arguments of their contemporaries in that they interpreted certain religious responses to sociocultural stress as impotent and passive. The term "autistic" was used to describe Native religions that mentally removed participants from the harsh realities of colonization and conflict. Coined in 1912, the psychiatric term was used more broadly outside its field of origin to describe a state of being out of touch with reason and reality.[115] Before the 1960s, the term was often associated with schizophrenia. But in an interesting twist, these studies suggested that such passive, "autistic" religion was a positive thing when it involved potentially rebellious Indians. Finally, various terms were used in these works to describe the Native movements. Words like "messianic," "nativistic," "millenarian," and "crisis cults" referred to different groups, and subcategories were devised to describe types of nativistic or other movements. At the same time, these different categories and classifications were almost always explained in the exact same way: as responses to cultural crisis and deprivation. In what follows, I briefly examine three articles, spanning the period from 1935 to 1943, to illustrate these themes.

In 1935, Harold Lasswell published "Collective Autism as a Consequence of Cultural Contact." Lasswell's study, which focused on the Peyote Way movement among the Taos Pueblo Indians, began with what would later read like a classic cultural crisis and deprivation theory statement. "The carriers of one culture may be deprived or indulged in consequence of their contact with the carriers of another culture," he wrote. "Deprivations may take the form of inflicted loss, threatened loss, or denied advantage."[116] Lasswell asserted that the negative repercussions for the deprived group involved in such cultural encounter included violence, intimidation, and disillusionment. But he added that "sometimes the carriers of the culture which is blocked are able to adapt to changed circumstances with comparative smoothness."[117] "Such instances," he suggested, "are of special importance to political thinkers whose principal preoccupation is with orderly change."[118] Lasswell argued that for the Taos Pueblo, the adoption of the "peyote cult signified an autistic reaction to culture blocking."[119] Specifically, it dampened what Lasswell termed "ameliorates," meaning in this case the tribe's collectivism. Conversely, the Peyote movement promoted individualism. "Concessions to individualism have proceeded, therefore," he argued, "within the patterns adapted to indigenous Pueblo culture."[120] In illustrating his assertion, Lasswell detailed peyote usage and the visions it induced, which he suggested were "privately enjoyed in a mild state of dissociation," yet practiced in the "company of others, which is congenial to the collectivism of Taos."[121] "Having been blocked by individualistic cultures of superior fighting technique," Lasswell concluded, "Taos has been proceeding gradually and smoothly toward the incorporation of individualistic traits."[122]

Lasswell's argument must be placed within the context of the colonization and subjugation of Native Americans, especially in the late nineteenth century and the first decades of the twentieth. "Indian schools," such as Carlisle mentioned at the beginning of the chapter, were established to acculturate and assimilate Native Americans—in Pratt's phrase, to "kill the Indian to save the man."[123] Native children were taken away from their families and tribal communities and placed in boarding schools, many set up along the lines of the military/training school model established by Pratt's Pennsylvania school. As noted by the scholar Joel Pfister, one explicit ideology promoted in the Indian schools was individualism.[124] He refers to Carlisle itself as an "individualizing factory" at which a primary component of "Americanization" was "individualization." Believing Native Americans to be too "tribal" and collectivist for American society, Indian schools sought to create civilized citizens and workers by making Native children into "rugged individuals."

Lasswell's article was published seventeen years after Carlisle closed its doors. Yet the concern for assimilating "collectivist" Indians by making them more individualistic remained. Lasswell viewed the Taos Pueblo incorporation of "individualistic traits" through Peyote religion as one "proceeding gradually and smoothly." It did not seem to bother him that this process occurred through what he described as a "cult" that promoted "collective autism," a movement literally offering peyote for the Indian masses to ease their cultural stresses and deprivations. Rather than seeing such a supposed "flight from reality" as negative, Lasswell implied that Peyote religion provided a useful service to both the triumphing nation and the defeated Natives. By pacifying and individualizing a subjugated minority, Lasswell seemed to suggest, Peyote religion assured the survival of the Taos Pueblo and guaranteed "orderly change" and lack of resistance within the nation's boundaries.

Two 1941 articles by Harvard University's Bernard Barber used Lasswell's 1935 piece to sound similar themes. In "Acculturation and Messianic Movements," published in the *American Sociological Review*, Barber examined both the 1870s–90s Ghost Dances and the post-1890 Peyote Cult movements in relation to the Navaho. Like Lasswell, Barber argued that deprivation and "harsh times" struck some Native Americans due to contact with whites, which caused their "old set of social and cultural norms" to be "undermined by the civilized culture."[125] Concurring with Phileo Nash's 1937 argument about tribal propensities to take up "Nativistic" cults, Barber suggested that the tribes most deprived and suffering were the ones most likely "predisposed to accept a doctrine of hope" offered by messianic movements such as the Ghost Dance.[126] "Correlatively," he continued, "the tribes that rejected the doctrine were in a state in which the values of their old life still functioned."[127]

According to Barber, the Navaho had initially ignored the Ghost Dance because "there was no social need of a redeemer."[128] The tribe was not suffering intense deprivation. But suggesting that their deprivation levels had increased markedly in the last fifteen years, he noted that "anti-white sentiment" and "revivalistic cults have appeared," as well as "a great increase in recourse to aboriginal ceremonials on all occasions."[129] One "revivalistic cult" the Navaho had taken up was Peyote religion. Like Lasswell, Barber saw the cult as adaptive. "Whereas the Ghost Dance doctrine had graphically described a reversion to the aboriginal state," Barber wrote, "the Peyote Cult crystallized around passive acceptance and resignation in the face of the existing deprivation."[130] The Peyote Cult was an "alternative," he asserted, "which seems better adapted to the existing phase of acculturation."[131]

In his *American Anthropologist* article, "A Socio-Cultural Interpretation of the Peyote Cult," Barber elaborated on the acculturative aspects of the religion. He argued that in contrast to the Ghost Dance, the Peyote Cult performed "certain adaptive functions."[132] For leaders of the religion, it provided "prestige and status, serving as a path to advancement."[133] For the broader community of participants, it offered "a mechanism for the dissolution of individual anxieties and a mode of social control."[134] As opposed to the Ghost Dance, "the doctrine of the Peyote Cult was peaceful, in no way did it threaten the white culture."[135] In comparing the two, Barber suggested in a footnote that the Peyote Cult was "even more autistic than the Ghost Dance."[136] For Barber, as for Lasswell, this was apparently a good thing.

In Barber's articles, the appearance of "messianic" and "revivalistic" movements in response to cultural contact, crisis, and deprivation were deemed nearly inevitable. While he noted that "the messianic movement is only one of several alternative responses" to deprivation, he asserted that "in the other direction, the relationship is more determinate; the messianic movement is comprehensible only as a response to widespread deprivation."[137] Barber left it to post–World War II scholars to follow through with that thought by arguing that religions with messianic figures and hopes—and perhaps all religions in general—stemmed from deprivations and cultural crises. This is the next chapter's subject.

4 | *Visions of the Disinherited*

The Origins of Religion, Deprivation, and the Usual Suspects after World War II

The 1995 *HarperCollins Dictionary of Religion*, the American Academy of Religion volume edited by Jonathan Z. Smith, contains entries on "nativistic movements" and "revitalization movements." Of nativistic movements, the unnamed entry writer suggests that "the term has enjoyed extended usage in ethnographies and theoretical sociological studies adopting an unstated disdain for nonwhite cultures and their rejection of Eurocentric values or Christianity."[1] The term refers to those movements that conquered and colonized peoples enacted in order to preserve their culture. After noting that groups ranging from cargo cults and Ghost Dancers to Irish Celts and Pueblos have been labeled nativistic, the writer concludes that "the pejorative overtones of the term render it useless for modern discussion; it reveals more about the user than about the phenomenon so labeled."[2]

The entry on revitalization movements follows a similar trajectory. "Although concerns for renewal and reform exist at the heart of most religions," the writer suggests, "the identifications of such efforts as revitalization movements has generally been limited to studies of conquered or colonized tribal peoples undertaking the reestablishment of their own culture in a conscious, organized fashion."[3] Using some of the same phrasing as the other entry, the writer attributes the mid-twentieth-century popularity of the term to "first, simple xenophobia, expressed in disdain for nonwhite cultures and their rejection of Eurocentric values or Christianity, and, second, a resistance to extension of the rubric 'religion' to non-Western or non-Christian groups."[4] "Its pejorative connotations and irresolvable imprecision," the writer concludes, "leave revitalization movements a term to be avoided."[5]

The criticisms leveled against these concepts—while well-intentioned—are only partly accurate. Native American new religions were indeed the focus of the earliest studies of nativistic movements. At the same time, Christian groups attracting the poor and working classes, such as Pentecostalism, also received attention in closely related "cultural crisis" theories. On a subconscious level, xenophobia and the scholarly craving to restrict the meaning of "religion" may certainly have been at issue. But the fears of, and accompanying desire for, assimilating, acculturating, and anesthetizing the marginalized masses—whether Native American, African American, or poor white—could have been an even more pressing, if equally unacknowledged, concern. But such psychological interpretations can never be more than suggestive.

We can't conclusively "prove" what moods and motivations drive scholars to make their arguments. But we do know that after World War II academics such as Anthony F. C. Wallace and Weston La Barre expanded theories of nativistic movements and crisis cults beyond indigenous peoples, colonized tribes, and dispossessed groups to apply to "religion" in general. Even in his earliest conception, Wallace suggested that all religions started as revitalization movements. La Barre similarly argued that in the origins of the Ghost Dance we could spy the birth of all religions. In addition, the post–World War II era witnessed what might be described as the "triumph of the deprived." This entailed no class warfare, no emergent social egalitarianism, and no cultural power shifts. Rather, this coup took place in the academic—particularly the social scientific—study of religion. Deprivation theories of religion emerged from earlier cultural crisis, revitalization, and nativistic movement studies to become a major—if not *the* major—explanatory trope in the 1960s and 1970s. Like the theories from whence they materialized, deprivation models most frequently featured the usual suspects: the so-called sects and cults of the poor, minority, indigenous, and otherwise dispossessed.[6]

In this chapter I examine social scientific explanations of religious affiliations after World War II. The amount of scholarship in this period is overwhelming. I do not attempt a comprehensive analysis of all crisis, revitalization, cargo cult, deprivation, and related studies. Instead, I focus on a selection of them, picking and choosing some of the most influential and representative. I begin where the last chapter ended by discussing Anthony F. C. Wallace's and Weston La Barre's continued interest in Native American new religions. But such a focus merely served as the starting block in these scholars' sprints for the origins of religion. This quest for origins wasn't exclusive to Wallace and La Barre but extended to other 1960s writers such as Charles Glock. His theory of the pivotal role played by deprivation well reflected its time period. Simply put, deprivation theories satisfactorily explained a variety of religious groups for many 1960s scholars, popular writers, and journalists. In the case of Glock, deprivation was seen as affecting all classes and races of religious believers. One movement that garnered particular attention during this period—and throughout the twentieth century—was Pentecostalism. Writers of various backgrounds and interests suggested that the attraction to Pentecostalism stemmed from the demonic, the depraved, and especially the deprived. Such sustained interest demands at least a brief case study, which this chapter provides. I conclude by examining some critiques of deprivation theories, specifically the work of Virginia Hine, Luther Gerlach, and Joel Martin.

Revitalizations, Deprivations, and the Origins of Religion

Religion scholar Tomoko Masuzawa correctly notes that most of those engaged in the contemporary study of religion have seemingly pledged a "voluntary renunciation of the pursuit of origin."[7] In contemporary religious studies, the search for the origins of religion appears to be an antiquated feature of late nineteenth- and early twentieth-century scholarship. But the query did not disappear with the deaths of E. B. Tylor, James Frazier, Emile Durkheim, and Sigmund Freud. The question was still posed—and answered—by some in post–World War II scholarship. Such theories of religion's origins initially surfaced in studies of Native American new religions but later materialized in examinations of cargo cults, millennial movements, sects, new religions, and other groups that scholars deemed marginal enough to need explaining.

One influential and widely cited article was Anthony F. C. Wallace's "Revitalization Movements," which appeared in a 1956 issue of *American Anthropologist*. In it, Wallace defined a revitalization movement as "a deliberate, organized, conscious effort by members of a society to construct a more satisfying culture."[8] He noted that this classification included what had previously been described as nativistic movements, cargo cults, messianic movements, mass movements, social movements, utopian movements, and several others. He asserted that "all these phenomena of major cultural-system innovation are characterized by a uniform process, for which I propose the term 'revitalization.'"[9]

Wallace blended psychological and sociological levels of analysis by suggesting that, like an individual, society itself could be "regarded as a definite kind of organism, and its culture is conceived as those patterns of learned behavior which certain 'parts' of the social organism or system (individual persons and groups of persons) characteristically display."[10] The ideal state that organisms work to remain in, Wallace posited, is one of homeostasis. Any stress upon a living organism results in its taking coordinated action to return it to a stable state. Wallace argued that revitalization movements appear when a society and its individuals enter a period of increased stress. During such times the established "mazeways," or mental conceptions of one's society, culture, and self, become distorted and ineffective. This leads individuals and the

society as a whole into a state of anxiety, conflict, deviance, and deteriora-
tion. Prophets appear during this period of "cultural distortion" and offer new
mazeways. Stress levels are reduced when a majority of the society embraces
a prophet's mazeway. Once they are content with the conceptions offered by
the prophet's revitalization movement, individuals and the society as a whole
resume stable "steady states."

For Wallace, revitalization movements were "recurrent features of human
history."[11] But even more, he argued, the world's religions emerged from revitalization movements. "Both Christianity and Mohammedanism, and possibly Buddhism as well," he asserted, "originated in revitalization movements."[12]
Then he pushed the claim further. "In fact," Wallace posited, "it can be argued
that all organized religions are relics of old revitalization movements, surviv-
ing in routinized form in stabilized cultures, and that religious phenomena
per se originated (if it is permissible still in this day and age to talk about the
'origins' of major elements of culture) in the revitalization process—i.e., in visions of a new way of life by individuals under extreme stress."[13]

For Wallace, the origins of all religion could be found in revitalization
movements. In turn, stress constituted the origins of all revitalization movements. In an essay published one year after "Revitalization Movements," Wallace detailed how cultural and socioeconomic crises often fomented revitalizations. "There is a type of social movement," he wrote, "precipitated not
by physical disaster but by socio-economic pressures, some of whose aspects
have a similarity to the disaster syndrome."[14] In cultures suffering from colonization, economic depression, or other factors, "a social crisis is reached in
which many people feel acutely uncomfortable, and there may be overt symp-
toms of widespread personal and social disorganization . . . in such sick societies, it not infrequently happens that religious prophets arise."[15]

Wallace's post–World War II theory of the origin of all religion was not
alone. Weston La Barre was an anthropologist who, like Wallace, utilized
psychological explanations. He also resembled Wallace in proposing to find
the origin of religion in stress, crisis, and anxiety. La Barre was a Yale Ph.D.
whose work extended through sixty years of the twentieth century. He conducted ethnography in North America, China, India, and Bolivia.[16] Perhaps
best known for his studies of southern snake-handling Pentecostals and Native American Peyotists, in 1970 La Barre published *The Ghost Dance: Origins
of Religion*.[17] Concurring with Bronislaw Malinowski's suggestion that there is
no cult without a crisis, La Barre wrote in language that resembled pre–World
War II scholarship when he suggested that the Ghost Dance was "a typical
crisis cult in being a largely fantasized 'autistic' solution" to the Natives' problems.[18] But he argued more broadly than earlier scholars such as Bernard Bar-

ber and Ralph Linton in suggesting that the Ghost Dance revealed something essential about culture and religion in general. Referring to the Ghost Dance as an abnormal, "grotesque acculturational cult," La Barre asserted that its importance for "a general theory of culture can hardly be overestimated, since it is so often in the study of pathological functioning (as in medicine and society) that we gain insight into normal functions."[19]

La Barre's conception of culture and of religion's place in it closely matched Wallace's. First, La Barre similarly envisioned culture as an organism. "A society's culture is a set of defense mechanisms, both technological and psychological," he asserted. "If technical means fail to protect people against anxiety and stress, then psychological means must be fabricated to maintain homeostasis."[20] Also like Wallace, La Barre viewed crisis and stress as necessary prerequisites for "cults" such as the Ghost Dance. During anxious times, charismatic leaders appear and offer stress reducers in the form of religious movements. "What is interesting," he suggested, "is that religions are always tailor-made, projectively, to fit current individual and group anxieties."[21] La Barre mirrored Wallace when he suggested that "all religions, perhaps, began as crisis cults, the response of society to problems the contemporary culture failed to resolve."[22] The tentativeness a reader might have perceived in La Barre's use of "perhaps" quickly disappeared a few lines down the page when he more boldly stated that "each religion is the Ghost Dance of a traumatized society."[23]

For La Barre, all religions spawned from cultural crisis, and all religions were at heart pathological. "In unbearable crisis situations," he asserted, "religious prophets are culture innovators who are able to contrive new social forms and new symbolisms to keep all men in the society from going individually insane; but what a monstrous pathology is the new 'normality!'"[24] Later, La Barre clarified that his "parallel between sacred culture and neurosis is not an idle one."[25] Nor did he reserve the "religion as pathology" argument for indigenous, minority, or lower-class religions. Arguing that Christianity grew out of the cultural crisis of the declining Roman Empire, La Barre suggested that "our sacred culture is the ghost hovering over dead Graeco-Judeo-Roman cultures, the ghost dance of our forgotten past."[26] Because of this, he continued, "our most sacred beliefs are the group-neurosis of our traditional society!"[27]

La Barre and Wallace shared negative assessments of religion. In his 1966 work, *Religion: An Anthropological View*, Wallace proposed that modern advances in scientific knowledge signaled that "the evolutionary future of religion is extinction."[28] In the last paragraph of *The Ghost Dance*, La Barre expressed hope for much the same. Stone Age and Neolithic humans may have needed magic, he wrote, but "can not man now know and accept his nature and limitations with equanimity, and receive with cool confidence and gladly the legacy of his manhood, without any antic self-cosening ghost dance? Can Atomic Age Man afford any less?"[29]

In their search for and seizure of religion's origin, both Wallace and La Barre followed in the tradition of late nineteenth- and early twentieth-century scholars such as James Frazier, E. B. Tylor, and Sigmund Freud. These writers predicted religion's demise with the advance of science. Freud, for example, called religion "the universal obsessional neurosis of humanity" and suggested that science would replace it.[30] But rather than seeing the birth of religion in the Oedipus complex and an act of primordial cannibalism, as Freud envisioned, Wallace and La Barre spied its origin in individual and cultural crises, particularly those spawned among the most dispossessed classes of people.[31]

But not all post–World War II scholarship that found the origin of religion in crises and stress had such negative assessments. Another scholar who looked for the origin of religion—or in this case, its "necessary precondition"—was the sociologist Charles Glock. While Glock suggested that deprivation was necessary for religion, he did not condemn it to the cultural junk heap or attest to its neurotic nature.[32] In his 1964 essay, "The Role of Deprivation in the Origin and Evolution of Religious Groups," Glock argued that "a necessary precondition for the rise of any organized social movement, whether it be religious or secular, is a situation of felt deprivation."[33] In using the word "felt," Glock suggested that deprivation could be relative. In a 1960 conference paper, the anthropologist David Aberle defined "relative deprivation" as "a negative discrepancy between legitimate expectation and actuality . . . not a particular state of affairs, but a difference between an anticipated state of affairs and a less agreeable actuality."[34] For Aberle, in other words, those groups and individuals who have historically been materially deprived may actually be less likely candidates for—in Wallace's term—a "revitalization movement" because they have no expectations for anything better. Instead, it is among those whose status has changed and no longer meets their expectations that such movements may be most attractive.

Glock mirrored Aberle by including in his analysis those who felt deprived of something. But he also suggested that some may be unwittingly propelled into movements by deprivations they possess but are not consciously aware of. For Glock, deprivation could be either conscious or unconscious, material or imagined. "Deprivation," he wrote, "refers to any and all ways that an individual or group may be, or feel, disadvantaged in comparison to other individuals or groups or to an internalized set of standards."[35] "It is primarily the attempt, then," Glock suggested, "to overcome some of the deprivation that

leads to social conflict and may ultimately lead to the formation or a new social or religious group."[36]

Glock identified five kinds of deprivation "to which individuals or groups
may be subject relative to others in society."[37] The first, economic deprivation,
could be either objective or subjective. "The person who appears economically privileged on objective criteria," Glock explained, "might nevertheless
perceive himself as economically deprived."[38] The second, social deprivation,
involved the prestige, power, and status the society awards to individuals or
groups for having certain characteristics and withholds from others. Three
examples Glock suggested for the 1960s United States were the preferences
for male over female, white over black, and Protestant over Catholic. Glock
dubbed the third type of deprivation "organismic," and he related it to the dif-
ferential mental and physical health of individuals. "It would include," he suggested, "persons suffering from neuroses and psychoses, the blind, the deaf,
the crippled, and the chronically ill."[39] Glock defined "ethical deprivation" as
the state of an individual who feels that "the dominant values of the society
no longer provide him with a meaningful way of organizing his life, and that it
is necessary for him to find an alternative."[40] He asserted that it usually arises
when other forms of deprivation are absent. Glock's final deprivation was psychic, "primarily a consequence of severe and unresolved social deprivation,"
in which the "individual is not missing the material advantages of life but has
been denied its psychic rewards."[41]

Having established his five-part taxonomy and asserted that all organized
social movements stemmed from such deficiencies, Glock then connected deprivation to religious movements. His argument resembled that of pre–World
War II writers who suggested that religious movements were born when "real"
actions failed to repair the damage brought on by cultural crisis. He wrote that
"religious resolutions are more likely to occur where the nature of deprivation
is inaccurately perceived or where those experiencing the deprivation are not
in a position to work directly at eliminating the causes."[42] Religious movements, especially in cases of economic, social, and organismic deprivation,
"are likely to compensate for feelings of deprivation rather than to eliminate
the causes."[43] Particularly in the case of religious groups addressing economic
deprivation, he argued, the salve is symbolic, because the "latent resentment
against society tends to be expressed in an ideology that rejects and radically
devalues the society."[44] Glock compared such purely symbolic and seemingly
ineffectual religious movements to secular organizations, which he suggested
were more likely to eliminate the actual causes of the deprivations.

Glock defined the varieties of deprivation and marked those that provoked
religious responses. He also placed a number of religious groups into his taxo-

nomic scheme. Certain American religions could be classified by the deprivations from which they stemmed. "Healing cults," for example, addressed organismic deprivation, while denominations such as the African Methodist Episcopalians, ethnic Lutherans, and Conservative Jews responded to social deprivations.[45] Other groups, including the Christian Scientists and Father Divine's Peace Mission, simultaneously addressed multiple deprivations, including social, economic, organismic, and psychic.[46] Movements such as Theosophy and Vedanta tended "to draw their membership from the severely socially deprived middle-class" who exhibited psychic deprivation.[47] Another type, represented by the "Black Muslims" (Nation of Islam), "exemplifies the kind of religious movement which grows out of economic deprivation (with its accompanying social deprivation)."[48]

Glock argued that church participation—regardless of the specific denomination or social class—functioned to relieve social deprivation. While he noted that this assertion was mostly theoretical, he added that "what little empirical evidence there is, however, suggests that churches tend to gain their greatest commitment from individuals who are most deprived of the rewards of the larger society."[49] "Thus," he continued, "it is the less gifted intellectually, the aged, women, and those without normal family lives who are most often actively involved in the church."[50]

Glock did not replicate La Barre's and Wallace's predictions of religion's demise. Yet his view of it as a compensator for deprivations—one that was mostly ineffective at instituting "real" material relief—implied that religion was seldom if ever an agent of positive change. Written in the midst of the church-led civil rights movement, Glock's argument seems constricted. He did suggest—again in line with some pre–World War II writers—that religion "plays an important role in the maintenance of personal and social integration."[51] He also noted that religion served many functions beyond relieving deprivations. He wrote that his argument "merely confirms one claim which religions make: that those who accept the faith will be relieved of the cares of the world."[52] Perhaps. But whether such relief was symbolic, temporary, and false, or real, material, and demonstrable was the question upon which Glock and religious believers would have likely disagreed.

By arguing that some form of deprivation was a necessary (though not the only) precondition for all organized religious movements, Glock's theory potentially broadened the scope of study beyond Native Americans, the poor, and new religions. For Wallace, every religion was a revitalization movement. For La Barre, every religion was the Ghost Dance. For Glock, every American denomination, sect, and new religion stemmed from deprivation. Yet the deprivations and cultural crises of Unitarian-Universalists, Presbyterians, Congregationalists, and other, more elite denominations garnered less attention.[53] Instead, emergent post–World War II deprivation theories focused on the usual suspects.

Triumph of the Deprived: The Usual Suspects

Deprivation theories peaked in studies of religion from the 1960s through the 1970s. Glock's argument that religions appealed to those deprived, disinherited, or otherwise fraught with crisis and anomie was more typical than innovative. In many studies, religion was the salve, the peyote, and the opium of the masses. But unlike Glock, most writers stopped short of suggesting that every religion was a canopy sheltering the dispossessed. Twentieth-century religion scholarship moved from biological to sociological explanations of religious preferences. But the groups garnering attention, needing explanation, and holding the academic gaze remained the same. Scholars explained sects, new religions, and the religions of indigenous peoples, racial minorities, and poor and rural whites with deprivation theories—just as their predecessors had utilized biological and evolutionary schemes to account for the same groups. Whether marginalized by colonial conquest, racial and economic inequalities, or social and religious exclusion, the usual suspects featured prominently in post–World War II explanations of religious preferences.

As seen in the second chapter, Native Americans provided the primary focus for nativistic, messianic, and cultural crisis theories before World War II. Such attention did not disappear after the war. After all, both Wallace and La Barre started with Native American new religions in developing their broader religion theories. But postwar studies expanded and internationalized cultural crisis and deprivation theories. Other indigenous colonized groups—including those encountered in World War II by American and Allied soldiers in the South Pacific—garnered attention. David Aberle's relative deprivation theory, for example, used Navaho, Iroquois, and other Native American groups as case studies. But it appeared in an edited volume, Sylvia Thrupp's *Millennial Dreams in Action* (originally published in 1962 and re-released with a different subtitle in 1970), that included Melanesian, Jamaican, African, Brazilian, and historical European and Chinese groups. Another work from the same period—and with a similar cast of characters—was the Italian scholar Vittorio Lanternari's *Religions of the Oppressed: A Study of Modern Messianic Cults*.[54]

Peter Worsley's *The Trumpet Shall Sound: A Study of "Cargo" Cults in Melanesia* provides one good example of scholarship applying deprivation and cultural crisis theories to indigenous religions. Originally published in 1957 and revised in 1968, *The Trumpet Shall Sound* examined a variety of South Pacific new religious movements in which a prophet predicted the end of the world and the return of ancestors or supernatural beings. The prophet also urged followers to construct shelters or otherwise prepare to receive the "cargo" the new era would provide. The term "cargo" referred to the literal freight that war planes dropped or late nineteenth-century missionaries left, such as food, tools, and clothing. But "cargo" also referred to less material forms of wealth, such as harmonious community and family relations.[55]

Dubbing Melanesian cargo cults "millenarian," Worsley defined the term as one that described "movements in which there is an expectation of, and preparation for, the coming period of supernatural bliss."[56] He expanded the discussion beyond Melanesian indigenous religions to account for most of the "usual suspects." Worsley argued that millenarian beliefs have recurred throughout history in every time and place, "precisely because they make such a strong appeal to the oppressed, the disinherited and the wretched."[57] He suggested that millenarianism could incite a revolutionary movement and posited that in "backward regions of Melanesia" it had a dynamic character.[58] But he also asserted that "where millenarism survives in countries with popular secular political organizations, it is generally escapist and quietist."[59] One such country was the United States, where "millenarian cults represent an escapist, passive trend and are principally confined to backward communities within the wider society: the White woodsman and the Negroes of the southern states of the USA or the frustrated urban Negro population which has thrown up figures like Father Divine."[60]

Such an assertion, complete with references to "backward communities," conjures the biological and evolutionary arguments early twentieth-century scholars proposed. Due to genetic deficiencies or low position on the human evolutionary ladder, such theories asserted, "backward" people were naturally attracted to "backward" religions. But Worsley saw no biological or evolutionary machinations at work. He argued, for example, that the "proliferation of Negro religious cults is not a product of any 'inherent religiosity.'"[61] Instead, he found the "cause" of black cults in the lack of participation African Americans were allowed in other American institutions. The factors Worsley identified were social.

But Worsley's argument that the religions of the American disinherited were passive and offered psychological balm in place of direct political action certainly mirrored earlier writers. Recall that Harold Lasswell, for example, named religions "autistic" when they did not stimulate remedial activism to allay deprivations. As seen in Glock's work, Worsley was not a lone voice in the postwar period. In asserting the passivity of American sects, Worsley quoted Elmer T. Clark's *Small Sects in American Christianity*, a 1949 work that was revised and published as *The Small Sects in America* in 1965. Clark was just one of dozens of religion scholars, journalists, and popular writers who found American sects and "cults" to be products of deprivation.

Following the church-sect typology built by Ernst Troeltsch and developed by H. Richard Niebuhr, Clark argued that all denominations began as sects and that in "the background of nearly all sects there is an economic influence."[62] Specifically, "these groups originate mainly among the religiously neglected poor, who find the conventional religion of their day unsuited to their social and psychological needs."[63] Clark's narrative of sect formation was essentially Niebuhr's: complacent, middle-class churches fail to address the needs of their lower-class parishioners, who then break off to form a sect of the disinherited. In these sects, members "elevate the necessities of their class—frugality, humility, and industry—into moral virtues and regard as sins the practices they are debarred from embracing."[64] Sects are thus "refuges of the poor."[65]

The cover of Clark's 1965 revised edition pronounced the book "an authentic study of almost 300 little-known groups." Averaging out to about one sect per page, Clark's scope ranged broadly. Seventh-Day Adventists, Negro Methodists, Quakers, Pentecostals, Father Divine, Shakers, Black Jews, Hard Shell Baptists, and the Temple of Yahweh were just a few of dozens that he listed in the chapter descriptions. While great attention to historical and theological detail would have been impossible for so many groups in a 256-page book, Clark's suggestion that "in the main features sects are much alike" meant that they could all be similarly classified and explained.[66] In fact, he asserted that "some sects are so nearly identical that the impartial student is unable to discover any differences, and in the case of many the differences are trivial."[67] As refuges for both the poor and, in Clark's terms, "the emotionally starved," the historical, theological, and ritual variations of different groups were explained away as irrelevant variations that all functioned to address deprivation.

Clark not only described the functions of all sects with the same theory but also indicted them with the same charge. He made the familiar critique that sects offered little more than a bandage to cover the gaping wounds of deprivation. "It is a strange fact," Clark wrote, "that these sects of the poor make little or no attempt to ameliorate the condition of their adherents."[68] He complained that they had no social reform plans, refused to work with labor, and dissuaded members from voting. Instead, they looked to ethereal solutions, "and they expect God to reward them in the world during the millennium or in heaven after death."[69]

Clark's arguments on the connections between sects, new religions, and socioeconomic and other deprivations was typical across many fields from the

1950s through the 1970s. Scholars of religion, religious apologists, and popular writers all argued that sects and cults were havens for the poor and deprived. For example, in *Challenge of the Sects* (1961), the mainline Protestant apologist Horton Davies suggested that sects should be conceived of and explained as "churches of the disinherited."[70] Yet Davies included, without caveat, chapters on Christian Scientists and Theosophists, both of whom had mostly middle- and upper-middle-class Cold War membership.[71] Writers for mass markets sounded the same trumpet. In *Faiths, Cults, and Sects of America: From Atheism to Zen* (1960), Richard Mathison asserted that cults were often "refuges for the poor" and that "unfortunates can turn away from the world and from a cult draw hope that some cosmic mechanism will in the near future place them above the rich and powerful."[72] For such dispossessed folks, "the immediate destruction of the world or the second coming are particularly attractive prospects."[73] Jehovah's Witnesses, for example, were "downtrodden and uneducated," while Elijah Muhammad attracted poor blacks from the worst slums for his "Black Muslim" movement.[74]

For some writers, it wasn't just the poor, but particular kinds of poor, who joined sects and cults. Mathison, for example, asserted that the newly poor were particular targets for "cult leaders." The cult's "strongest appeal is not to the abject poor who have never known better times but to the 'new poor' with memories of power, comfort or even wealth."[75] In arguing this, Mathison cited Eric Hoffer, a former longshoreman turned pop sociologist. In his influential 1951 book, *The True Believer*, Hoffer asserted that those most likely to join any mass movement were not the "abject poor." Hoffer claimed that the downtrodden of inner-city slums remain "smug in their decay" and "shudder at the thought of life outside their familiar cesspool."[76] Nor did mass movements appeal to the "creative" poor or those impoverished who had strong family ties. Instead, it was "usually those whose poverty is relatively recent, the 'new poor,' who throb with the ferment of frustration" and "respond to every rising mass movement."[77]

Such arguments were not just the province of popular writers. As seen in Aberle and Glock, some scholars suggested that the feelings of deprivation leading one into a religious movement were sometimes relative to individual expectations. Psychologist E. M. Pattison asserted that sects practicing faith healing and glossolalia particularly appealed to the "marginalized middle-class," while sociologist Gary Schwartz posited that Adventists and Pentecostals were made up of those precariously perched between the lower and middle classes.[78] But regardless of the precise economic place of their memberships, sects and new religions were consistently depicted as havens for the deprived.

In addition to indigenous peoples and sectarian and new religious movements, other minority religions—particularly African American ones—remained the usual suspects explained through deprivation and cultural crisis theories. As seen in Glock and in Clark, even the African Methodist Episcopal Church and Black Baptists were explained via deprivation models. But the theory was especially prominent in accounting for new religions attracting African Americans. In 1960, for example, the liberal Protestant *Christian Century* titled an editorial "Despair Serves Purposes of Bizarre Cults." In it, the unnamed writer suggested that poverty and inequality drove black Jamaicans to Rastafarianism and black Americans to the Nation of Islam. Like the "gaunt, ragged, sickly people" of Kingston, the writer asserted, "our own great cities are spotted with 'Back-to-the-Wall' slums in which desperate people will turn to any leader who offers escape."[79]

As I have argued elsewhere, the Nation of Islam's fiery racial rhetoric, critique of Christianity, and demographics made it a menacing specter of otherness for predominantly white, middle- and upper-middle-class journalists.[80] The new religious movement, which combined millennialist Evangelical Protestantism, Islam, and the prophecies and proclamations of founder W. D. Fard and leader Elijah Muhammad, also garnered scholarly attention. Nation of Islam members—largely first- and second-generation southern migrants to the North who were both African American and poor—made it an obvious target for deprivation explanations by writers such as Glock, Clark, and Mathison. In *Black Muslims in America* (1961), C. Eric Lincoln utilized deprivation-style motifs and Hoffer's "true believer" typology to argue that the movement "represents one attempt to break out of this bondage of discrimination and despair, which threatens the peace and casts a dark shadow over the happiness and prosperity of all America."[81] For Lincoln, the poverty and related deprivations driving blacks into the Nation of Islam resulted from historical white racism and inequality. He was not alone in this assessment. In an article appearing three years after Lincoln's book, James Laue suggested that the Black Muslims were best viewed as a revitalization movement.[82] Seeing a new religion filled with frustrated individuals desiring access to what white Americans had, Laue interpreted the Black Muslims in light of Anthony F. C. Wallace's theory. "Just as the emergence of the Peyote cult offered a more readily syncretic alternative for frustrated and hostile American Indians," Laue argued, "so the Lost-Found Nation of Islam presents today a workable and sufficiently flexible identity for an ever-expanding group of militantly disenchanted Negro Americans."[83]

The final usual suspect appearing in post–World War II deprivation theories was the poor rural white. The bane of the rural church sociologists discussed in chapter 2, rural whites remained in the eye of postwar scholars and writers on religion. In the mid-to-late 1960s, for example, minister Jack Weller continued several trends discussed in the second chapter. First Weller, like Frederick Morgan Davenport, concentrated his focus on rural white Appalachia. Second, Weller's observations—while presented as ethnography—emerged from his pastoral position in a West Virginia Presbyterian Church. Like Warren Wilson, Weller was a mainline Protestant pastor placed into a geographic region filled with Evangelical, Pentecostal, and otherwise non-mainline Protestants. Compared to Wilson, however, Weller's assessment of what he observed was far less negative. What Wilson had attributed to genetic deficiency, Weller ascribed to socioeconomic and other material circumstances. Recall that Wilson argued that rural revivalism could be attributed to the high percentage of "morons and inferior humans" and the "domination of the subnormal" in the countryside.[84] For Weller, the Appalachian mountaineer lived in "a tight environment and an economy that denied him room to develop freely."[85] Such conditions meant that "for many people their only escape is religion, the church, the flight from the cold reality around them, the emotional binge."[86] "I am indeed no follower of Karl Marx," noted Weller, "yet I understand plainly his thesis when he notes that the economic factor has a central place in the determination of the character of all areas of life, including the religious area."[87]

Weller argued that religion functioned to temporarily release rural Appalachians from their hellish existence. "For many people among the dispossessed," he wrote, "religious services provide the way to escape life for a few hours, the way to find a fleeting glimpse of hope, joy, and release in the midst of a life of despair, sadness, and grinding bondage."[88] Given this, he did not view ecstatic religious practices as signs of depravity. Instead, Weller asserted that "emotional explosions in church no doubt keep many a man or woman sane."[89]

Weller's assessment did not have the sting of Wilson's. Nor did his affirmation of Marx include adopting a Marxian critique of religion. At the same time, his descriptions shared much with earlier writings. The title of Weller's 1965 book, *Yesterday's People: Life in Contemporary Appalachia*, suggested a group suffering from cultural, technological, and religious lag in a modernizing world. The Appalachian religion scholar Deborah McCauley argues that theologically liberal Protestants in particular "historically and consistently interpreted the worship practices, belief systems and church traditions of mountain people as the religion of a subculture of poverty and the product of powerlessness and alienation."[90] Weller's work would seem to fit this description. He described mountaineer religion as traditional, fatalistic, and individualistic. He suggested that it was "a crutch for times of trouble but is not much use in daily life."[91] Finally, Weller's descriptions of mountaineer beliefs and practices as ignorant and superstitious resembled those of George Cutten, Warren Wilson, H. Richard Niebuhr, and other earlier writers. Explaining the propensity toward Fundamentalism, he asserted that "never having been trained in the use of words, or in the understanding of subtle differences between ideas, mountain people have never appreciated anything but a simple literalistic belief in the Scriptures."[92] He also suggested that rural Appalachians viewed the Bible as "a magical book," one revered, though misquoted to suit "common prejudices."[93] In fact, Weller claimed, "such use of the Bible, coupled with the mountaineer's individualism, results in a folk religion, not in a Biblical Christianity."[94] This folk religion was self-centered and "based on sentiment, tradition, superstition, and personal feelings, all reinforcing the patterns of the culture."[95] While he explained the religion of "yesterday's people" through the idiom of socioeconomic deprivation, Weller's conclusions shared much with those earlier writers who used biological and evolutionary analysis. Viewing rural white Appalachian religion as fatalistic, otherworldly, and socially passive, Weller implicitly condemned it.[96]

The use of socioeconomic deprivation theories to explain rural white religious preferences geographically extended beyond Appalachia into the rest of the United States. Such theories also stretched in time beyond the 1960s and into the 1990s. In 1993 it was initially not a specific religion, but rural white Fundamentalist belief in underground satanic cults, that garnered sociologist Jeffrey Victor's attention. During the 1980s and early 1990s, small-town newspapers across the United States reported rumors about local, underground satanist groups who mutilated animals, desecrated cemeteries, and left cryptic graffiti on the walls of abandoned farmhouses. Rumors also spread that the groups threatened to abduct and sacrifice children. On occasion, parents and other citizens reacted to these rumors by keeping children home from school and patrolling the streets. Victor identified sixty-two of these panic-inducing rumors in the United States from 1982 through 1992.[97] In every case, investigators found no evidence to support the rumors. In explaining why some believed them, Victor was one of a number of sociologists, folklorists, and criminologists who suggested that the rumors had roots in cultural crisis and socioeconomic deprivation.[98]

Victor argued that the rumors about subversive satanic cults should be viewed as contemporary legends that symbolically revealed the communities' anxieties over socioeconomic stress and the breakdown of nuclear family structures. In making this argument, Victor shared some of the ambivalence toward the rural population demonstrated by earlier rural church sociologists. He asserted that Fundamentalism, combined with an unquestioning patriotism, led rural whites to deflect blame away from the government for socioeconomic inequalities. Thus, "economically stressed blue-collar workers are those people who are most likely to believe the Satanic cult rumors."[99] In other words, Victor suggested that deprived, rural, white Fundamentalists believed that satanic cults were threatening them because they couldn't psychologically admit that their government had abandoned them. Similar to Jack Weller's "yesterday's people" and, from chapter 2, Louis Binder's "backward communities," Victor viewed working-class, rural, white Fundamentalists as those particularly troubled by modernity, pluralism, and change. Alienated and feeling powerless, believers in satanic cults embarked on a moral campaign, one that was "essentially a symbolic crusade aimed at the reaffirmation of traditional cultural values of obedience to family and religious authority."[100] Conversely, Victor argued that those critical of such rumors were "groups of people who hold modernist values, or at least, people who don't feel threatened by contemporary social change."[101]

Whether the focus was on rural whites, African Americans, sects, new religions, or indigenous peoples, many postwar writers explained their beliefs and practices through deprivation theories. In these interpretations it was a lack or deficit of some kind—social, economic, psychological, cultural—that attracted people to certain religions. Once in the movement, members found symbolic succor for their woes, but no real material relief from their deprivations. Instead, in the eyes of many scholars, it was as if the usual suspects had ingested a placebo, a false cure that shielded them from identifying and ameliorating their real troubles.

Explaining God's Peculiar People: Visions of Pentecostalism

Among the usual suspects, one specific religious movement dominated scholarly literature. It is no exaggeration to suggest that one could trace the twentieth-century history of theories of religious affiliation by singularly focusing on Pentecostalism. Many of the scholars examined in this and previous chapters made Pentecostalism a focal subject. Some, such as John Holt, carefully described Pentecostal theology.[102] Others—one immediately thinks of George Barton Cutten in his 1927 volume *Speaking with Tongues*—seemed unaware that the people they discussed and explained were Pentecostals. To give a thorough narrative of the ways scholars have envisioned Pentecostalism would fill a book. Here, I instead offer a skeletal outline of three trajectories that explanations of Pentecostalism followed. The first, the demonic, generally came not from academics but from religious detractors who suggested that gifts of the spirit, such as speaking in tongues, were signs of demonic possession. Examples include Alma White, the Holiness minister and Ku Klux Klan apologist. In her book *Demons and Tongues*, she sought to uncover Pentecostalism's "satanic Tongues delusion."[103] The second line of explanation, the depraved, included interpretations by earlier writers such as Cutten. This line of theory asserted that those who spoke in tongues and demonstrated charismatic gifts of the spirit did so because of inherent intellectual inferiority, bad genes, evolutionary backwardness, or some other biological deficiency.

The third line of interpretation—and the one most pertinent to this chapter—was the deprived. As noted by the historian Grant Wacker, "the presumption that Pentecostalism arose as a more or less functional adaptation to social and cultural disequilibrium has acquired the status of an orthodoxy."[104] Sociological, historical, and psychological studies concurred in suggesting that Pentecostalism was a religion of the dispossessed. Such arguments were based upon a combination of factors, including the movement's history and practices. Pentecostal rhetoric, which often touted the movement's pariah status in the world, also fueled deprivation theory's fire.

Pentecostalism formed in the first few years of the twentieth century.[105] The movement "officially" started in 1901 at Charles Parham's Bethel Bible College in Topeka, Kansas. But it garnered national attention through 1906 press coverage of William J. Seymour's multiracial Azusa Street Temple congregation in Los Angeles. The Azusa Street Revival, as it came to be known, attracted journalists and the curious who wanted to see the reported divine healings, dancing in the spirit, and speaking in tongues. It also attracted religious seekers from all over the country. Coming from Holiness and other congregations, many of these visitors took the new Pentecostal faith home with them. Thus a small, but visible, movement was born.

The historian Edith Blumhofer has dubbed the theology of one early Pentecostal denomination "Fundamentalism with a difference."[106] In other words, the Assemblies of God, as well as many other Pentecostals, shared much with Fundamentalists. Both were biblical literalists, more often than not held premillennialist views of history, and espoused moral codes that promoted social conservatism and a general wariness toward the world. But the difference was significant enough that it made Fundamentalists the most strident historical opponents of Pentecostalism. Pentecostalism's distinction entailed a focus on gifts of the spirit, especially speaking in tongues. Many—but certainly not all—early Pentecostals came out of Holiness backgrounds. Based in the writings of John Wesley and emerging from the mid-nineteenth-century Methodist movement, Holiness believers held to a doctrine of "Second Blessing," also called "Entire Sanctification."[107] This was the belief that there is a distinct, postconversion event (thus a "second blessing") that makes individuals free of all voluntary sins. Starting with Parham, early Holiness Pentecostals contended that Baptism of the Holy Ghost was a sign of the Second Blessing. But more important for the movement, Baptism of the Holy Ghost was physically evidenced by speaking in tongues.

Pentecostals originally thought that speaking in tongues—also referred to as "glossolalia"—was the God-given ability to speak in a foreign language unknown to the orator. This is called "xenoglossia." Grant Wacker notes that this early interpretation changed to the view that the "tongues" being spoken was usually not a foreign language, but instead a divine one imparted to the believer by God.[108] Pentecostals looked to the biblical verses of Acts 2:1–4 to support their belief in tongues and 1 Corinthians 12–14 to support their belief in the gifts of the spirit. Along with "unknown tongues," that passage lists eight other gifts: wisdom, knowledge, faith, miracles, prophecy, discernment of false spirits, interpretation of tongues, and healing. While Pentecostals found all of these important, speaking in tongues was of primary concern to even non-Holiness Pentecostals.

By the end of the twentieth century, Pentecostalism was the fastest-growing style of Christianity in the United States and the world. Wacker notes that over two hundred different Pentecostal groups now dot the American landscape.[109] The movement comes in a variety of theological forms. In addition to Holiness Pentecostals, who adhere to the doctrine of the Second Blessing, there are "finished work" Pentecostals, such as the Assemblies of God, who deny a second, distinct postconversion experience of Entire Sanctification. Pentecostals also divide between Trinitarian and Oneness believers, the latter being those who do not believe that God manifests as a tripartite being. Another branch of the movement that today consists of only several hundred members are snake-handling Holiness Pentecostals. Mostly restricted to southern Appalachia, these believers look to verses in the King James Version, Mark 16:17–20, which among other things, suggest that the faithful shall take up serpents and drink poisons. Despite their small numbers, snake-handling Holiness Pentecostals have garnered much scholarly and journalistic attention.[110] Finally, beginning in the 1960s, Pentecostalism influenced the birth of the charismatic movement. Charismatics, who may be independent Evangelicals, Roman Catholics, or mainline Protestants such as Episcopalians, embrace the Pentecostal view that the gifts of the spirit are accessible to contemporary believers and should be sought.[111]

Two aspects of Pentecostalism attracted scholars who used deprivation and cultural crisis theories. First, ecstatic ritual practices, such as speaking in tongues, dancing in the spirit, and faith healing, drew those researchers who argued, in the spirit of the anthropologist I. M. Lewis, that "possession works to help the interests of the weak and downtrodden who have otherwise few effective means to press their claims for attention and respect."[112] The second aspect of Pentecostalism garnering scholars' attention was the movement's demographics. Famously dubbed "the vision of the disinherited" in Robert Mapes Anderson's book of the same title, scholars viewed Pentecostals as society's dregs. Early journalistic accounts blended exoticism, class stereotypes, and folkloric rumor. One 1906 newspaper, for example, warned that local Pentecostals were planning child sacrifices.[113] As noted by Wacker, marginalization was not purely an outsider's perspective. Pentecostals often used a rhetoric that stressed their pariah status. Sometimes, he argues, Pentecostals "repeatedly emphasized their own social marginality."[114] At other times, they "went out of their way to stress the respectability of their social placement."[115] In accounting for Pentecostalism, scholars inevitably focused on the marginality and ignored the cases of respectability. They also ignored the fact—stressed by Wacker—that early twentieth-century Pentecostals looked much like a "typical American" of the time: largely lower- or working-class.[116]

Deprivation theories appeared in sociological, historical, and psychological studies of Pentecostalism. As seen in this and previous chapters, the list of scholars utilizing deprivation theories to discuss Pentecostalism is long. From the 1940s through the 1970s, John Holt, Liston Pope, Elmer Clark, Gary Schwartz, and a plethora of others suggested that the movement appealed especially to the deprived. Even scholars who criticized their peers' explanations sometimes left the deprivation aspect of their accounts untouched. For example, in 1961 the sociologist Benton Johnson attacked the view that "Holiness sects" functioned as an opium that offered "underprivileged groups an emotional and otherworldly escape from the realities that beset them."[117] Instead, he suggested that such groups actually presented a tangible remedy, namely, "the socializing of marginal, lower class groups in the values commonly called middle class, or more broadly, in the dominant, institutionalized values of the larger society."[118] But in answering the question, "what impels individuals to become members of Holiness sects?" Johnson agreed with his peers that "there is likely to be an experience of heightened frustration or deprivation."[119] Concurring with John Holt's assertion that those attracted to Holiness and Pentecostal groups were rural agrarians thrust into urban industrial modernity, Johnson wrote that the theology of the Holiness religion "enables the lower class individual to deny that he is really on the bottom in any meaningful sense."[120]

Johnson's view that Pentecostalism functioned to assimilate members into American middle-class society was similar to Bernard Barber's and Harold

Lasswell's assessments of Native American new religions discussed in chapter 3. All three agreed that certain movements could assist in the process of assimilating disinherited populations. For Barber and Lasswell, Peyote religion could work to acculturate defeated and collectivist Native Americans into the colonizer's more individualistic culture. For Johnson, "Holiness sects" assimilated the rural white poor into American middle-class values. Peyote religion also functioned to quell the potential for revolt. While Johnson did not suggest this for the Pentecostals he dubbed "Holiness sects," others did note how the movement seemed to prohibit labor organizing and class insurrection. Johnson's critique of Pentecostalism as an escapist fantasy would be a minority one for many years. Instead, deprivation theorists continued to assert that movement participants remained unconscious of their own motivations and ineffective in remedying their ills.

Deprivation theory played a framing role in Robert Mapes Anderson's historical narrative, *Vision of the Disinherited: The Making of American Pentecostalism*. Pentecostalism, he argued, "may be viewed as one small part of a widespread, long-term protest against the whole thrust of modern urban-industrial capitalist society."[121] But unlike Benton Johnson, Anderson saw the religious part of this protest as ineffective. "Pentecostalism," he argued, "deflected social protest from effective expression, and channeled it into the harmless backwaters of religious ideology."[122] The most thorough history of Pentecostalism of its era, *Vision of the Disinherited* told what had become a familiar story of the rural agrarian poor who were thrust into an urban industrial environment, experiencing this culture shock and its accompanying deprivations amid a national economic decline. Such material circumstances made a group of people who were already predisposed to join an ecstatic millennialist movement doubly primed. "For the Pentecostals, as for many adherents of similar religious movements," Anderson suggested, "ecstasy was a mode of adjustment to highly unstable circumstances over which they had little or no control."[123] Glossolalia and other physically demonstrative behaviors, he posited, were in part responses to harsh material conditions, which they could do little to ameliorate. "When men cannot adjust to their environment by reason and action," he wrote, "they fall back upon symbolic manipulation and the inner world of desire and imagination."[124] Similar to his assessment of ecstatic worship practices, Anderson saw millennialist belief as "inimical to the real life interests of the Pentecostals."[125] In sum, he concluded that "the radical social impulse inherent in the vision of the disinherited was transformed into social passivity, ecstatic escape, and finally, a most conservative conformity."[126]

Psychological studies, like sociological and historical ones, used deprivation theories to explain Pentecostals. Many of these blended socioeconomic
deprivation models with psychoanalysis. Weston La Barre—perhaps unsur-
prisingly, given his argument about the origins of religion—found a mixture
of sexual repression, the Oedipal complex, and harsh material circumstances
at work in the Holiness Pentecostal snake-handlers of the North Carolina
piedmont. Referring to the largely mill-worker membership of a Durham-
area church, La Barre suggested that these "rural primitive tribesmen" demonstrated a psychopathology in handling phallic snakes.[127] Key to La Barre's
analysis were the unconscious motivations that drove believers. "The pain-
ful thing to us, who are accustomed to a higher degree of sophisticated self-
awareness," La Barre confided in his readers, "is that because of the pressures
of their sadly neurotic and archaic and unhappy culture, these people have to
have what satisfactions they can without any psychological self-possession,
without any knowledge of who they are, and what they are like, and what they
are really doing."[128]

Psychologist William Wood, like La Barre, mixed social and psychological
deprivation theories in his 1965 study of southern Pentecostals in a place he
dubbed "Hilltown." Wood's main tool of analysis in *Culture and Personality
Aspects of the Pentecostal Holiness Religion* was the Rorschach test, in which
individuals were asked what they see in a series of ink blots. Among his conclusions, presented as thirteen distinct hypotheses, "Hypothesis VII" stressed
that "Pentecostalism attracts uncertain, threatened, inadequately organized
persons with strong motivation to reach a state of satisfactory interpersonal
relatedness and personal integrity."[129] To demonstrate that Pentecostals lacked
such things as "an adequately structured value attitude system," Wood added
to his Rorschach test findings several observations. Apparently unaware that
Christian testimonials for centuries had followed set narrative structures that
required such things as preconversion wretchedness, Wood presented as evidence the fact that believers testified publicly in church and privately to him
that their previous lives had been unhappy.[130] To this he also added that Pentecostal homes and neighborhoods seemed particularly "disorganized," adding
that "social disorganization occurs frequently with personality failure."[131]

Similar to Johnson, who suggested that the movement might provide an
inroad into middle-class values, Wood believed Pentecostalism might function to alleviate some psychological problems. With tentative phrasing, Wood
asserted that "if I conclude that Pentecostalism attracts persons seeking organization within themselves and between the persons, attitudes and values
in their socio-cultural environment and that it has something to offer these

persons in satisfying their drives, then Pentecostalism is a potential solution to some of the personality problems which are a by-product of certain socio-cultural conditions."[132]

La Barre's and Wood's work on Pentecostals appeared in the 1960s. But even one later psychological study that explicitly critiqued deprivation theories concluded by proposing what amounted to one. In his 1984 article, "Glossolalia and the Psychology of the Self and Narcissism," John Donald Castelein focused on the Pentecostal and charismatic practice of speaking in tongues. He argued that "glossolalists can no longer be viewed as suffering from psychopathological disorders or from sociological deprivation."[133] Castelein, who reported that he had spoken in tongues for about a year "on a daily basis," asserted that studies of glossolalia suggest that it "is not limited to any economic, educational, racial, social, or religious group in any one geographical area or century."[134] But after discounting theories of psychopathology or socioeconomic hardship, Castelein replaced them with another deprivation. Speaking in tongues, he argued, "profitably may be seen to function as a therapeutic practice for people who predominantly already have a conservative religious background but suffer from narcissistic disorders."[135] Specifically, "by means of speaking in tongues they seek to integrate their deficient self (frustrated in the modern secular world), by reacquiring a vivid experience of what they believe to be the supernatural."[136] Castelein, who resembled Anton T. Boisen in his biographical connection to his subject, found a new deprivation: the narcissistic, deficient self. And like Wood and La Barre, Castelein mixed a bit of depravity back into Pentecostalism's vision of the disinherited.

Not everyone, of course, viewed Pentecostalism solely as a haven for the demonic, depraved, and deprived. Despite their pariah rhetoric, Pentecostals themselves obviously saw things differently and responded to critics in sermons, books, and other media. A common Pentecostal/charismatic apologetic involved charging the critics with weak, inauthentic, and overly intellectualized faith. In *Quenching the Spirit* (1992), for example, William De Artega asserted that those who deny the authenticity of gifts of the spirit, such as speaking in tongues, belong to the "perennial heresy" of "Pharisaism."[137] Arguing that such detractors have been present throughout Christian history, De Artega suggested that "the Pharisees restrict the flow of spiritual experiences until religion becomes a purely intellectual and theological exercise, and the Spirit is quenched."[138]

Not just Pentecostals but also some scholars have taken exception. As noted above, the historian Grant Wacker critiqued deprivation theories by suggesting that early Pentecostals demographically resembled the rest of the United States. If they suffered deprivations, it was from the same harsh material conditions faced by the majority of early twentieth-century Americans. One can also identify a trajectory, starting in the 1960s, of scholarship examining glossolalia from cultural and neuroscience perspectives. Such studies as Felicitas Goodman's *Speaking in Tongues* (1972) were more interested in the physiology of glossolalic utterances and how it was culturally "learned."[139] But the earliest general critiques of deprivation theories came from two University of Minnesota scholars who focused on Pentecostalism.

Deprivation's Critics

Deprivation theories of religion were prominent after World War II. But they also had their critics. Critique proceeded along two paths. First, some argued that deprivation theories were simplistic and almost impossible to test. They reduced religious belief and practice to a single variable, ignoring the complex interaction of factors at play. Second, some scholars critiqued deprivation theories for denying religious participants any agency. Deprivation schemes often suggested that individuals were attracted to religious movements because they were compelled by forces outside their control and consciousness. In this view, religious people did not know the *real* motivations that led to their commitments. Ostensible belief in the truth of a particular theology or ritual was secondary to the often veiled needs wrought by deprivation. These two streams of criticism often combined. But many critics of deprivation theories refused to dismiss them outright, suggesting that deprivations likely played a role in religious preferences.[140]

Early criticism of deprivation theories in the 1960s and 1970s came from two scholars, the University of Minnesota anthropology professor Luther P. Gerlach and his former graduate student Virginia H. Hine. Their focus was Pentecostalism, but they went beyond their specific subject to attack deprivation theory in general. Both contributed chapters to Irving Zaretsky and Mark Leone's large 1974 volume of social scientific studies, *Religious Movements in Contemporary America*. In "Pentecostalism: Revolution or Counter-Revolution?" Gerlach argued that the logic of deprivation theories was circular and depended upon the misrecognition of believers as to their true motives for commitment. "How do we know," Gerlach queried, "that people are sufficiently deprived, disorganized, devitalized, or defective enough to join or start a movement or a sect?"[141] "Easy!," he sarcastically answered himself. "You know that they have reached this condition after they do join or start this activity."[142] "If an informant explains his religious behavior and the growth of the movement as the will of God," Gerlach continued, "the typical anthropologist smiles knowingly and searches for the 'real reason.'"[143]

Gerlach argued that the "real" reason the anthropologist discovered depended upon whom he was studying:

> If the "subjects" of his study are those anthropology once called primitive and now call peasants or "peoples of . . . ," then he displays a commitment to cultural relativity, and explains their behavior as eufunctional or some such thing. If the "subjects" of his study are North American, but are members of a racial minority group or have not yet made it into "the middle class," then he explains their behavior as a consequence of deprivation or disorganization. And if they are "normal" middle class in all but religious behavior, then he explains their behavior as a consequence of personality defect.[144]

In an examination of American and Haitian Pentecostal and charismatic groups, Gerlach suggested that factors other than deprivation played an important role. These included movement organization, recruitment techniques, group ideology, perception of opposition to the group, and the processes by which people commit to the group. Gerlach argued that studies have tended to see religion more as a product of social and individual change than as a producer. Yet, he asserted, it can be both. "Religion can serve as a force to generate personal transformation and revolutionary social change," he wrote, "or as a force to maintain the existing social order and provide therapy to reintegrate persons into this order."[145]

In the same volume, Virginia Hine contributed another sustained critique. In "The Deprivation and Disorganization Theories of Social Movements," Hine focused on three explanatory schemes. Disorganization theories looked for the causes of religious commitment in personal and societal disorder. These included cultural crisis theories. Deprivation models, Hine suggested, were nearly universal in studies of ecstatic and emotional religions. The third, the deviant/defective individual model, suggested neurotic and even psychopathological sources of belief and practice. Using the same data as Gerlach, Hine argued that these theories failed to explain participation in Pentecostal groups. Well, almost. While Hine suggested that Pentecostal membership could not be explained through economic, disorganization, or pathological models, one particular form of deprivation figured into the argument. "It may be said," Hine wrote, "that relative deprivation of status, or power as we have defined this concept, is associated with participation in the Pentecostal movement."[146] At the same time, she suggested that power deprivation should not be seen as causing this religious preference but rather "facilitating" it.[147] She concluded that "a far more satisfying explanation of an individual's conversion to Pentecostalism as well as other types of movements can be found in a study of recruitment patterns."[148]

Gerlach's and Hine's chapters were based in a larger project focusing on Pentecostal and Black Power movements, published in 1970 under the title *People, Power, Change: Movements of Social Transformation.*[149] Their concentration on the ways social movements—including religious ones—can effect individual and cultural change appeared at a time when many social events and intellectual currents converged. The 1960s and early 1970s saw the birth of organized social movements protesting the Vietnam War, fighting for the equal rights of women, and continuing the struggle for African Americans' civil rights. In addition, some Catholic and Protestant theologians had begun to embrace social activism. Beginning with Roman Catholics in Latin America and later moving into some U.S. Protestant and Catholic theological discourse, liberation theology asserted that Christianity was a religion of the oppressed and that its job was to actively ameliorate the social inequities and injustices causing such oppression. In 1970, for example, theologian James Cone argued that his black liberation theology arose from the oppressed status of African Americans. "The task of black theology, then," wrote Cone, "is to analyze the nature of the gospel of Jesus Christ in the light of oppressed blacks so they will see the gospel as inseparable from their humiliated condition, and as bestowing on them the necessary power to break the chains of oppression."[150] Given such discourse, Gerlach's and Hine's scholarship, with its embrace of "power deprivation," seems partly a product of its time.

But Gerlach's and Hine's critiques of deprivation, disorganization, and "defective individual" theories continue to be pertinent. They pointed out the circularity of such models. They criticized deprivation theory's exclusion of variables like recruitment techniques and social networks. Within their work one can also see how such theories are unable to account for those who fit the "deprived" demographic but do not belong to the movement in question, or conversely, those who do not meet the characteristics yet are group members. Contemporary criticisms of deprivation theories continue to include citations of Hine's and Gerlach's contributions. For example, Stephen Cook's critique of deprivation explanations of biblical apocalyptic texts cites Hine several times.[151] Other examinations of Pentecostalism have also used Gerlach and Hine to argue against deprivation theories.[152]

In addition to Pentecostals, other usual suspects such as Native Americans have garnered attention from deprivation's critics. The historian Joel Martin, for example, has offered an alternative, nondeprivationist interpretation of one Native American prophetic movement. In *Sacred Revolt* (1991), Martin examines a Native American religious group that emerged, like the later Ghost Dance and Peyote movements, out of the colonial situation created by white invasion. On 27 March 1814, an army of thousands of whites, Cherokees, and Muskogees surrounded the Native town of Tohopeka in central Alabama. Within the town limits resided one thousand Muskogee rebels, known as "Redsticks" because of their painted tomahawks. By the end of that day, over eight hundred rebels were dead and their millennialist movement was squelched.

Martin suggests that his goal in understanding the Redstick revolt is "to appreciate the Muskogees as subjects of their own history and ultimately to grasp how and why a great number of them came to rebel against the United States and fight at Tohopeka."[153] In doing this, Martin elaborates on the prophetic visions of cosmic renewal and the enactment of certain rituals that gave "meaning to significant acts of rebellion."[154] He argues that the revolt should be viewed as a collective rite of passage "performed on a grand scale."[155] Occurring in a complex situation of intense cultural contacts, pan–Native American movements, the newly received visions of some Muskogee shamans, and a portentous series of earthquakes, Martin argues, the prophetic movement was an act of purification that initiated Muskogee participants into what was becoming a new social, economic, and symbolic world.

Criticizing the view that colonialism and the deprivations that came with it were the sole causes of the Muskogee movement, Martin stresses the creativity and power that new rituals and shamanic visions offered. He acknowledges that his argument faces seemingly contradictory observations from the comparative study of other Native American prophetic religions. Following a trajectory identified by scholars such as Wallace, La Barre, and others, such movements usually occurred a couple of generations after initial contact with Europeans, emerged in the context of full-fledged colonialism, and positively correlated with a period of severe depletion of food, land, and other resources. Martin agrees that "colonialism may have been a necessary precondition of these movements" but adds that "colonialism and the deprivation that colonial relations produced were probably not the only causes."[156] After all, he notes, most Muskogees faced deprivation, but only some chose to join the movement and participate in the revolt. Given this, Martin asserts that positive factors of human agency—such as creativity—played a role in commitment. "In addition to the land loss and game depletion," he suggests, "we should also call attention to the impact and power of new visions, visions discerned through ecstatic contact with spirits of water, earth, and sky, and amplified in communal discussions."[157]

Martin charges that deprivation theory "focuses so narrowly on negative experiences that it neglects to consider that these movements may have been motivated by positive experiences, visions, and hopes, some derived from the contact context, others springing from renewed connection with tradition, and still others supported by new modes of pan–Native American coopera-tion."[158] He also asserts that deprivation models deny the human agency, and thus the humanity, of those they explain. His argument, in contrast, "affirms the full humanity of Native Americans by assuming that they were much more than victims of history—they were also actors in it."[159]

By factoring human agency and creativity into the Redstick revolt, Mar-tin refuses to simplistically reduce a Native American religious movement into a predictable reaction to harsh material deprivation and cultural crisis. At the same time, he judiciously does not deny that the Muskogees—though actors with agency—were thrown into a play that they had not chosen to be in. This is crucial. In attempting to give voice and agency to the oppressed and marginalized, deprivation theory's critics risk downplaying the violence of constraint and habit forced upon subjects by material conditions—condi-tions imposed upon them by colonizers, enslavers, and laissez-faire capitalist markets. To propose an alternative to the deprivation, cultural crisis, evolu-tionary, and biologically deterministic theories examined in the first part of this book, we must find a language with which to discuss the complex connec-tions between human agency, cultural constraint, material conditions, social locations, and religion. This is something I hope to have modestly begun work on in the first chapter and will return to in the conclusion. In the next section I initiate the process of putting some class back into the interdisciplinary study of American religions.

Part II

Putting Some Class
in American Religion

5 | Some Theologies of Class in American Religious History

Throughout this work I have argued that class matters in the study of religion in general and American religions in particular. Such an assertion begs the question of how one goes about studying class and religion. In the first chapter I proposed a three-part conception of class that is potentially useful for the study of religion. In part 1 of the book, I suggested that a cultural history of the study of American religion reveals how "class" was tied to classifications and explanations of religious preferences. In the next chapter I present an ethnographic study that fronts possible interactions between religion and class at the congregational level. This chapter reflects my initial attempt at identifying some recurrent religious explanations of social differentiation in American history. I call these cosmologies, some of which are explicit and systematic and others that are implicit and fragmentary, "theologies of class."

Specifically, in this chapter I name and describe four recurring theologies of class in American religious history. The first, which I call "divine hierarchies," is closely tied to Calvinist predestination and suggests that socioeconomic differences are divinely ordained. The second, "economic Arminianism," emerges amidst nineteenth-century Evangelicalism, Republicanism, and the development of industrial class relations. Asserting that all human beings have the free will to progress in both religious and financial endeavors, economic Arminianism is the most dominant class theology today and can be seen in movements as variant as the prosperity gospel and New Age channeling. The third recurring theology, "social harmony," was represented in many Protestant Social Gospel writings as well as a Roman Catholic statement on labor and capital, Pope Leo XIII's *Rerum Novarum*. With roots in antebellum notions of the ideal society as a "harmony of interests" among differentiated unequals, proponents of this class theology argued that laborers and capitalist owners in the emerging industrial economy shared mutual, rather than opposing, interests and goals. While some criticized Gilded Age robber barons for their exploitative practices, adherents to this view consistently upheld capitalism, private property, and profits as biblically sanctioned. The fourth theology, "the class-conscious Christ," took a rather different view. Espoused by some Gilded Age supporters of the working class, this theology envisioned Jesus as champion of laborers and enemy of capitalism. Rather than a harmony of interests, proponents of the class-conscious Christ viewed labor and capital relations as inherently conflictual. At times, they even envisioned such conflict as a literal battle between good and evil.

In identifying these four recurrent theologies of class, I broaden the term "theology" beyond explicit treatises on the nature of God (or gods) and the universe, to include more implicit and less methodical visions of the world and the supernatural orders revealed in nineteenth-century labor song-poems, early twentieth-century motivational sermons, and twenty-first-century channeling websites. Whether book-length works or short songs, these sources are textual and focused on the social order. But, as the religious studies scholar R. Marie Griffith has argued, theologies are not mere textual abstractions; they are also disciplinary implements literally inscribed onto our bodies. In *Born Again Bodies: Flesh and Spirit in American Christianity*, Griffith states that religion "has been central to the creation of American bodies."[1] Contesting previous scholarship that ignores religion's influence on modern American views of and obsessions with the body, Griffith examines religious conceptions of the corporeal body from early modern Puritans to contemporary devotional diet literature. She argues for the influence of New Thought and Evangelical Protestantism, suggesting that religious fascination with the body has not been one of repulsion, as some previous studies have asserted, but rather one of its regenerative possibilities. Making one's body new, or "born again," correlates with the belief that physical bodies mirror the state and true character of one's soul. The connection of inner character and external appearance, Griffith notes, makes the body a historically contested site in which race, gender, and class figure prominently.

Taking Griffith's arguments to heart, I end the chapter by posing the question of how theologies of class might also be embodied. I do this by comparing Peter Cartwright's and Charles Grandison Finney's interpretations of antebellum ecstatic religious behaviors. In brief, I suggest that their differing conclusions on what constituted "authentic" and "inauthentic" physical manifestations during the Second Great Awakening revivals may be partly attributed to emerging class differences. These could be seen in shifting attitudes toward emotional control and acceptable bodily gestures in the mid-nineteenth century.

Caveats

In addition to describing here what I argue, I must also offer several caveats about what this chapter does not do. First, my focus departs from the two most traveled paths in examining class in American religious history. The first route asks the question of whether "religion" has been supportive of or oppressive toward labor and the working class in American history. Much of this scholarship has been inspired by the cultural Marxism of scholars such as E. P. Thompson, whose classic study *The Making of the English Working Class* suggested that certain religious theologies—specifically Methodism—ambivalently tended to support the status quo while simultaneously being "indirectly responsible for a growth in self-confidence and capacity for organization of working people."[2]

In the American context, the answers to this question have been similarly ambivalent and mixed. For example, Paul Johnson argued in *A Shopkeeper's Millennium* that antebellum revivals in Rochester, New York, aided the ownership class to the detriment of working people. The Evangelicalism of the Second Great Awakening revivals, Johnson contended, "was order-inducing, repressive, and quintessentially bourgeois."[3] He asserted that Evangelical revivalism's belief that "every man was spiritually free and self-governing enabled masters to present a relationship that denied human interdependence as the realization of Christian ideals."[4] A somewhat more nuanced view can be seen in Herbert Gutman's study of Protestantism and labor in the Gilded Age. Gutman concedes that much support of laissez-faire capitalism can be found among nineteenth-century religious leaders. But he adds that Protestantism, along with Republicanism, was one preindustrial "tradition" that "especially offered the discontented nineteenth-century American worker a transcendent and sanctioning 'notion of right.'"[5] Similarly, Ken Fones-Wolf has examined how post–Civil War Philadelphia workers used religion to critique capitalism, while William Sutton has described how antebellum Evangelical journeymen workers in Baltimore had a variety of responses to the developing market economy, ranging "from reluctant assimilation to violent rejection of industrial capitalism."[6] Stepping outside of such Protestant-focused scholarship, Evelyn Savidge Sterne has suggested that in Rhode Island, Providence's Catholic churches provided crucial spaces for labor and political organizing among working-class and immigrant communities in the late nineteenth and early twentieth centuries.[7] In sum, these studies reveal that simple statements about the relationship between religion and labor cannot be made. Simply put, religion played a significant role in both promoting *and* obstructing labor concerns in the nineteenth and early twentieth centuries.

A second and somewhat related path taken by studies of class in American religious history examines and debates the influence of religion in developing class distinctions and class consciousness among what would become nineteenth-century working- and middle-class Americans. Historian Jama Lazerow, for example, detailed the influential religious culture of antebellum working-class New Englanders.[8] Looking at the same era and region, Teresa Anne Murphy argued that "religion and reform structured the discourse of labor activism in antebellum New England and distinguished it from labor movements elsewhere."[9] Mark Schantz has similarly suggested that religious culture "played a decisive role in the process of class formation in antebellum Providence, Rhode Island."[10] While this research trajectory, like the previous one, asks interesting questions and provides useful case studies, in this chapter I move away from such foci and instead make an initial attempt at identifying some recurrent religious explanations of social differentiation.

A second caveat acknowledges, but contests, the criticism that by using "theologies of class" I utilize a term to describe the ideas of people who had no concept of "class." But this criticism is only true if one embraces the very narrow, Marxist-infused, definition of class I argued against in the first chapter. New England Puritans and even early Jacksonian Americans usually did not distinguish classes by position within the means of production.[11] At the same time, no single group or period in American history existed without a language of social differentiation. In tracing social taxonomies in Revolutionary and nineteenth-century America, Martin Burke examines how "class" eventually replaced terms like "orders," "ranks," and "sorts."[12] While the word "class" may not have entered the English language until the early 1600s, terms of social differentiation existed long before.[13]

The final caveat addresses the critique that my theologies of class typology is selective and ahistorical. For example, one could accurately posit that too many of my examples are dead white male Protestants, while another could charge that any of my theological categories—if one grants that they could be said to exist at all—could change dramatically over time and in particular contexts. I concur to a point with these criticisms, but it is not my intention here to produce a thorough historical analysis of change over time that describes the subtleties of argumentation within one category, or the changing conceptions over time in one individual author. Instead, my goal here is to provide an intentionally broad and unsubtle starting point for discussion and debate. By using a Weberian "ideal typology" of theologies of class, I hope to open a heretofore absent conversation on recurring religious explanations of social differentiation in American history, not make any final or complete statement on the subject.

Divine Hierarchies

Many American religion textbooks include discussions of—if not quotations from—John Winthrop's 1630 "Model of Christian Charity" sermon. The Puritan lawyer gave the exposition aboard the *Arbella*, a ship filled with English Puritans and docked at what would become the Massachusetts Bay Colony.[14] Because it includes references to the passengers being entered into a covenant with God to act as a "city upon a hill" with "the eyes of all people upon us," Winthrop's sermon has been used in texts as representative of, in the words of the historian Edwin Gaustad, the "characteristic features of the 'Puritan mind' and 'the New England way.'"[15] But in stressing the covenant theology and self-perception of Puritans as God's New Israel, most textbook writers ignore Winthrop's opening lines, in which he succinctly states that God had established a divinely ordained social hierarchy. "God Almighty in His most holy and wise providence," Winthrop began, "hath so disposed of the condition of mankind as in all times some must be rich, some poor; some high and eminent in power and dignity, others mean and in subjection."[16] Much of the sermon that followed detailed the reasons for such social differentiation. As such, it serves as one of the best examples in American religious history of the theology of class I call "divine hierarchies."

First, Winthrop suggested that God produced a differentiated and unequal human society "to hold conformity with the rest of His works, being delighted to show forth the glory of His wisdom in the variety and difference of the creatures and the glory of His power, in ordering all these differences for the preservation and good of the whole."[17] In other words, Winthrop's view—and the Calvinist New England Puritan view, inasmuch as Winthrop could be said to partly represent it—was that God had ordered the cosmos along the lines of distinctions, hierarchies, and varieties. In what is, in effect, an early precursor to the nineteenth-century "harmony of interests" conception of society, inherent inequalities and differences promote the general good and advance God's earthly work.

The second reason Winthrop mentioned for God's divine hierarchy was that inequality allowed God to "have the more occasion to manifest the work of His Spirit: first, upon the wicked in moderating and restraining them, so that the rich and mighty should not eat up the poor, nor the poor and despised rise up against their superiors and shake off their yokes."[18] Being a Calvinist predestinarian, Winthrop's conception of agency was more focused on God's desire to impart different types of grace onto individuals of different stations than it was on any human free will to act morally. Thus, divinely ordained inequality between individuals allowed God to exercise "His graces in them—as in the great ones, their love, mercy, gentleness, temperance, etc., in the poor and inferior sort, their faith, patience, obedience, etc."[19] As David Chidester notes in what may be the only textbook discussion of this passage, Winthrop was asserting that "different virtues were appropriate to different stations in life."[20] While the rich could, with God's grace, practice love and mercy, the poor saints were preordained to develop patience and obedience.

Winthrop's third reason for divinely ordained hierarchy repeated the emergent harmony of interests conception, suggesting that "every man might have need of the other, and from hence they might be all knit more nearly together in the bond of brotherly affection."[21] "From hence," he continued, "it appears plainly that no man is made more honorable than another or more wealthy, etc., out of any particular and singular respect to himself, but for the glory of his creator and the common good of the creature, man."[22] "This harmony of mutual need," comments Chidester, "served to weave together a unified religious community."[23] He adds that "it is also clear that such a theocentric solution justified a hierarchy of needs and gave religious aura to social inequalities."[24]

While I strongly concur with the majority of Chidester's sermon analysis, I suggest that rather than being a mere "religious aura" rationalizing social differentiation, Winthrop's theology of divine hierarchies must be acknowledged as an inherent part of his religion. The divine origin of social inequality has long standing in Christian history. As noted by Gary Day, Augustine suggested that human inequalities stemmed from Adam and Eve's "Fall" in the Garden of Eden. "From that fateful event," Day writes, "came the division of mankind into masters and servants, the institution of private property and its consequent inequalities, and the impossibility of ever realizing a truly harmonious society without the need for laws."[25] It is certainly likely that Winthrop's sermon—given before the faithful set foot upon the soil of their new community—was a reminder to listeners to keep to their stations because the Massachusetts Bay Colony would not be communal, egalitarian, or democratic. But it was also a message deeply embedded in the heart of his Puritan theology.[26] Indeed, most of the notable conflicts in New England Puritan history—whether the 1630s "antinomian" controversies, the later Quaker persecutions, or the 1680s clergy crackdown on lay folk practices—involved charges that individuals were overstepping the bounds that God's divine hierarchy had allotted them.[27]

In some ways, the Calvinism of the New England Puritans appeared to have an "elective affinity" with the theology of divine hierarchies. Their predestinarian beliefs suggested that God made humans with no free will to act on their own. Before the world existed, God had determined who would be rich, poor, saved, and damned. All were dependent upon God's grace, and if it was offered, none could resist it. At the same time, if you were divinely destined to deprivations on earth and hell after death, there was similarly nothing that could be done. The other three theologies of class I examine here appear after the rise of Evangelical Arminianism during the Second Great Awakening and include some notion of free will. But the theology of divine hierarchies did not disappear with the decline of Puritan Calvinism. I suggest that a transformed theology of hierarchies reappeared with particular force in Gilded Age assertions that social inequalities and class distinctions were part of the natural evolutionary order and necessary for the progress of humanity.

The social Darwinism of the Gilded Age, closely related to the early twentieth-century eugenics writings discussed in the second chapter, asserted that social differentiation was biologically based. In other words, the genetically less-endowed were those most likely to be poor, while the richest reflected the best genetic stock. An example of this "scientistic" theology of class can be seen in Andrew Carnegie's famous 1889 essay, "The Gospel of Wealth."[28] An atheist, Carnegie presented what might be described as the naturalistic and nondeistic version of fellow robber baron John D. Rockefeller's famous statement "God gave me my money."[29] Inequality, for Carnegie, was essential for human progress. "The contrast between the place of the millionaire and the cottage of the laborers with us today," Carnegie wrote, "measures the change that has come with civilization."[30] "It is well, nay, essential," he continued, "for the progress of the race that the houses of some should be homes for all that is highest and best in literature and the arts and for all the refinements of civilization, rather than that none should be so."[31] For Carnegie, the self-made millionaire son of working-class Scots from Dunfermline, the law of capitalist market competition provided the tool by which humanity evolved. He acknowledged that such a "law may be sometimes hard for the individual" but posited that "it is best for the race, because it insures survival of the fittest in every department."[32] Natural selection in human evolution, rather than any God, provided the agency in Carnegie's hierarchical theology of social differentiation.

Though differing over the existence of supernatural powers, both Winthrop's theology of divine hierarchy and Carnegie's evolutionary "survival of the fittest" explanation of social differentiation posited that the machinations of class inequality lay outside of individual human agency. While Winthrop asserted that God determined one's social status, Carnegie's self-made men apparently succeeded because they were the most biologically fit. One point over which Carnegie and his Puritan forebear differed, however, was on the proper relations between rich and poor. Winthrop suggested that humanity's divinely ordained hierarchy required those at the top to provide charity and support for those on the bottom, so that "every man might have need of the other, and from hence they might be all knit more nearly together in the bond of brotherly affection."[33] Carnegie's social Darwinism conversely led him to assert that "one of the serious obstacles to the improvement of our race is indiscriminate charity."[34] In Carnegie's historical imaginings, "civilization took its start from the day when the capable, industrious workman said to his incompetent and lazy fellow, 'if thou dost not sow, thou shalt not reap,' and thus ended primitive communism by separating the drones from the bees."[35] He suggested that in "bestowing charity, the main consideration should be to help those who will help themselves."[36] Thus, Carnegie the philanthropist funded the building of 2,800 libraries and numerous educational endowments with the view that "those worthy of assistance, except in rare cases, seldom require assistance."[37]

Economic Arminianism

The Second Great Awakening, a series of religious revivals spanning the 1790s through the 1830s, changed the face of American religion. Geographically, the movement swept the United States, from the frontier meetings of Cane Ridge, Kentucky, to the northeastern city revivals spurred by ministers such as Charles Grandison Finney. The revivals led to the marked growth of Baptists and Methodists and the later birth or expansion of several new religions, such as Mormonism, the Millerites, and the Shakers. The Second Great Awakening spurred what the historian Nathan Hatch calls the "democratization of American Christianity" by putting into practice Martin Luther's "priesthood of all believers," resulting in the rise of lay preaching, prophesying, and revelations.[38] It also signaled the decline of Calvinist predestinarian beliefs and the concomitant rise of the Arminian ideas that God wants to save the souls of all who repent and that sinners have free will to accept or reject faith. Thus, argues the sociologist George Thomas, nineteenth-century Evangelical revivalism held an elective affinity with rising antebellum Republicanism and free market capitalism in that all three shared, among other things, a belief in "the autonomy of the individual as a rational decision-making entity."[39]

The theology of class I call "economic Arminianism" developed within nineteenth-century Evangelical revivalism. In this cosmology, individuals held responsibility for both their heavenly and earthly fates. One's poverty or wealth, like one's damnation or salvation, was a matter of individual free will. Stretching from antebellum and post–Civil War writers to contemporary prosperity gospel ministers and New Age channels, economic Arminianism has been the most prominent and malleable theology of social differentiation in American religious history.

Free will, the idea that all individuals act autonomously of their own volition, is the crucial component of economic Arminianism. In 1870, Henry Ward Beecher delivered a sermon titled "Individual Responsibility."[40] Beecher was a popular mid-nineteenth-century Congregationalist minister whose ideas, many religious historians argue, both mirrored and shaped white middle-class Protestantism.[41] The subject of "Individual Responsibility" was free will. For Beecher, God placed upon every human "the responsibility of using faculties with which he has been endowed, in their own spheres; putting him to find out the truth, to guide himself by that which he finds out; giving him ample helps, collateral suggestions, pattern, counsel and law, giving him none of these things in such a peremptory form as to supersede his own individual liberty and responsibility for finding that which is right, and then doing that which he has found out."[42] In Beecher's theology, free will was God's gift of sovereignty for every human individual. "I am pope of my own senses," Beecher proclaimed, "I am sovereign of my own faculties; and it is designed, either that I should form a judgment, and act according to it, or that I should take the penalties and consequences."[43]

Beecher's free will Evangelical Arminianism meant that while Christianity "lets us have all manner of helps," "liberty is the essential element of it."[44] God, in his view, had planted "ample helps" to lead humanity to the truth, but the ultimate responsibility to discover and adhere to the truth lay upon each individual. Declaring Christianity a "charter of liberty," Beecher's sermon followed a familiar post–Civil War path of positioning his own form of Protestantism as democratic and as the opposite of the supposedly undemocratic and autocratic faiths of Judaism and Roman Catholicism.[45] He declared that Judaism was too rigid in laws and institutions and charged Roman Catholicism with being too paternal. For Beecher a paternal religion, like a paternal government, was dangerous because it trumped God-given free will, "providing for men, and not leaving them to provide for themselves."[46]

The primacy of free will in Beecher's theology allowed him to place blame upon individuals for their faults, shortcomings, and social locations. If God had indeed given all people the freedom to act and multiple clues as to the divine truth, who else but the individual could be responsible? Beecher lamented that "the earth is burdened with worthless population" and even suggested that "if you could only make a good selection of men, there would be nothing so good as killing, in this world."[47] Given these views, it is not surprising that Beecher's form of economic Arminianism led him to view poverty as both a sign and a result of individual sin, rather than something related to any social structural circumstances. "'Looking comprehensively through city and town and village and country,'" the historian Sidney Mead quotes Beecher from one mid-1870s sermon, "'the general truth will stand, that no man in this land suffers from poverty unless it be more than his fault—unless it be his sin.'"[48]

Economic Arminianism, as seen in Beecher, asserts that poverty often relates to individual shortcomings, if not sinfulness. In this theology of class, the converse also holds true. In other words, gaining wealth could be just as much a sign of God's approval and favor as poverty is a sign of one's sinfulness. "If you can honestly attain unto riches . . . it is our Christian and godly duty to do so," exclaimed Russell Conwell in his famous "Acres of Diamonds" speech.[49] A Baptist minister and founder of Temple University, in the late nineteenth and early twentieth centuries Conwell preached a "gospel of wealth," which asserted that God wanted his followers to be rich. For Conwell, making money through honest means was simultaneously to "preach the gospel."[50] "It is an awful mistake," he declared, "of these poor people to think you must be awfully poor in order to be pious."[51]

Conwell's gospel of wealth focused on the Christian's duty to become rich. But he also offered a Beecherlike condemnation of the poor. Poverty, in his articulation, was God's punishment for individual sin. Conwell suggested that he sympathized with the poor, "but the number of poor who are to be with is very small."[52] "To sympathize with a man whom God has punished for his sins," he elaborated, "thus to help him when God would still continue a just punishment, is to do wrong, no doubt about it, and we do that more than we help those who are deserving."[53] Reflecting the same trust in American free market capitalism as Beecher, Conwell could conclude that there "is not a poor person in the United States who was not made poor by his own shortcomings, or by the shortcomings of someone else. It is all wrong to be poor, anyhow."[54]

Late twentieth-century and contemporary economic Arminianism follows the trajectories seen in Beecher and Conwell. In his 1993 study of Christian Right authors, the political scientist Michael Lienesch found arguments that mirrored the economic Arminianism of their nineteenth-century forbears. Lienesch quotes writer Davis Chilton's assertion that "'siding with the poor is not automatic with God . . . nor should it be with His people.'"[55] Another Christian Right author, Larry Burkett, mirrors Conwell's statement that poverty is God's punishment for sin. In helping the poor who are undeserving, Lienesch quotes Burkett, "'you may well be interfering with God's plan for them.'"[56] Lienesch finds other writers asserting connections between poverty and "wickedness" and being unsaved and impoverished.[57] He argues and demonstrates that many of the authors view economic equality as unbiblical and perhaps satanic. Simultaneously, they believe they find in scripture evidence that Jesus, Moses, and other biblical figures were wealthy champions of capitalism.[58]

While one could rightly suggest that Christian Right authors provide a unique case for the amalgamation of conservative social values, laissez-faire capitalism, and Evangelical religion, it would be incorrect to suggest that economic Arminianism can only be found among such explicitly political ideologues. It also appears outside of Protestant Christianity. One example is the contemporary channeling movement, which is usually placed within the collection of various practices dubbed "New Age."[59] Channeling is the process of communicating with a nonphysical entity for the purpose of attaining wisdom and knowledge. While channels themselves benefit from the entity's wisdom, they usually act as mediating consultants who impart counseling and advice to paying clients. Contemporary New Age channels resemble nineteenth-century Spiritualist mediums, with one important difference: whereas mediums were usually called upon to contact deceased human beings, channels enter into trances and take on the personas of divine and wise beings. The teachings given by channels in possession trances usually contain similar themes: humans are good, they create their own realities, and they have the divine within them.

Channeling became visible in the 1980s with the appearance of J. Z. Knight, who continues to channel the enlightened being "Ramtha" and has approximately three thousand client-devotees who pay for her services. The interested can participate in seminars and sessions at "Ramtha's School of Enlightenment," based in Washington state. According to the center's website, the "four cornerstones" of Ramtha's teaching are "1) the statement 'you are God'; 2) the directive to make the unknown known; 3) the concept that consciousness and energy create the nature of reality; and 4) the challenge to conquer yourself."[60] In an introductory booklet that can be accessed from the website, the unnamed author suggests that "the human is best described as consciousness and energy creating the nature of reality."[61] Because humans create their own realities, "it is absurd to argue for our limitations when we are, as consciousness and energy, the ones who created them."[62] The belief that human beings have the free will to create the reality in which they live—even including things like illness, accidents, and economic status—has historical connections to New Thought movements such as Christian Science and Father Divine's Peace Mission movement. It also taps into the economic Arminianism seen in Beecher, Conwell, and others.

In his study of New Age channelers, the anthropologist Michael Brown suggests that the movement's commonly held view that individuals create their own reality leads to two recurrent interpretations of sickness, poverty, and misfortune. "The first," Brown writes, "is that they occur because the victims cannot or will not envision the world in ways that protect them from misfortune. Calamity originates in a failure of individual attitude or thought."[63] "Poverty exists, in other words," Brown explains, "because poor people think impoverished thoughts."[64] The second interpretation fronted by channels follows the logic of Conwell's and Burkett's arguments that the poor are so because God is punishing them for sin. Brown notes that most channels believe in reincarnation and multiple lives and thus posit the explanation that "victims of illness or misadventure have chosen their fate, usually at a 'deep soul level' beneath everyday awareness."[65] Together, such explanations form an economic Arminian theology of class that parallels Protestant versions.[66]

Perhaps the most prominent example of economic Arminianism in the late twentieth and early twenty-first centuries is a form of the prosperity gospel known as the Word of Faith movement. The sociologist and former Word of Faith believer Milmon Harrison places the origins of the movement in a mix of Holiness, Pentecostal, and New Thought traditions.[67] Harrison suggests that the nondenominational movement, promoted by E. W. Kenyon, Kenneth Hagin, Reverend Ike, Creflo Dollar, Frederick Price, and the Trinity Broadcasting Network, has broad appeal and is increasingly influential in some forms of African American Protestantism. He describes Word of Faith's three core beliefs as "the principle of knowing who you are in Christ; the practice of positive confession (and positive mental attitude); and a worldview that emphasizes material prosperity and physical health as the divine right of every Christian."[68] This latter principle, that every Christian should expect wealth and good health, resembles Conwell's assertion that becoming rich is a form of preaching the gospel. Also similar to Conwell's views on charity is what Harrison suggests is a much-repeated Word of Faith message attributed to Reverend Ike: "The best thing you can do for the poor is not become one of them."[69]

As an example of economic Arminianism, Word of Faith theology suggests that each individual has the God-given free will to be economically successful. Focusing on the power of positive thinking, the movement encourages members to "name it and claim it" by repeating positive affirmations and prayers. Conversely, negative thinking corresponds to poverty, illness, and misfortune. In one interview, Harrison asks a believer who did she think was to blame for one's suffering in life. "You!" she answered. "Your faith must not have been strong enough, you must have been outside the will of God . . . It's your fault."[70]

In *The Great Investment: Faith, Family, and Finance*, Bishop T. D. Jakes offers a tempered version of economic Arminianism inflected with Word of Faith theology. Born working-class in Charleston, West Virginia, Jakes rose to prominence through a popular television ministry and several books, including the bestseller *Woman, Thou Art Loosed!* A 2005 biography dubbed him "America's New Preacher," while a 2006 *Atlantic Monthly* article suggested that he was "perhaps the most influential black leader in America today."[71] In *The Great Investment*, Jakes criticizes both the "monk" and the "prosperity preacher," asserting that they have equally "failed to understand the essence of Christianity."[72] At the same time, the economic Arminianism that emerges in the book suggests that Jakes actually views the "monk" as more removed from "authentic" Christianity than the "prosperity preacher."

"I want to prove that God is not against being affluent," writes Jakes.[73] In his theology of class, God "gives us the power to get wealth."[74] "That power," Jakes asserts, "is in your will. It is in your talents. It is in your creativity."[75] He describes God as a businessman and suggests that the Holy Spirit can inspire individuals to develop business plans.[76] "God is not offended by opulence," Jakes states, "or He would never have created Heaven with gold streets."[77]

In Jakes's brand of economic Arminianism, God has granted all with the talents and free will to attain wealth and prosperity. He adheres to a doctrine of "supernatural returns" in which believers will be financially blessed when they tithe and make offerings.[78] Money, for Jakes, is "neither evil nor good."[79] The morality of money lies in what kinds of *personal* benefits and services one spends it on. "That same hundred dollar bill," he writes, "can feed a crack habit or put food on a table, pay for a prostitute, or buy your wife a bottle of perfume."[80] For Jakes—as for Conwell, Beecher, and others—poverty, passivity, and individual sacrifice do not equate with godliness. "God," he asserts, "blesses the actions of men and women who are not afraid to make a move."[81] Jakes asserts that God gives more wealth to those who already have it because, as a businessman, "He is not going to do business with someone who shows no sign of potential return. He invests in people who demonstrate an ability to handle what he has given them."[82]

When Jakes does take issue with his straw prosperity preacher, the point of contention involves proper financial stewardship of one's riches, rather than any problem inherent in gospel of wealth theology. When God blesses you, he writes, "there is a greater and greater need to be a good steward."[83] For Jakes this stewardship is individually, rather than socially, focused. While it includes church tithing, it also entails establishing a "portfolio and estate planning that allows you to have the greatest impact with what God has given you."[84] "It is a tragic misappropriation of God's blessings," he elaborates, "when those who acquire wealth begin to drive luxury cars but drive home to trailers or cheap efficiency apartments."[85] When Jakes declares that "prayer is essential, but faith without works is dead," the next sentence clears up any confusion the reader might have about whether "works" should entail social activism: "You must have a plan for your financial well-being, and it needs to include where you are, where you want to go, and how you will maintain what you have when you get there."[86]

Social Harmony

I call the third recurrent theology of class "social harmony." Prominent in the Gilded Age among some writers associated with the Social Gospel, this theology of social differentiation acknowledged potential conflicts between labor and capital, yet suggested that opposing parties shared mutual, rather than opposing, interests and goals. Such a conception of social relations in some ways resembled the Puritan theology of divine hierarchies. All persons in society had their station and its associated tasks. Only by fulfilling these tasks would social harmony be upheld. There were social class differences, but all classes depended upon each other. However, social harmony theology differed from the divine hierarchy cosmology in asserting that individuals had the free will to move into different social locations. Laborers could become business owners, and investing entrepreneurs could fall into the working class. In social harmony theology, capitalism entailed no inherent class conflict, private property and profits were biblically based, and the key to solving labor disputes lay in reminding opposing parties of their differing God-given obligations toward one another.

Though my examples here come from Gilded Age writings, aspects of the theology of social harmony also appear in earlier decades. In his study of emergent "languages of class" in antebellum America, the historian Stephen Rice argues that Americans "who were coming to perceive themselves (and be perceived by others) as middle-class in the decades before 1860 consolidated their authority and minimized the potential for class conflict in part by representing the social relations of the workplace as necessarily cooperative rather than oppositional."[87] They did this, he suggests, "by participating in a popular discourse on mechanization in which they defined the relation between proprietors (and the overseers, foremen, or managers they employed) and wageworkers as analogous to three other sets of relations: between head and hand, mind and body, and human and machine."[88] Here, then, one sees emergent linkages between physicality and the working class and between intellectual aptitude and the middle, managerial, and ownership classes. As suggested throughout this work, these linkages would by the twentieth century become naturalized and fixed to such an extent that they guided scholars' interpretations of religious preferences.

The discourse identified by Rice represented a workplace version of a larger ideology that the historian Martin Burke identifies as the "harmony of interests." Burke notes that between the 1830s and 1850s "an intellectual community of professors, politicians, educators, and journalists continued to disseminate the doctrine of the harmony of interests, and to argue that the republic's social arrangements were in accord with the dictates of nature."[89] This ideology, promoted by figures such as the Baptist minister Francis Wayland, played down socioeconomic differences and suggested that "classes were constantly being made and remade by the constant choices of free individuals in the marketplace."[90]

As noted by the historian Robert Handy, what contemporary scholars usually define as the "Social Gospel" are writings and activities of a select group of progressive ministers who came out of a much larger and more variant movement known as "social Christianity."[91] While Gilded Age social Christianity had both conservative and radical arms, Handy describes the progressive Social Gospelers as having attitudes that "were essentially middle-class, combining a call for social action with an emphasis on the importance of the individual, his rights, and responsibilities."[92] One progressive Social Gospel writer who provides a good example of social harmony theology is Washington Gladden.

The harmony of interests worldview reveals itself in Gladden's suggestion that "the relations of men to one another in society are not contractual, but vital and organic; that we are members of one another; that no man reaches perfection or happiness apart from his fellow men; that no man liveth to himself; and none dieth to himself."[93] Because of this, Gladden argued, "the broad equities of Christ's rule" demanded that both laborers and capitalists get their own fair shares.[94] Thus, Gladden suggested that churches shouldn't necessarily takes sides in labor–capital disputes but rather offer what might be described as biblically based mediation.[95] Citing the scriptural dictum to "love thy neighbor as thyself," he asserted that "it must be possible to shape the organization of our industries in such a way that it shall be the daily habit of the workman to think of the interest of the employer, and of the employer to think of the interest of the workman."[96]

Inherent in Gladden's theology of social harmony was support of capitalism and private property. For Gladden, increasing wealth was not problematic, but actually "a blessing to mankind."[97] He suggested that "one effect produced by Christianity upon an uncivilized people receiving it is to multiply the wealth of that people."[98] "Christianity cannot be hostile to the production of wealth," he reasoned, "without making war upon itself; for it is the one grand cause of the production of wealth in modern times." Like late twentieth-century Christian Right authors and other economic Arminians, Gladden asserted that the early Christians were not communistic but rather owned private property that they voluntarily chose to share.[99] "I think that for the natural development of human character, and the stable and fruitful organization of human society," he wrote, "it is necessary to have private property firmly safeguarded and private enterprise strongly encouraged by the state."[100] Given the developmental importance and biblical basis of property and wealth, any attempt at redistribution "among the poor, by the power of the state, of the goods of the rich, would be a blunder so nearly criminal in its dimensions as fairly to justify Fouque's paradox . . . no one who clearly apprehends the drift of Christian teaching on the subject would ever think of such a thing."[101]

Gladden's attitude toward the poor shared elements with both the divine hierarchy and the economic Arminian theologies. Mirroring the Puritan theology of divine hierarchies, he asserted of the poor that "we have them always with us."[102] And like many economic Arminians, Gladden distinguished between deserving and undeserving poor. He suggested that giving money to "actual or incipient paupers" only harms them, while "helpless invalids, old people, and little children who are destitute have a special claim on those who have abundance."[103] The "church," Gladden lamented, "bred paupers by the thousand; by their careless and unquestioning doles they have paved the way for whole families to enter the steep and slimy path of beggary; they have aided and abetted parents in training up their children for mendicancy and crime."[104] To rectify this situation, he urged churches to utilize social science to discover how to best help the poor.[105]

Gladden provides a good example of the theology of social harmony, but other Social Gospel writers and documents do too. For example, in 1912 the Federal Council of Churches produced a "Social Creed of the Christian Churches" that jointly upheld the rights of both employees and employers to organize and earn the income due to them.[106] Even Walter Rauschenbusch, who was generally more socialistic and critical of capitalism than Gladden, said of capitalism that "in so far as our present economic order is simply the perfecting of human association, Christianity can have no quarrel with it."[107] But the theology of social harmony was not the sole province of progressive Protestantism. American Catholic responses to Pope Leo XIII's *Rerum Novarum*, an 1891 encyclical on labor, socialism, and the condition of the working classes under capitalism, provide another Gilded Age example of this theology.

Rerum Novarum, translated into English as *On the Condition of Labor*, promoted a theology of social harmony: it condemned socialism, upheld labor's right to unionize, declared private property sacred, and denied any "natural" conflict between socioeconomic classes. Pope Leo XIII presented an explicit harmony of interests conception. Mirroring earlier conceptions, *Rerum Novarum* envisioned society as a human body made up of different parts working harmoniously together. Because of this, the Pope suggested that to assume there was an inherent conflict between rich and poor was a "capital evil."[108] "This is so abhorrent to reason and truth that the exact opposite is true," read the encyclical. "For just as in the human body the different members harmonize with one another, whence it arises that disposition of parts and proportion in the human figure rightly called symmetry, so likewise nature has commanded in the case of the State that the two classes mentioned should agree harmoniously and should properly form equally balanced counterparts to each other."[109] "Each," it continued, "needs the other completely: neither capital can do without labor, nor labor without capital."[110]

In *Rerum Novarum*'s related attack on socialism, older notions of divinely instituted hierarchies merged with social harmony theology. Contrary to socialism's view of equality, the Pope asserted, "a condition of human existence must be borne with, namely, that in civil society the lowest cannot be made equal to the highest."[111] To struggle against such inequalities, the Pope suggested, was to struggle against God's natural order. "There are truly very great and very many natural differences among men," wrote Leo XIII. "Neither the talents, nor the skill, nor the health, nor the capacities of all are the same, and unequal fortune follows of itself upon necessary inequality in respect to these endowments."[112] "And clearly this condition of things is adapted to benefit both individuals and the community," he continued, "for to carry on its affairs community life requires varied aptitudes and diverse services, and to perform these diverse services men are impelled most by differences in individual property holdings."[113]

Like Gladden's theology of applied Christianity, *Rerum Novarum* upheld the rights of workers to organize, while simultaneously declaring the moral and developmental necessity of private property. "To own goods privately," Pope Leo asserted, was "necessary for human life."[114] Private property was not only in accord with God and nature, but "the right of private property must be regarded as sacred."[115] Any socialist proposal to redistribute property was therefore a "remedy openly in conflict with justice, inasmuch as nature confers on man the right to possess things privately as his own."[116]

Unlike Protestant proponents of both economic Arminianism and social harmony, *Rerum Novarum* defended charity and almsgiving. Pope Leo XIII wrote that "when the demands of necessity and propriety have been met, it is a duty to give to the poor out of that which remains."[117] And while nineteenth- and twentieth-century Protestants from Beecher and Gladden to Conwell and Burkett distinguished "deserving" from "undeserving" poor, the Pope noted that the Roman Catholic Church even provided alms "for the wretched poor."[118] No state institutions or "human devices," he wrote, "can ever be found to supplant Christian charity, which gives itself entirely for the benefit of others."[119]

The historian Jay Dolan suggests that the initial American Catholic response to *Rerum Novarum* was "quite favorable" but short-lived, in that "within a few years it was put on the shelf to gather dust."[120] Dolan asserts that, like most papal encyclicals, *Rerum Novarum* "was open to a variety of interpretations: it had an anti-capitalist, pro-labor perspective as well as an antisocialist, pro-private property perspective."[121] He further argues that "American bishops and priests focused on the latter and ignored the Pope's criticism of capitalism and his call for social reform."[122] Two early American responses to the encyclical appeared in the September 1891 issue of *Catholic World*. Though differing in focus and temper, both the Reverend Morgan M. Sheedy's "The Encyclical and American Iron-Workers and Coal-Miners" and the Reverend J. L. Spalding's "Socialism and Labor" upheld the theology of social harmony inherent in *Rerum Novarum*.

Sheedy asserted that the Pope had released the document in "this fateful hour to teach the world the true social gospel."[123] For Sheedy, the papacy was the "only international power to-day in existence possessed of sufficient authority and strength, sufficiently sure of itself, and rich in light and energy, to attempt the supreme task of reconciling the contending forces of society."[124] He suggested that the Pope displayed "fatherly tenderness and sympathy" in addressing the pressing problems of the day, and he focused much of the discussion in his article on the religious labor organizations and trajectories of worker–management arbitration that the encyclical suggested.[125] *Rerum Novarum*, Sheedy stressed, "did not array class against class" but rather "points out the line of duty for each to follow, while it aims to strengthen right relations between labor and capital."[126] As such, it stood as a unifying "message of peace and good-will to all men," one that "lays down the eternal principles of right and justice for the guidance of rich and poor, worker and capitalist."[127]

While Sheedy's essay concentrated on the encyclical's messages concerning labor organizing and work disputes, Spalding's article focused on proving the falsity of socialist arguments about inherent class differences and conflict in American society. In doing this, he added to and amended *Rerum Novarum* in a way that called into question the existence of "classes," while simultaneously suggesting an American class of "undeserving poor." Contrary to socialist views, Spalding asserted, there was no chasm "between the enormously rich and the very poor, but there is a gradation of possession from the beggar to the great capitalist."[128] For Spalding, the actual "social gulf is not between rich men and steady, thrifty laborers, but rather between these latter and the crowd of loafers and criminals."[129] Sounding like American Protestants who held to economic Arminian views, Spalding asserted that "the cause of this disparity of condition is moral rather than economic, whoever observes may see; and this fact gives emphasis to the great truth that all real amelioration in the lot of human beings depends on their religious, moral, and intellectual state."[130] In other words, it was personal sinfulness, rather than social-structural inequalities, that accounted for one's poverty-stricken state.

Spalding suggested that because owning private property was not criminal, but natural and thus divinely ordained, "wealth however great, if it be honestly acquired and justly used, must be respected."[131] Using rhetoric that resembled the workers-as-hands and owners-as-heads analogy identified by the historian Stephen Rice, Spalding asserted that capitalism and capitalists were necessary, because "without the genius of inventors and discoverers, without the foresight and enterprise of investors and capitalists, there would be little for laborers to do, and society would drift into general poverty."[132] Likewise necessary was unequal wage distribution for differing kinds of work. Recalling *Rerum Novarum*'s declaration that human society was divinely designed to be unequal, Spalding asserted that it simply wasn't part of human nature to find socialist goals of equality appealing.[133] "If all receive the same reward, whatever their labor," Spalding wrote, "spontaneity would come to an end and progress would cease, and such an equality would finally come to be a universal equality in indolence, poverty, and low thinking; while from an ethical point of view, it would seem to be unjust that the same reward should be given to every kind of labor."[134] It was only when both workers and owners realized their places and their obligations to each other, when "all unite for the common good of the whole people," Spalding surmised, that "a new era will dawn."[135] Like *Rerum Novarum* itself, and like the theology of social harmony it promoted, Spalding's essay followed the harmony of interests view that suggested—to use the Catholic Reverend James Cleary's 1893 remark about the encyclical—"religion's duty is to teach the rich the responsibilities of wealth and the poor respect for law and order."[136]

The Class-Conscious Christ

In his 2004 book, *Blue Collar Jesus*, Indianapolis Methodist minister Darren Cushman Wood presents an argument that shares much with the theology

penter. White, like the labor-songwriters, asserted Jesus's working-class roots. "Jesus," the head resident of New York's Trinity House wrote, "belongs to the proletariat by birthright" and is the "proletariat's lord by divinest right."[154] The book's frontispiece painting by Balfour Ker, which portrayed Jesus as a contemporary carpenter at work, concurred. For White, Jesus's sayings provided "evidence of a working-class consciousness," and his quick death on the cross stemmed from a lifetime of working-class deprivations.[155] "The home of penury in which he had been born," White surmised, "with its wearing toil begun too early, its limited and uncertain food supplies, and the harassments to which a fine-grained workingman was submitted by the absolutism which was upon the people, conspired not to the making of a sleek and happy animal."[156]

The carpenter's message, for White, was a revolutionary one addressed to the masses. He described the "life of the poor in that age as one long crucifixion."[157] Coming from "working-class Galilee," Jesus spoke to the downtrodden and "declared war on the capitalism of his day, because capitalism declared war on him."[158] In White's theology the Sermon on the Mount became a call to "class solidarity" directed at workers.[159] Jesus, for White, was no pacifist, but a labor and human rights activist who "sought to breed a type of man that would look oppression in the face and wring its neck."[160] White's Jesus "looked upon any large accumulation of goods as an impediment" and considered the "over-rich as distinct objects of pity."[161] "Jesus announced 'good news,'" he declared, "namely, that heaven is passionately on the side of the people against the despotic tendencies of property; and under that leadership a messianic passion for men is announcing itself."[162]

Though far from the contemporaneous theologies of economic Arminianism and social harmony, White's portrayal of Jesus as a class revolutionary shared at least two Protestant prejudices of its time. First, White's anti-Catholicism emerged in his assertion that the Holy Roman Empire suppressed "every tendency to independence of thought."[163] In a slight twist on such nativism, White viewed Paul as the prime culprit who helped Rome "annex" Christianity and make it docile.[164] Paul, he wrote, was an elite and antidemocratic "stockholder in Rome's world corporation."[165] For White it was Paul who first began the "process of Romanizing the man of Nazareth," concealing Jesus's revolutionary message and creating a Christianity that serviced the empire.[166]

A second notion that White shared with some of his nonrevolutionary Protestant contemporaries was the dislike of charity and the related belief that a dangerous class of undeserving poor threatened society. White hoped that the working class, "stiffened by manly fibre" and "refusing the doles of charity," would be "the saviours of a civilization threatened with dry rot."[167] But he also warned of a looming threat. "There is a danger to civilization," White cautioned.[168] This menace was not posed by "the agitator type of working-man," he explained, but rather "the rabble underneath, who have no desire for freedom, and are content with the bread line."[169] White described this "vast underworld population" as "brainless, heartless, soulless," and he advised that "devoid of respect for themselves, when comes the hour of opportunity they will be devoid of respect for others."[170]

The Call of the Carpenter also contained three arguments that were some-what unique, given the time and the social and religious locations from which White wrote. First, White argued that Mary, the mother of Jesus, played the primary role in fomenting her son's class consciousness. White minimized father Joseph's influence and portrayed Mary as a strong and independent revolutionary fighting the oppression of the Roman Empire. Joseph "lacked . . . the aggressive temperament which the times demanded," he asserted, pro-posing instead that "this element came from Mary . . . hers was the brain that dared conceive, hers the spirit that dared to execute."[171] "Sensing a child within her," he envisioned, "Mary feels herself equal to the Roman Empire; and she announces that the days of despotism are numbered."[172] In White's view, Mary influenced Jesus, his brother James, and John the Baptist to speak against "the economic oppressions of the day."[173] He criticized views of Mary that portrayed her as one held passively in the "bounds of feminine retire-ment," claiming that "if Mary had been the conventional, the starchly deco-rous creature which some would prefer her to have been, Christianity would never have been born."[174]

Second, White found Mary's and Jesus's revolutionary spirits fomented not just by material circumstances but also biology. "Galilee," he asserted, "was the heart of the most intense race ever known," and one must "take ac-count of the aboriginal energy of spirit in that Jewish blood."[175] Using the eugenics-inflected language of his time, White asserted that "a Jew is congeni-tally unfit for a servile lot—as the capitalist class of old discovered."[176] Early twentieth-century eugenics tended to be anti-Semitic. But White envisioned Jewish genes and culture as the pinnacle of revolutionary consciousness. For White, "Israel stood for the value of man, against the overweening influence of property."[177] In his rendering, ancient Jewish society was democratic, egali-tarian, peasant-free, and governed by mass meetings.[178] He declared the Book of Psalms the "hymnbook of democracy" and asserted that "Jesus planned to make the Jews the nucleus of a federation of the world's proletariat against the world's oppressor."[179] In considering the impetus for Jesus and his teachings, White surmised that "it was not an accident that the most aggressive democrat in history was born in Galilee, of a race the most tenaciously democratical in human annals."[180]

A third unique aspect of *The Call of the Carpenter* was White's critique of the theological image of God as father. White asserted that a "paternal despotism flows copiously from that dogma."[181] He cited three major problems with the concept: first, it was unscriptural; second, it was false; and third, it offered religious support for economic and political despotism.[182] He elaborated:

> Theology has a way of translating itself into economic magnitudes, and this is particularly so with the most stupendous doctrine that ever sought to impose itself on the human mind—the doctrine, namely, that the physical universe is ruled over by a personage who created it, owns it, and personally runs it. Put a boss at the top of the universe, and the idea of bossism will trickle down to every human relationship. Subserviency to an absolute ruler in the skies, how beneficent that ruler may be, paves the way for subserviency to an absolute ruler upon earth.[183]

In contrast, White offered a focus on the person of Jesus that would be a "theology acceptable to the democracy; and it is a theology founded on exact scriptural science."[184] "A fraternal relationship between God and man, in which the former is man's elder brother," White suggested, "is an education in self-respect, and makes an earthly despot impossible."[185]

Embodied Theologies of Class

Despite the variation in their conclusions, all four theologies of class discussed above share something in common: each engaged the question of social differentiation through texts. In sermons, songs, articles, and books, most of the authors promoted views about social bodies that they considered "scriptural." At the same time, none of them addressed individual, corporeal bodies. While my sources in this final section are also textual, their focus is on physical bodies. Theologies of class do not just entail explanations of social differentiation but also notions of civility, etiquette, and bodily comportment. In other words, theologies of class are embodied.

The historian Edward Kilsdonk argues that from the 1820s through the 1850s members of the emerging Evangelical Protestant middle class defined themselves not by focusing on income and wealth but rather by "selectively choosing styles of deportment and public conduct while attaching moral values to their actions."[186] Their belief in the need for restraint and self-control in emotions and bodily movements was part of a larger cultural trend noted by the historian John Kasson.[187] The work of the social theorist Beverley Skeggs seems to concur, in that it was in the nineteenth century that the working class came to be associated with excess, emotion, and lack of self-control, while the middle class became linked with denial, reason, and self-restraint.[188] Such discourses helped produce the differentiations of social class still present today.

In what follows, I examine the writings of two figures of the Second Great Awakening. I suggest that Peter Cartwright's and Charles Grandison Finney's commentaries on ecstatic revival behaviors were not just reflections of emerging class constructions but implements of such conceptions. In their delineations of "authentic" and "false" physical manifestations, both ministers expressed concern over maintaining ecclesiastical authority, restraining personal judgment, and promoting "true" religion. In doing this, both men—but especially Finney—suggested standards of bodily adornment, physical movement, and emotional disposition that simultaneously reflected and helped construct emergent social-class distinctions.

The Jerks as Judgment: Peter Cartwright

Peter Cartwright, perhaps the most famous Methodist itinerant rider, devoted a chapter of his 1856 autobiography to the Second Great Awakening frontier camp revivals.[189] A frequent preacher at such events in Kentucky, Tennessee, and the Carolinas, Cartwright described meetings that lasted three to four weeks. "I have seen more than a hundred sinners fall like dead men under one powerful sermon," Cartwright wrote, "and I have seen and heard more than five hundred Christians all shouting aloud the high praises of God at once; and I will venture to assert that many happy thousands were awakened and converted to God at these camp-meetings."[190]

Cartwright's recounting of early Second Great Awakening frontier revivals is filled with descriptions of ecstatic religious behaviors and his assessments of them. In general, he believed that many of the physical manifestations he witnessed were authentic, God-driven actions. Cartwright dubbed one of the physical manifestations he observed "the jerks." During meetings, both saints and sinners, he reported, "would be taken under a warm song or sermon, and seized with a convulsive jerking all over, which they could not by any possibility avoid, and the more they resisted the more they jerked."[191] For Cartwright, these jerks were a "judgment sent from God, first, to bring sinners to repentance; and secondly, to show professors that God could work with or without means, and that he could work over and above means, and do whatever seemeth him good, to the glory of his grace and the salvation of the world."[192] He asserted that this judgment was brought upon sinners as varied as rude children and unrepentant drunks.[193] But it was also a punishment that God imposed upon the wealthy and arrogant in order to humble them. "To see those proud young gentlemen and young ladies, dressed in their silks, jewelry, and prunella, from toe to toe, take the jerks, would often excite my risibilities," he wrote.[194] "The first jerk or so," he continued, "you would see their fine bonnets, caps, and combs fly; and so sudden would be the jerking of the head that their long loose hair would crack as loud as a wagoneer's whip."[195]

Cartwright did not think that all the physical manifestations he observed were supernaturally inspired. Although he generally thought the jerks to be authentic acts of God, Cartwright did suspect some jerking exercises to be inauthentic activities of people susceptible to suggestion. "There is no doubt in my mind," he commented, "that with weakminded, ignorant, and superstitious persons, there was a great deal of sympathetic feeling with many that claimed to be under the influence of this jerking exercise."[196] For Cartwright, "true" jerks were always involuntary and could be stopped by impassioned prayers.[197]

Cartwright had more reservations about other ecstatic religious behaviors. He asserted that members of his own denomination, the Methodists, did a good job keeping the camp revivals "moderately balanced." On the other hand, he accused some participants—particularly Presbyterians—of having "indulged in some extravagancies that were hard to control."[198] The "exercises" that "Methodist ministers generally preached against" included running, jumping, and barking.[199] But Cartwright singled out trance states that led to prophesying for particular scrutiny. "From these wild exercises," he related, "another great evil arose from the heated and wild imaginations of some."[200] Cartwright described individuals who fell into trances and saw visions of heaven, hell, God, angels, the devil, and the damned. "They would prophesy," he wrote, "and under the pretense of Divine inspiration, predict the time of the end of the world, and the ushering of the great millennium."[201] To oppose these prophecies, Cartwright asserted, was to "meet the clamor of the multitude" and even have the visionary "denounce the dreadful judgments of God against him."[202]

In reading Cartwright's descriptions of the camp meeting battles between prophets and preachers, one must first recognize that these were contestations over the authenticity of heartfelt religious beliefs and practices. In other words, the debates that revival participants engaged in over prophecies and physical "excitements" were theological disputes about the nature of human and divine interactions. At the same time, they also revealed conflicts over ministerial and lay authority. The belief developing during the Second Great Awakening in the "priesthood of all believers" suggested that any person could be called by God to minister and thus usurped hierarchical distinctions between clergy and laity. If God directly inspired individual believers, then couldn't anyone—regardless of education, training, and station—receive visions, revelations, and prophecies? And if this were so, how could one discern true from false prophecy?

While certainly not his focus, Cartwright's writing also touched on two issues relating to class. First, he saw the jerks as a judgment that God occasionally imposed on the wealthy and proud. An initial interpretation of such stories might suggest an underlying theology that reversed statuses in the spiritual world: the poor and humble stood closer to salvation than the rich and gaudy. While mid-twentieth-century deprivation theorists might assume this was a theology of the dispossessed, Kilsdonk suggests that many nineteenth-century Americans were equally "apprehensive" about displays of fashion because they were viewed as an "emblem of the secular world."[203] He relates that Baptists and Methodists, in particular, shared popular tales in the parlor and from the pulpit of how "fashionable observers at religious meetings were overcome by the spirit but were unable to experience conversion until they divested themselves of their finery."[204] Kilsdonk notes that such tales even appeared in Presbyterian Charles Grandison Finney's revival sermons. The view that, to use Kilsdonk's phrasing, there was a "spiritual danger of a concentration on outward finery at the expense of the inner adornments" was apparently as much an emergent aspect of middle-class Evangelical anxiety as it was a lower-class theology of resentment.

There is, I argue, a second way that Cartwright's descriptions of Second Great Awakening revivals may be analyzed in terms of class. In declaring some jerking manifestations as coming directly from God, Cartwright expressed a view that contrasted with emerging middle-class conceptions of physical and emotional deportment. The reason, self-control, and restraint that was becoming associated with a "middle-class disposition" precluded Cartwright's beloved jerks, as well as other demonstrative exercises. Instead, and as seen in the writings of Charles Grandison Finney, authentic religious experiences for the emergent middle class were supposed to be intellectual rather than emotional and practically invisible versus physically demonstrative.

Objectionable Excitements and Fanaticism: Charles Grandison Finney

Comparisons between Peter Cartwright and Charles Grandison Finney have tended to stress—if not exaggerate—their differences. Cartwright, the Methodist itinerant, had little formal education and lived on the American "frontier" in Illinois. Finney was an educated lawyer who became the minister of a well-heeled urban Presbyterian church and later served as an Oberlin College professor. But the two also had some similar life experiences. Though he had less education, Cartwright was no backwoods provincial. Starting in the 1820s, he embarked on a long political career that made him as much a public figure as Finney. And though Finney was a lawyer, scholar, and New York minister, he spent more than a decade as an itinerant minister, just as Cartwright had.[205] In their writings, both show concern over the importance of maintaining ministerial authority and discerning true from false excitements. On the latter, however, the two differed in ways that related to emergent class constructs.

Two of the many things that Charles Grandison Finney is well known for are his 1835 work *Lectures on Revivals of Religion* and that Second Great Awakening innovation known as the "anxious bench." In *Lectures*, Finney asserted that a revival was not a God-given miracle but rather a planned human event that succeeded through "the result of the right use of the appropriate means."[206] One of these "means" was the anxious bench. The historian Charles Lippy suggests that this innovation served as the place in Finney's church "where those who felt the stirring of the Spirit could gather."[207] It resembled the "pen" of frontier revivals. But the ecstatic behaviors of the frontier revivals were not Finney's goal. While he did believe that God endowed religious believers with spiritual and physical experiences, his view of what behaviors were authentic was much more constricted than those of Cartwright or other frontier itinerants. The historian Nathan Hatch argues that Finney's historical importance lies in his transformation of camp meeting revivalism into a form suitable to emerging northeastern middle-class tastes. Hatch dubs Finney a "bridge between cultures" who "conveyed the indigenous methods of popular culture to the middle class."[208] He suggests that Finney "trimmed away some rough edges" of revivalism for his middle-class audience, preaching "the same themes but with less ardor."[209]

I suggest that Finney's "trimming" of the "rough edges" of revivalism also entailed taming ecstatic religious behaviors. For Finney, authentic religious experience never involved uncontrolled emotions or bodies. In a series of letters dated from May to July of 1845, Finney laid out his distinctions between "authentic" religious events, "objectionable" excitements, and "fanaticism." "In every age of the church," he suggested, "cases have occurred in which persons have had such clear manifestations of divine truth as to prostrate their physical strength entirely."[210] Citing the biblical examples of Daniel and Saul of Tarsus, Finney asserted that God occasionally induced religious experiences that entailed physical reactions. But such events, he argued, never manifested in any ecstatic, demonstrative behaviors. For Finney such excitements always enlightened the individuals' intellect and allowed them to comprehend with exceeding clarity. At the same time, the event at most physically rendered believers quiet and still, as if paralyzed. He elaborated:

> The mind seems not to be conscious of any unusual excitement of its own sensibility; but on the contrary, seems to itself to be calm and its state seems peculiar only because truth is seen with unusual clearness. Manifestly there is no such effervescence of the sensibility as produces tears, or any of the usual manifestations of an excited imagination or deeply moved feelings. There is not that gush of feeling which distracts the thoughts, but the mind sees truth unveiled, and in such relations as really to take away all bodily strength, while the mind looks in upon the unveiled glories of the Godhead.[211]

For Finney, then, an authentic God-induced excitement was not a judgment—as it was for Cartwright—but an enriching clarity of thought accompanied by temporary physical paralysis. Finney suggested that one way to discern whether such experiences were real involved seeing if the individuals converted and changed their lives. "I do not recollect any clearly marked case of its kind," he assured, "in which it was not afterwards manifest that the love of God had been deeply shed abroad in the heart, the will greatly subdued, and the whole character greatly and most desirably modified."[212]

In addition to such authentic religious excitements, Finney described in his letters what he considered two inauthentic behaviors. The first, "objectionable excitements," entailed irrational emotions, uncontrollable physical activity, and anti-intellectual sentiments.[213] Their catalyst was human instrumentality, often in the form of sermons that employed "exciting measures" and "very exciting illustrations," which tended to "agitate and strain the nervous system until the sensibility seems to gush forth like a flood of water, and for the time completely overwhelm and drown the intelligence."[214] Finney dubbed the second type of inauthentic behavior "fanaticism." He defined it as "a state of mind in which the malign emotions take control of the will, and hurry the individual away into an outrageous and vindictive effort to sustain what he calls right and truth."[215] Such dogmatism, Finney confided, was frequently satanically inspired.[216] He believed that the people most likely to fall under the spell of such fanaticism had a "strong and ultra democratic tendency of mind, anti-conservative to the extreme and strongly tending to misrule."[217] These susceptible sorts were prone to regard "the visible church as Babylon, and all men as on the high road to hell who do not come out to denounce her."[218]

In Finney's demarcation of authentic and inauthentic religious experience lay emergent discourses about the interrelations between emotions, bodily deportment, and class. Finney did not invent these. As noted earlier in this chapter, discourses concurrent with Finney's likened factory owners to the brain and laborers to the hand. At the same time, Finney's classification of religious excitements offered a new *possibility* of homologous ordering of religious practice that mirrored emerging class distinctions. In other words, Finney's categories provided a potential language of class distinction within the religious field. Emotive "objectionable excitements" could be tied to the lower class and certain religions, while intellectually stimulating and emotionally restrained worship could be correlated to middle- and upper-class people and their religions. And this is exactly what happened. The developing nineteenth-century connections between reason, control, restraint, and the middle and upper classes—and conversely, between emotionalism, excess, and the working class—became so naturalized by the twentieth century that, as seen in part 1 of this book, much of the historical and social scientific scholarship on religion accepted these articulations as natural.

6 | *In the Field*

Deprivation, Class, and the Usual Suspects at Two Holiness Pentecostal Assemblies

One chilly April day in 1973, Matt Wray woke to find himself alone in his rural New Hampshire house. His Pentecostal brothers and mother were gone and their beds left unmade. Though morning light filled the house, Wray's alarm clock read 3:05 A.M.—it had stopped in the night. He fell to the floor, stricken by fear. "Jesus had taken my family away," Wray writes in his recounting. "The Rapture had occurred while I slept."[1] Wray was certain that the Second Coming had taken place and that he had been left behind. He blamed himself. "I felt the crushing weight of my sins," Wray remembers, "the guilty shame of having abandoned Jesus."[2] It wasn't until he looked out the window and saw activity at his church across the street that he realized he had merely overslept. The rapture hadn't occurred. His family couldn't wake him and had left him to sleep while they attended an early morning Easter Sunday service.

As an adult removed from his Pentecostal roots, Wray explains his childhood beliefs in terms of his family's poverty. "Though not all the members of our church were poor," he writes, "poverty was primary among the social conditions which helped shape our religious identity."[3] "In general," Wray asserts, "charismatic Christianity brings a sense of spiritual power and righteousness to those who, because of their positions within capitalist economic structures, suffer from a fundamental lack of social and economic power."[4]

Wray's explanation of his Pentecostal background is a familiar one. As seen in chapter 4 of this book, scholars such as Robert Mapes Anderson proposed deprivationist explanations of the movement. In *Vision of the Disinherited* Anderson suggested, with supporting demographic evidence, that Pentecostalism attracted those from the lower social classes. In explaining why, he asserted that those with the least power and influence in society were attracted to (1) theologies that promise them rewards in the afterlife and (2) ecstatic ritual practices (like speaking in tongues) that give them an elevated spiritual status in their congregations. Here, in the final chapter of the book, I seek to

C. C. Bradshaw broke out of the choruses of country- and rockabilly-tinged gospels to say "praise Him!" into the microphone. In both churches, my pew neighbors raised their hands high, closed their eyes, and repeated, "praise the Lord!" and "hallelujah!"

But the forms that praise took in the two assemblies were not confined to verbal utterances, songs, sermons, and physical gestures. Holiness Pentecostalism has historically urged that praise manifest itself in believers' everyday lives. Holiness codes concerning clothing, grooming, alcohol and tobacco consumption, and restrictions on entertainments such as music, television, and movies existed in both churches. These regulations literally inscribed the faith onto believers' bodies. When Pastor John referred to the coat of praise, then, the reference not only signified verbal laudations to God but the actual coats and garments worn by members.

In addition to religious speech, gesture, and personal appearance, the church décor added a component of praise. At Holiness Road, colorful stained glass depictions of Jesus served as polychromatic bursts of glory in an otherwise austere brown interior. Brown Hill punctuated its colorful interior with a large banner that announced "The Holy Spirit is Welcome Here." Even the geographical placement of Holiness Road—intended or not—served as a reminder of the Holiness Pentecostal worldview. The church sat on the outskirts of Jefferson, on the major rural route leading to Centerville. In Holiness Pentecostalism, the road to sanctity, redemption, and heaven is a long and arduous one. *Once saved* never implies *always saved*: one can always "fall off the wagon," so to speak, and lose the Second Blessing. Also called "Entire Sanctification," the Second Blessing entails a postconversion experience—demonstrated in Holiness Pentecostalism by speaking in tongues—that is supposed to make the believer free of all voluntary sin. Despite the inevitable potholes that cause some to temporarily fall from such grace, they believe that staying on the holiness road will eventually lead them to the city of God.

The primary manifestation of praise at both Holiness Road and Brown Hill entailed ecstatic rituals that, for believers, physically demonstrated the "gifts of the spirit." In both churches, clapping hands, speaking in tongues, dancing in the spirit, and other physical gestures signaled the presence of the Holy Ghost. While these activities were forms of praise, they were also literal contacts between the human and the divine. The human, in praising God, is touched and blessed by God.

Both churches were positioned on the outskirts of Jefferson. According to some accounts, Jefferson's first Pentecostal assembly consisted of Appalachian migrants who, after World War I, met in an abandoned turkey coop on Gobbler's Nob. Whether or not this oral narrative is historically accurate, it

certainly holds a legendary truth consonant with Jefferson's Holiness Pentecostals. The movement's history in Jefferson is entwined with the story of uprooted Appalachians who came to the small Ohio River valley city in search
of work. These migrants settled in Jefferson's hilly areas and built small, ethnic
neighborhoods that included Pentecostal churches. Even in the 1990s, when I
conducted my fieldwork, certain parts of Jefferson were still known as "Appalachian" or "Kentucky" neighborhoods. These are the places you find the bulk
of the city's Holiness Pentecostal churches.

Jefferson sits in a hilly spot of the Ohio River valley. Founded as a frontier
outpost in the 1790s, the city was listed in the 1990 census with a population
of a little more than 61,000, down from a high of nearly 68,000 in 1970. By
the mid-1990s, it was apparent the city was in a slow decline. The decreasing
population mirrored a loss of industrial jobs. Smaller, burgeoning towns surrounding Jefferson that were closer to the interstates took business and people
away from the city. According to a February 1994 local radio newscast, Jefferson had one of the highest unemployment rates in the state for a city of its
size.

It was the city's impressive post–World War I industrial growth that originally attracted southern Appalachians. According to one study, Jefferson fac-
tories sent representatives into eastern Kentucky to recruit laborers. Some
even provided trains to transport workers.[10] Appalachian migration to Jefferson slowed during World War II but gathered new momentum in the late
1940s that lasted through the 1960s. And this pattern was not particular to
Jefferson. The Great Migration, from the 1910s through the 1960s, brought
millions of African Americans from the Jim Crow South into urban industrial northern cities.[11] At the same time, as noted by the Appalachia scholar
Thomas Wagner, as many as seven million Appalachian migrants moved into
Ohio, Pennsylvania, Indiana, Michigan, and Illinois.[12]

As of April 1994, Jefferson had twenty-one Pentecostal churches. Most of
these were concentrated in three areas of the city. Two, Gobbler's Nob and
Miller Woods, were areas of Appalachian settlement. The third district, located in the city's second ward, was predominantly African American.

The Brown Hill Church of God

Brown Hill sat two miles east of downtown Jefferson on Brown Road. The
church complex was situated in a liminal area that marked the transition from
a residential setting to one of open fields and farms. On both sides of the
church sat housing developments flanked by cornfields. Rosehill Cemetery
stood across the road.

The building was a tan brick structure surrounded by a large manicured lawn and a large asphalt parking lot. Attached to the east side of the church was a two-story complex that housed preschoolers during the weekdays. Anyone who passed by the church on Brown Road was greeted by white lettering on the church announcing the assembly's name. About fifty feet off the road, along the driveway leading to the parking lot, a white sign proclaimed the last name of Brown Hill's "family of the week" in black block letters.

Congregants entered the building through four sets of glass double doors. Inside, the church was styled as an auditorium. The narthex encircled three sides of the auditorium seating area. The walls of the narthex were cream-colored and the carpeting was brown. Four sets of dark-brown wood doors separated the narthex from the seats. Inside the auditorium, five rows of pews, padded with red cloth cushions that matched the auditorium carpeting, angled toward the stage, and there was a balcony. Like the narthex, the auditorium walls were cream.

The stage held a number of things: seating for about fifty people; an area for the eight to fifteen people who played in the brass, electric, and percussion band; a grand piano; an electric organ; a centered plastic lectern; and several additional seats for associate pastors on the right side of the stage. On occasion, a telephone sat on a table by the associate pastors' chairs. Flanking the stage were rectangular stained glass windows featuring purple and tan colors. The windows shared an identical, somewhat abstract design that appeared to represent wheat. On the left side and behind the stage was the large banner reading "The Holy Spirit is Welcome Here." The stage was four steps higher than the front pews. In front of the stage, on both sides, sat six-foot-tall green plants.

Sunday Morning Services at Brown Hill

During my observation period, attendance at Brown Hill ranged from approximately 350 to 600 people. The assembly was mostly white, with an average of five to ten nonwhites (mainly African Americans) per service. The social historian Mickey Crews suggests that the contemporary Church of God (Cleveland, TN), with which Brown Hill was affiliated, has about 4 percent African American membership.[13] The historian Grant Wacker notes that Pentecostal churches—like those of other American denominations—are generally divided along lines of race and class.[14] Brown Hill, like Jefferson's churches as a whole, was no exception.

The gender ratio on a given Sunday morning was usually three women for every two men. More than 50 percent of the assembly appeared to be in their late forties or older. About 10 percent were children, another 10 percent were in their teens or early twenties, and about 30 percent were between twenty-five and forty-five. In one conversation an assistant pastor stated that while there had been a recent appearance of new people who had little or no Pentecostal background, most of the members still had parents and grandparents who were members.

The majority of the men in the assembly consistently dressed in two- or three-piece blue, brown, or gray suits. Most wore their hair short and were clean-shaven. A few sported mustaches. Never in my visits did I see a woman wear anything but a dress. Many did, however, wear necklaces, earrings, bracelets, and facial cosmetics. A small contingent of older women, present at every service, followed holiness codes that prohibited jewelry and hair cuts. These women wore their long hair in buns. The pastors—all male—wore suits similar to those worn by other men in the assembly. The choir was robed in pink and white gowns.

The first-time visitor at Brown Hill might have perceived the service to be random or at least very loosely structured. No bulletins described activities, no hymnals sat in the pews, and no formalized liturgy existed. But repeated visits to Brown Hill revealed a consistent pattern. Each service began with music and singing. Next, the pastor welcomed worshipers and led the group in prayer. Offering was then taken up, followed by announcements and the "Family of the Week" presentation. After these events came more music and singing, followed by the day's sermon. Every service ended with an altar call, which occasionally entailed healings at the front of the stage. Services usually lasted one hour.

Every Brown Hill meeting began and ended with contemporary Christian music in the style of Michael W. Smith, with songs set in two-four time that utilized keyboards, guitars, drums, bass, and brass instruments. Some songs were faster, some slower. Structurally, choruses were emphasized and repeated for longer periods than verses. One particular song, "I'm Blessed," started almost every service. Those in the pews usually responded to the opening songs by standing and clapping. Many knew the lyrics and sang along. Some in the pews raised their hands and rapidly spoke prayers. Others raised their hands and repeated phrases such as "praise Jesus" and "hallelujah." In general, these prayers and praises increased when upbeat, faster-paced songs were played.

On occasion, services would move out of this typical structure. Every Sunday, Pastor Timothy John invariably started the morning by saying, "I feel the Holy Spirit is with us here today." But on some mornings this claim seemed to be more the case than on others. At one particular service, Pastor John welcomed the "Golden Hillers Amazing Grace Choir." The group was made up of church members who were over fifty years old. This choir was not attired in the church's standard robes but in dress shirts, slacks, and dresses. John introduced the group by remarking that they "have a way of bringing out the Spirit in people." "In fact," he added, "I don't think I've ever seen them perform without someone in the audience getting the Spirit."

As the music—even faster-paced than usual—began, John told the congregation to stand and raise their hands in praise. About 90 percent of the assembly complied. While everyone remained in the pews, many clapped and energetically moved to the music. A man close to me stood with his hands in the air and spoke rapidly. A group of five women and two men stood together in the front-middle row of pews and vocalized loudly while swinging their arms. Their body movements were out of rhythm with the music and their speech may have been glossolalic, though I was not close enough to them to be able to say this for certain. On stage, the female lead vocalist began to speak in tongues during the song's choruses. Her utterances were accompanied by ecstatic physical gestures, including rapid head jerks and body jolts that made her look like she was being shocked. When the song ended, the lead vocalist and the pew participants stopped their ecstatic worship activities.

Following the song, the keyboardist played a slow melody that accompanied Pastor John's request for those who needed healing to come to the front. A number of people—largely older women—did. Five male assistants proceeded to lay their hands on participants' backs while John put oil on their foreheads. Each time he applied oil John briefly spoke in tongues before moving to the next person. In the pews, the majority kept their hands raised. The woman directly in front of me cried loudly, moved her hands up and down, and sang. After about ten minutes, John announced that the choir would perform another song.

The Golden Hillers again performed a fast-paced, repetitive tune. The enthusiasm of many in the congregation became more pronounced. The most ecstatic activities, however, were on the stage itself. The female lead vocalist again spoke in tongues and convulsed during the choruses. After each convulsion, in which her whole body jerked again as if being shocked, a quick glossolalic burst erupted from her, followed by silence and no movement, and then more tongues. Each time she spoke in tongues her eyes closed and her body became stiff and still. Seated behind the lead singer in the choir seats was Brother K., who began moving in his chair. With eyes closed, he stood and danced his way out of the choir aisle and onto the stage. In doing this, the gray-haired man fell three times, only to be helped up each time by one of the other male singers. At the end of the ten-minute song, Brother K. opened his eyes, looked around, and went back to his seat. With the music over, an assistant pastor stepped to the lectern and remarked, "I've seen some praising the Lord by dancing and that's just fine." "Psalm 150," he continued, "talks about dancing to praise the Lord." He then introduced Pastor John and noted that his sermon would be about praising the Lord.

Brown Hill Church of God sermons, like the services, followed a predictable structure. The exposition began with a comical story that was used to introduce the talk's theme. For example, a sermon about Christ appearing when all hope is gone started with the story of a woman who thought that as long as she had checks in her checkbook, she had money in the bank. After the humorous story, John named the sermon's theme and read Bible verses that addressed it. This formed the bulk of the sermon. Nearly every sermon ended with a sad personal story. It was not unusual for John to repeat the same narrative in different sermons. For example, he related the story of his wife's miscarriage three times in a three-month span. The basic sermon structure remained the same, even on the occasion of a talk by a visiting pastor. His exposition was about falling into the hands of God. It began with a humorous childhood recollection and ended with the frightening personal account of a destructive Arkansas tornado. During the horrific tale, the visiting pastor mirrored John's preaching style in that he cried and briefly spoke in tongues.

Sermons at Brown Hill usually had one of two themes. The first, found in most every sermon, was a general call to praise God. The second, less frequent subject entailed listing the problems in contemporary society, which John dubbed "Godless." In the nine-month period of observation, John gave three sermons condemning homosexuality. In each, he declared it a sin and a sign of demon possession. He also paired abortion with homosexuality in these three sermons, suggesting that both illustrated the fallen state of the modern world.

Holiness Road Pentecostal Church

Holiness Road was located four miles northeast of downtown Jefferson on Route 4. The area immediately surrounding the church was rural, consisting of open fields and a farmhouse about one thousand feet behind the church. Trees were sparse. Across the four lane road stood a Church of Christ. About one-half mile down the road, toward Jefferson, new subdivisions gave evidence that the city was expanding toward Holiness Road.

The church was surrounded by a parking lot. The building was one hundred feet long and rectangular. Large tan cement bricks and gray concrete made up its exterior. By the road, a glass-and-brick sign announced the church's name, the pastor's name, and the service hours. Behind the building sat an open-sided pole barn. Though it looked like the kind of structure some churches have for outdoor revivals or picnics, during my period of observation it was being used to store an aging mower, used tires, old desks, wooden boards, and other items.

One entered the church through two glass doors that faced the road. The small vestibule had stairs on the left that led to basement toilets and Sunday school classrooms. One entered the worship and seating area through two brown doors. Inside, two rows of fifteen pews sat on each side of the room. The pews, like the ceiling, were dark brown wood. The carpet was burgundy. The walls were cream white, and four stained glass windows—mostly decorated with depictions of Jesus—adorned each side.

The brown lectern and attached microphone sat in the middle front of the stage. Also on the stage stood a piano, two acoustic guitars, amplifiers, and folding chairs. The wall behind the stage was covered with brown paneling, though in its center faux rocks made a line from ceiling to stage floor.

Sunday Morning Services at Holiness Road Pentecostal Church

During my period of observation, Sunday morning service attendance ranged from about fifty-five to eighty people. The assembly was almost exclusively white. Only once during my nine-month span of observation did I see anyone who wasn't white. On that occasion, a white mother brought her racially mixed infant.

Twice as many women as men usually attended services. About 55 percent of the assembly appeared to be in their late forties or older. About 15 percent consisted of children, 10 percent could have been classified as young adults, and about 20 percent looked to be between twenty-five and forty-five years of age. From references made by formal speakers and those conversing in the pews, it appeared that many in the church were related and that, on a given Sunday, three generations of one family might be present.

In terms of clothing, the males dressed in a variety of colors but almost invariably wore dress shirts and dress pants. About one of every four men wore ties and/or three-piece suits. No men in any service I observed had any facial hair or wore their hair long. Every woman in every meeting wore a dress. Though men and women in the assembly sported wedding rings, practically none of the women had other jewelry or makeup. All the women kept their hair long and unstyled, though most of the older women kept their hair in buns.

Holiness Road services had even less visible structure than Brown Hill services. No bulletins, robed choirs, or formalized liturgy existed. The pastor's assistants were only recognizable as such when they occasionally sat on the stage. At the same time, repeated observation of Holiness Road services did reveal a predictable pattern. Sunday morning services started right after Bible study classes. Since they both occurred in the main worship area, they often bled into each other. The start of the service was signaled by music. On occasion the pastor, C. C. Bradshaw, performed healings during the initial music. After the music, assistants took up the offering, which was followed by more music and then the sermon. After the sermon, altar call and pew prayers occurred, with occasional healings at the front of the stage. The meetings lasted from fifty to seventy-five minutes, with the performance of country-and-western and rockabilly-tinged gospel tunes—with enthusiastic assembly participation—taking up about half of the service time. On several occasions in which the congregation's participation was especially enthusiastic, the offering was skipped. The following description of one service illustrates the structure of the event and the style of the assembly's participation.

One morning I entered the church at 10:55 A.M. and walked into the adult Bible study class. A brown-haired man spoke for three to five minutes about a Bible verse and then stopped abruptly in midsentence and introduced Pastor C. C. Bradshaw. A gray-haired man of fifty-five or more years, Bradshaw related the Bible verse (unnamed after my entrance) to a narrative about a man who had come into Holiness Road wearing a sweat suit and "wanting a prayer." Bradshaw said that he "and a few of the brothers" prayed over him, after which the man thanked them and left. Bradshaw then asked for anyone who needed a prayer to join him up front. After the invitation, the musicians began to play "Joy Unspeakable." This signaled the beginning of the service.

With an acoustic guitar, Bradshaw played the song with a decidedly country-and-western flavor. He was accompanied by a drummer, electric guitarist, electric bassist, and the youth pastor on another acoustic guitar. During the song, three women walked up to the left side of the stage and four men gathered on the right side. As I became more acquainted with the church, I realized that these first people were the day's pastoral assistants who would meet those of their sex who came forward for healing and prayer. The women stayed on the left side of the stage and the men on the right. On this particular morning, nine women and two men went forward to their respective sides for prayer. Three of the women went up carrying or walking with children.

During the initial music, nearly the whole assembly—except me—was energetic in its worship. For fifteen minutes, a gray-haired woman six rows in front of me flexed her back and neck muscles, alternately stiffening and relaxing them while she waved her arms and uttered what sounded like moans of pained ecstasy. The bodies of four women who had gone to the front shook when they raised their hands into the air and shouted praise. Soon the four began vocalizing a wavelike pattern of sounds, like humming, in unison. For me, their alternating high and low pitches of moaning and chanting proved to be a mesmerizing combination.

During the first song, Bradshaw moved back and forth between the men on the right of the stage and the women on the left. When the music stopped, he directed his attention to the four women who hummed in unison. "We don't stand on our strength, we stand on His!" Bradshaw said as he stood over them. "We have the victory," he added, "hallelujah!" After Bradshaw said this, the women abruptly stopped their vocalizing.

During the second song, "I Cross the River Jordan," the enthusiasm in the pews grew stronger. A woman who looked to be in her twenties rose from her seat and ran three laps around the outside aisles of the pews. As she ran past me, I heard her speaking in tongues. At the end of the third run, she stopped, leaned her face against the wall to the far right of the stage, and remained there until the song ended. Offering plates were then passed around without any announcement.

Following the offering, the band performed "Child of the King." Like the two previous numbers, the song was up-tempo, country-and-western, lengthy, and repetitious. Many women raised their hands and shouted praises to God. The graying woman directly in front of me cried as she tightened and released her hand muscles, making fists while she prayed with closed eyes. An older woman walked around the outside of the pews saying, "thank you Lord," as tears streamed down her face.

The men, with a few exceptions, worshiped in less demonstrative ways. One spoke in glossolalia and shouted on occasion, but this was unusual among the men. After more music, Brother Bradshaw—as members called him—began his sermon by quoting Psalm 81, which urges believers to sing aloud and praise God with voice and instrument.

The sermons at Holiness Road, unlike those at Brown Hill, followed no typical structure. Bradshaw often spoke extemporaneously, waiting for God to give him the day's message. Despite the lack of predictable order, though, certain motifs appeared in nearly every sermon. Personal testimonials about human suffering, general comments on the world's sinful state, and assertions that God holds the answer to individual and global problems filled almost every sermon.

First, stories about human suffering abounded in Holiness Road sermons by Bradshaw, as well as his one-time guest speaker, Brother James. Bradshaw began many sermons with attention-grabbing statements. "Stood over a casket yesterday," he began one sermon. "One son left—a drinker," he continued.

"He stood over the casket and cried, 'Daddy, I'm gonna make something out of myself.' But the Lord will have to give him a hand," Bradshaw suggested. He began another sermon by recounting his mother's death and his current assurance that she was now in heaven. "Where she is now," he said in a loud, tearful tone, "makes her little old shack look like a pigsty."

Brother James, in his guest sermon at Holiness Road, also gave personal testimony of human suffering. "What more?" James exclaimed. "I can't give the boys all they need—no suits, no money—but Jesus can give it to them." His sermon, which I return to later, contained tales of five deaths of the faithless and his own fight for life in a hospital critical care ward. "While you're gasping for air and there's no air there," James recounted, "you'll wish you were saved!"

A second theme in Holiness Road sermons entailed the world's fallen, sinful state. "America's goofing up today," Bradshaw lamented one Sunday morning. "TV and video games have made our children into a generation of spectators." On another occasion, Brother Bradshaw prayed to "help those [who are] into the various forms of worldly entertainment." In addition to these condemnations of American popular culture, he also looked to troubling world events as signs that the world as we knew it was nearing its end. In one sermon, Bradshaw referred to violence in the Philippines and the first Gulf War as signs that the apocalyptic battle between God and Satan was at hand:

> In the Philippines today there is a sense of ensuing judgment. Here in the U.S. there's a sense of portending judgment, some here today may know it. Even sinners know it. Doom can't roll in until the light of the world is gone. The heinous leader of Iraq opened up the oil caps in the Persian Gulf. I saw camels in *National Geographic* walking around in the goo and darkness. It was localized because of brave countries fighting it. The fire's out now, but a new fire's getting ready to rage.

The third recurring sermon theme was God as the solution to individual and global problems. In one sermon, Bradshaw suggested that God had blessed the congregation and America with the "finest wheat," and people had only to accept the grain. One example of the "finest wheat" given that morning appeared in a narrative about "Brother Teffy back in West Virginia." Bradshaw related that Teffy loved honey. One day, when walking in the woods in search of it, Teffy asked his companion to kneel and pray with him. Soon after their prayer they saw a hole in the tree in front of them glistening in the sun with honey. Bradshaw said that Teffy knew he had the finest wheat, and that the Holiness Road congregation should remember that they did too.

These three recurring subjects were usually—though not always—sup-

and loudly spoke in tongues. When she began, every participant in the church stopped praying, praising, or engaging in other gestures to focus attention on her. I had never seen her speak—in tongues or English—during my previous visits, and from the response in the pews I wondered if it was rare. Bradshaw interpreted his wife's message. He closed his eyes and said that everyone present that morning should "take the Lord's word to heed." This action had the effect of calming the worshipers and moving the service out of the music segment and into Bradshaw's sermon.

Poloma dubs the second type of ritual style the "Evangelistic Service" and suggests that it entails "ritual practices that emphasize personal testimonies."[17] Such services feature testimonies about healing, visions, and answered prayers. The majority of Brown Hill sermons contained a story of answered prayers. Pastor John's tearful personal testimony of the miraculous adoption of a daughter after his wife's stillbirth and his story of a woman healed of AIDS through conversion and prayer provided two examples. This type of testimony was less frequent at Holiness Road. Bradshaw once made the remark, for example, that "Brother Kilbourn went back to the doctor last week and his tumor disappeared through the will of Jesus." But comments like this were infrequent, and in neither church was time set aside for the people in the pews to give testimonies. As will be seen in the discussion below, Holiness Road sermons more often stressed the bad things that happened to the unsaved, rather than the good that believers garnered.

Poloma terms the third ritual type "Neo-liturgical," which is similar in several ways to her "Old-style Pentecostal" classification.[18] Neo-liturgical style includes gestures such as formalized calls-and-responses in the form of "amens" and "hallelujahs," prescribed greetings of one's pew neighbor, set team performances by assistant pastors, and professional quality musicians and staging. These features accurately describe the most recognizable element of Brown Hill's Sunday services. Pastor John asked the assembly to "praise God by clapping your hands" and also to "turn to the person next to you and tell them the Holy Spirit is here today." Brown Hill services were taped for both radio and television broadcast, and the church featured a "media ministry."

Neo-liturgical practices—at least as Poloma defines them—were virtually absent at the Holiness Road Pentecostal Church. Holiness Road had no media ministry, and while many of the musicians were quite accomplished, the concept of the "professional church band" was negated by the presence of others who were less trained but felt God calling them to go on stage and play. In addition, Brother Bradshaw seldom asked the congregants for "amens" or shouts of praise. While the Holiness Road participants were generally enthusiastic, they received no explicit call from the pulpit to be so.

Poloma's fourth category, "Communal Experiences," closely mirrors anthropologist Victor Turner's concept of "communitas."[19] For Turner, communitas entailed the communal experience of unstructured, egalitarian relationships.[20] In such types of Pentecostal rituals, Poloma argues, the "order of the
service is set aside, the offering forgotten, and the congregation collectively
responds as 'the power of the Holy Spirit' takes over the service."[21] These types
of services were much more frequent at Holiness Road. On some occasions,
offerings were forgotten at ecstatic worship services. When such enthusiastic
meetings erupted, over half the morning service entailed singing, speaking
in tongues, healings, dancing in the spirit, and other gestures. Such occasions
were very rare at Brown Hill, with the sole example being the Golden Hillers
performance described above.

While Poloma's categories consist of Weberian ideal types that, in actual
cases, may bleed into each other, they are still useful for comparing Brown
Hill and Holiness Road. As already noted above, Holiness Road presented
a more ecstatic, less structured, and less formalized style of Holiness Pentecostalism than Brown Hill Church of God. But one similarity the assemblies shared was the sort of people who were most likely to speak in tongues,
dance in the spirit, and exhibit other ecstatic worship behaviors. Similar to the
ethnographic observations made in American Pentecostal churches by Elaine
Lawless, Troy Abell, and Felicitas Goodman, I observed that those most likely
to speak in tongues at both Brown Hill and Holiness Road were women.[22] In
addition, my observations concur with Abell's that it was older participants—
both female and male—who were most likely to speak in tongues and demonstrate other ecstatic worship gestures. In both churches, whenever males who
were not clergy spoke in tongues or worshipped with marked enthusiasm,
they were older men. In addition, Abell suggests two different styles of glossolalia. He argues that the first, which he calls "dissociative," occurs during what
in earlier decades would have been called "altered states of consciousness."
The second, "stylized tongues," seems to occur in a nondissociative state. No
physical behaviors accompany these tongues, which often come in the middle
of sentences and last a few seconds.[23] Stylized tongues were most common at
Brown Hill and were voiced by Pastor John during sermons. The majority of
glossolalia at Holiness Road, in contrast, appeared to be dissociative, accompanied by ecstatic bodily movements and gestures.

Sermon Tones in the Two Assemblies

In *Verbal Art as Performance*, the folklorist Richard Bauman argues that public speech may be thought of as a performance. The act of speaking to certain

groups under specific circumstances lends itself to the same types of evaluations and accountability as a dramatic presentation. Listeners judge the speaker on accuracy, authenticity, and engagement. For example, how one tells a joke will be as much of a factor in eliciting laughter as its punch-line. Likewise, the ability to scare listeners with a ghost story involves the way one performs the story, the context it is told in, and the demographics of the listeners.

The folklorist Elaine Lawless references Bauman's ideas in her analysis of the "spiritual life stories" of female Holiness Pentecostal preachers. Lawless argues that their autobiographical narratives must contain certain motifs and follow predictable patterns to be validated as authentic by their assemblies and to justify the taking of the pastor's role by a female.[24] For example, a woman who told her congregation that she had always wanted to be a preacher would not, according to Lawless, have her authority accepted by the group. Instead, a female Pentecostal pastor's story invariably requires God's calling her to the ministry, her rejection of the calling because she was a "just a woman," God's continued command to preach, and the woman's eventual acquiescence to God's demands.

Bauman and Lawless offer useful approaches for comparing sermons at Brown Hill and Holiness Road. Sermons are performances. Positive and enthusiastic response from the pews may partly gauge the consonance of the sermon's content and delivery with the congregation's assumptions, expectations, concerns, and values. In other words, positively received sermons may reveal something about the church's corporate disposition or, to use the social theorist Pierre Bourdieu's term, "habitus."[25] The habitus, as a "system of lasting, transposable dispositions," bears the features of past and present social locations and "functions at every moment as a matrix of perceptions, appreciations, and actions."[26] Of course, one must stress that successful sermons may only *partly* reveal something about the congregational habitus because a variety of factors play a role in participant response. What looks like enthusiasm may be politeness. What appears to be apathy may have more to do with circumstances apart from the sermon and its delivery. Even more, any congregation—no matter how demographically homogeneous—includes a variety of individuals with differing perceptions. One must be careful not to make too much of participant response.

At the same time, one expects different reactions to performances that coincide with or that violate congregational norms and expectations. One example of the latter occurred at the only subdued service I attended at Holiness Road. That meeting began with a young man singing two slow songs while playing solo acoustic guitar, versus the standard, upbeat, full-band rockabilly and country-and-western style of music. Brother Bradshaw then announced that a family of guest singers from a neighboring state would sing. The group consisted of a father, three boys, and one girl. While the music was slightly more upbeat, only one person in the pews clapped for the group. The rest were still and silent. I noticed that the girl stood at the same microphone as the boys. With the exception of Bradshaw's laying healing hands on females who came forward, this was the only time I had ever seen members of both sexes near each other on or near the stage. I couldn't help but wonder whether the different musical style and the violation of sex separation on the stage combined to dampen the congregation's enthusiasm.

Sermons at both Brown Hill and Holiness Road contained themes of praise, faith in God, and the fallen state of the world. Both pastors delivered animated sermons. At the same time, there were marked differences. Structurally, Brown Hill sermons followed a strict pattern, while Holiness Road sermons were less formalized and less predictable. But this difference was overshadowed by a starker one. The sermon tone differed dramatically. In brief, Brown Hill sermons were conversational, personal, humorous, sentimental, and reassuring. Holiness Road sermons were very serious, seldom if ever humorous, and rarely reassuring. Brown Hill sermons focused on the good that God does for believers. Holiness Road sermons focused on the struggles believers faced and the damnation and pain sinners were assured. An example of this difference can be seen by comparing sermons broaching the same subject: car accidents.

Pastor John started one September morning sermon with the question, "have you ever been confused?" Following the story of a boy who forgot his lines in a Christian school play, John told the congregants that his friend worked in insurance and handled car accident claims. "You read through some of those car insurance claims and boy," John observed, "you see a lot of confusion there." He proceeded to read eight quotes from some of the claims. Half of them involved a pedestrian getting hit. "'The pedestrian didn't know which way to go,'" he read, "'so I hit him.'" He read another: "'First he ran left, then he ran right, then I hit him.'" These stories, used to illustrate confusion, garnered much laughter from the assembly. "Jesus takes care of you" was the sermon theme. John ended it by repeating the story of his wife's miscarriage and the adoption of their daughter, who, John said "came by the supernatural." "I don't know why bad things happen to good people," he remarked, "but Jesus will come to you." Following the sermon, an unusually large number of people—thirty-two—more than I typically saw during the period of my observation, went forward for the altar call. The majority were older women.

Car accidents appeared in the sermon as humorous illustrations of confusion. Despite the fact that pedestrians were struck and presumably injured, congregants laughed. The sermon ended with the usual reassuring note that Jesus takes care of believers. At the same time, John never suggested that Jesus took care of the injured pedestrians. They helped introduce his narrative through humor but dropped out of the sermon early. As such, John's utilization of car accidents contrasted dramatically with the use of the same subject in one Holiness Road sermon given by Brother James, whose guest talk replicated the tone and style of Bradshaw's weekly addresses. James's theme was "you can't reject God."

The sermon contained descriptions of hell, the story of James's conversion in a hospital bed, and six tales of people suffering terrible fates when they rejected God. Three of these featured car accidents, one involved a helicopter crash, one an illness, and another a suicide. The first car accident involved three teenagers who left a church service before it was over and were killed on the road five hundred feet from the church doors. Told as a memorate, meaning a personal experience story containing supernatural elements, James said that he had been preaching, and the Holy Ghost had warned him that this would occur if the teens rejected God. The second story involved a drunk man who died in a car wreck, his intoxication making him unable to pray for forgiveness before his death. The third story concerned a girl he encountered in Alabama who was terribly injured in an accident the night after she refused to pray during his service. In five of the six stories, James said that the Holy Ghost had warned him that these victims had one "last chance" to repent or face injury, death, and eternal torment in hell.

After the sermon, more than half the assembly went to the front during altar call. James singled out women and the few youth in attendance to come forward. "Now I'm not getting the feeling this morning," James stated, "but I could imagine a lady here at Holiness Road dying; I can imagine myself getting called a few days from now about it." In addition to such portentous statements, James looked at specific congregants, walked off the stage toward them, and spoke directly to them, saying "go, please go!" Most who went forward during altar call that morning shook and cried.

While this example involved a guest speaker, Brother James, it followed the tone of Brother Bradshaw's sermons, which similarly warned listeners to not be sure of anything, especially one's state of sanctification. This contrasted sharply to the sermons at Brown Hill, whose congregants consistently heard humorous and sentimental reassurances that God would always take care of them.

Explaining the Differences: The Deprivationist View and Its Shortcomings

Pentecostalism, as seen in chapter 4, has long been interpreted as a religion of the deprived. In examining the Brown Hill Church of God and the Holiness Road Pentecostal Church, a deprivation theorist might suggest that Holiness Road participants suffered more deprivation than congregants at Brown Hill. Perhaps they were poorer, older, less healthy, and endured more "culture shock" from the dislocations of migration from rural Appalachia to urban Jefferson. These factors, the deprivationist might postulate, would account for the greater number of ecstatic ritual gestures, stricter holiness codes, and harsher sermon tones at Holiness Road.

A deprivation theorist might also point out that women and older congregants in both assemblies were the most likely to speak in tongues, dance in the spirit, and engage in other ecstatic worship behaviors. The anthropologist I. M. Lewis argues that "possession works to help the interests of the weak and downtrodden who have otherwise few effective means to press their claims for attention and respect."[27] A deprivationist might posit that ecstatic worship behaviors such as glossolalia allowed the two groups with the least power in the two churches and the larger society to gain spiritual status. Recall that in Holiness Pentecostal theology, speaking in tongues is a sign of Entire Sanctification, a physical demonstration that the individual is free of all voluntary sin. Being in such a state of holiness grants one a superior religious rank.

The deprivationist could also use this argument corporately in comparing the two churches. Holiness Road, a church of the rural working class, was more ecstatic than Brown Hill, a congregation of an emerging suburban middle class. In addition to ritual behaviors, the argument could also explain the differences in church decorum, personal dress, and sermon tone. In *Sect Ideologies and Social Status*, Gary Schwartz makes the Weberian argument that a church's rituals, symbols, and messages reflect and validate its members' social locations. "In a very subtle fashion," Schwartz suggests, "the lifestyle of a class or community gains religious attributes."[28] In this interpretation, Holiness Road congregants followed strict dress codes because they could not afford the more expensive and elaborate clothing that many Brown Hill members wore. Likewise, Brown Hill congregants engaged less in ecstatic worship because they had relatively more economic effect on, control over, and power in their lives and community.

A deprivation theorist could also use this line of argument to explain the differences in sermon tone. The sociologist Max Weber argued that groups and individuals seek theological legitimacy for their worldly success or fail-

hibit ecstatic worship behaviors at both churches. Rather then their low status as older people, the fact that they may have had more experience and history with the religious tradition could account for their more frequent speaking in tongues, dancing in the spirit, and other gestures.

A second variable that may partly explain congregational differences involves music and sermon deliveries. There were both similarities and differences in the styles of Pastor John and Brother Bradshaw. Both spoke with charismatic intonations and inflections. Both paced, jumped, stamped, shook, flailed, and sang during sermons. At the same time, Bradshaw gave his sermons in a rhythmic, songlike delivery, which John did not use. Bradshaw's sermons tended to become faster as they progressed, and he would enhance the rhythmic nature of them by ending every line with an "ah" sound. Bradshaw's speed and repetition, coupled with his songlike delivery, may have been more effective as "driving speech" that encouraged ecstatic worship. In addition, Holiness Road's music tended to be louder, faster, and more repetitive. In their studies of glossolalia and other Pentecostal gestures, Felicitas Goodman, Troy Abell, and Cyril Williams have all noted that music, service rhythm, and the physical quality of the altar call directly correlate to the amount of ecstatic worship and speaking in tongues in a given meeting.[31] Goodman termed these energetic aspects of Pentecostal ritual "driving" elements.[32] Both Goodman and Abell suggest that driving assists participants in entering a dissociative state in which such gestures as speaking in tongues, rocking, dancing, and shaking occur.[33] Whether or not congregants entered into altered, dissociative states of consciousness, one could conclude that the driving elements of pastoral style and music were much stronger at Holiness Road.

The third factor one must weigh involves congregational affiliation. Brown Hill Church of God belonged to a national denomination, the Church of God (Cleveland, TN). Holiness Road was independent and entirely self-governing. In brief, the milieu of Brown Hill's services was partly the result of a larger national institution marked by growth and accommodation, while the Holiness Road assembly had not been subject to the changing trends and bureaucracy of any extralocal institution. The Church of God (Cleveland, TN)—which is one of the fastest growing denominations in the United States—historically has developed a tightly controlled bureaucracy that resulted in much conformity between organizational goals and individual congregations.[34]

In *The Church of God: A Social History*, the scholar Mickey Crews suggests that the history of the denomination shows a slow accommodation and acculturation toward larger American cultural styles and trends. In the 1910s and 1920s, the Church of God sanctioned snake-handling and followed strict holiness codes that even included a ban on wedding rings (because they are jewelry). Gradually, and especially after World War II, Crews explains, the denomination softened its attitude toward "worldly" activities such as spectator sports, television, clothing, jewelry, and members' enlistment in the United States military. He suggests that an influx of more economically affluent non-Pentecostals into the denomination after World War II spurred this change.

One specific case of such accommodation relevant to the Jefferson churches is the changing stance of the Church of God hierarchy toward dress and appearance. Before World War II, Crews notes, leaders admonished female members—to whom the codes are primarily addressed—to "not dress in a manner that would attract people's attention."[35] In 1933, the General Assembly voted that all female members must wear dresses that "came to the elbows and ankles."[36] In 1934, the resolution was reworded so that those not conforming to the standards could be expelled from the denomination. According to Crews, the rule didn't work because "as new fashions became popular, Church of God women, like many American females, bought and wore dresses that were shorter and more revealing."[37]

By the 1940s, the Church of God began officially relaxing holiness dress codes. One resolution that year adopted a statement calling for women to dress "according to New Testament standards," yet it chose not to define what those standards were. While one 1968 Executive Council declaration responded to the youth counterculture by prohibiting "low-cut, sleeveless dresses, mini-skirts, shorts, slacks, and jeans," a 1976 statement returned to nonspecificity, saying members should "conform to the scripture relative to outward adornment and to the use of cosmetics."[38]

The Church of God's dicta concerning holiness dress codes might be described as "accommodation through ambiguity." The marked growth of the denomination since the mid-1960s has made enforcement of specific dress codes virtually impossible. The resulting 1976 Executive Council statement allowed the church to keep its holiness concerns yet has also instituted a flexibility that opens congregations to new members unfamiliar with historical Holiness churches.[39] The Brown Hill position on appearance and dress, found in the denomination's undated pamphlet *Our Statements of Faith*, available in the church lobby, well illustrates this:

APPEARANCE AND DRESS

Our life, character, and self-image are reflected by our apparel and mode of dress. The admonition of Scripture, "Be not conformed to this world," reminds us that our manner of dress must be modest and decent (Romans 12:2; I Thessalonians 5:22, 23). It is not displeasing to God for us to dress well and be well-groomed. However, above all we must seek spiritual beauty, which does not come from outward adornment with jewelry, expensive clothes or cosmetics, but from good works, chaste conversation, and a meek and quiet spirit (Philippians 4:8; I Peter 3:3–5).[40]

If one examines the biblical texts cited as authoritative, they urge believers to not conform to the world, to abstain from the appearance of evil, and to think about and praise honesty, truth, purity, and other related characteristics. Only in 1 Peter can one find specific dress restrictions. Examining the translation most common at Brown Hill—the King James Version[41]—the passage urges wives to be in subjection to their husbands and, if they must adorn themselves, to "let it not be that outward adorning of plaiting the hair, and of wearing gold, or of putting on of apparel; But let it be the hidden man of the heart, in that which is not corruptible, even the ornament of a meek and quiet spirit, which is in the sight of God of great price." The Church of God statement leaves the permissible middle point between "modest" and "well-dressed" up to each member. At Brown Hill, many women use makeup and jewelry—including gold. Crews's social history of the Church of God suggests that the variety of dress and appearance at Brown Hill likely mirrors changes in the national denomination as a whole. One Brown Hill assistant pastor, whom I asked about the differences in holiness code adherence between his church and Holiness Road, suggested that assemblies with too strict holiness codes "will lose souls." He noted that he would like to see more people at Brown Hill "practicing holiness" in the way they dressed but added that there had to be a "happy medium" between "gaining souls for the Lord and keeping holiness."

In contrast, the majority of Holiness Road participants followed stricter holiness dress and appearance codes. Though the claim would be hard to corroborate, one nonmember suggested to me that Holiness Road had actually become more strict since the congregation split apart in the 1970s. Being independent, the congregation engaged in practices unique to the assembly. The sex separation on and in front of the stage during worship was one such example. A female member told me that she had not seen the practice at other churches that Holiness Road was "in fellowship with." "I know for myself," she added, "when I am down praying I would rather be surrounded by other women than by a bunch of men."

Since the early twentieth-century writings of Max Weber, Ernst Troelstch, and H. Richard Niebuhr, some social scientists have argued that institutional organization leads to routinization of religious behaviors. Margaret Poloma, for example, has suggested that institutionalization led to the tempering and routinization of charismatic worship within the Assemblies of God denomi-

nation and in the Toronto Blessing movement of the 1990s.[42] The more structured services, formulaic sermons, and less charismatic worship at Brown
Hill contrasted with the more ecstatic, expository, and open style of Holiness
Road. These differences are at least partly attributable to each assembly's institutional versus independent status. Combining such factors as institutional
affiliation with the number of new faces in the pews and different music and
sermon delivery styles, one can begin to see that deprivation theories or other
psychological explanations are not necessary to account for the differences
between Brown Hill and Holiness Road. But what about the place of class in
understanding the two assemblies?

Class in the Assemblies

In the previous section I intentionally left class out of the discussion. At the
same time, most outside observers would immediately see "class" writ large
in the cars, clothing, decorum, music, speech, worship, and other aspects of
the two assemblies. I would concur with such observers that both churches
were predominantly working-class. At the same time, many of Jefferson's congregations were working-class, but of course most of them were not Holiness Pentecostal. Rather than discussing class by looking at Brown Hill and
Holiness Road in contrast to other local churches, I suggest that we compare
the two. Given the arguments set forth in chapter 1, class may emerge in two
ways. First, did either of the congregations consciously nurture a subcultural
identity that included a class component? Second, how might class have constrained or permitted religious repertoires and thus resulted in differing congregational styles? In addressing these questions, my answers should be taken
as propositions for consideration and discussion.

In the first chapter I suggested that one way to conceive of class is to view
it as a tool of self-definition ascribed to one's group or person. Neither Brown
Hill nor Holiness Road actively or explicitly nurtured a class identity. At the
same time, class identification latently emerged. Recall that C. C. Bradshaw's
discussion of his mother's place in heaven making her "little old shack look
like a pigsty" suggested a modest earthly abode. Likewise, Brother James's
guest sermon contained several class references. He marked his personal testimony with allusions to being poor. He called himself the "thirty-third heir
of thirty heirs" to an old Kentucky coal mine and declared in another part of
the talk, "I can't give the boys all they need—no suits, no money—but Jesus
can give it to them." On both occasions, class appeared in a sermon that mentioned Kentucky. In a process of inexplicit articulation, such rhetoric linked
Appalachian, lower-class, and Holiness Pentecostal identities. At the same

time, tales of suffering and misfortune were seldom explicitly linked to socio-economic locations.

Like Holiness Road, public speech at the Brown Hill Church of God exhibited little subcultural identification with class. In fact—and unlike Holiness Road—explicit class references never appeared in my nine months of Brown Hill observations. When suffering and misfortune surfaced in Pastor John's sermons, they were never linked to socioeconomic locations. Rather, problems such as AIDS or miscarriages were explained in terms of what John assumed to be either "lifestyle choices" or medical problems that crossed class boundaries. Similarly, references to Appalachian background appeared only once, and with a different tone and reaction. In one sermon, John smiled as he referred to Kentucky as a "holy land" that some in the assembly returned to for holidays. Many in the assembly quietly laughed as the amused pastor looked at the congregation, half-shook his head, and repeated his phrase. I am certain that such a statement at Holiness Road would not be given with a smile nor received with chuckles. Rather than something reflexively humorous, such a statement at Holiness Road would likely be taken more as a matter of fact. When Brother Bradshaw referred to Brother Teffy in Kentucky, the place was a secondary fact in the story. Teffy's love of honey was primary and this is what brought smiles to listeners' faces.

Class as a subcultural identity was present but muted and latent in both assemblies. Class or socioeconomic hardship never explicitly appeared in Brown Hill sermons, songs, or testimonies. While such topics did appear at Holiness Road, they did not dominate public speech and were closely intertwined with other identities, such as Appalachian. But did class relate to the religious styles, or repertoires, of the two churches? How might class have permitted or constrained the congregations in terms of worship styles, behavioral codes, sermons, and testimonies? To engage these questions, it is necessary to return to my third conception of class, as well as the notion of "class culture."

As noted in the first chapter, my conception of class as availability and constraint closely resembles Bourdieu's concept of habitus, that "system of lasting, transposable dispositions which, integrating past experiences, functions at every moment as a matrix of perceptions, appreciations, and actions."[43] While this definition seems particularly applicable to individuals, Bourdieu also examines social groupings. "Classes on paper," as he dubs such social scientific taxonomies, are "sets of agents who occupy similar positions and who, being placed in similar conditions and subjected to similar conditionings, have every likelihood of having similar dispositions and interests and therefore of producing similar practices and adopting similar stances."[44] Drawing on Bourdieu's habitus model, the sociologist Fred Rose uses the term "class culture." With one caveat, I find his definition useful. Rose defines class culture as "beliefs, attitudes, and understandings, symbols, social practices, and rituals throughout the life cycle that are characteristic of positions within the production process."[45] My exception to this definition is that narrowly tying the concept to the Marxian definition of class as inherently about "positions within the production process" underestimates important and primary class variables such as education, wealth, and income. Here I adopt and slightly adapt "class culture" to mean the range of cultural repertoires (styles, objects, tools, and strategies) found among a particular group of people who are related by similar social locations and material conditions.

Rose's model of class culture in some ways resembles sociologist Ann Swidler's concept of "cultural repertoire." For Rose, "social class shapes social movements through the medium of class culture," but classes are not homogeneous, and "class is not correlated with any one set of ideas or politics."[46] Instead, class cultures, like cultural repertoires, work more on the level of structure, strategy, and form rather than content. In other words, members of a specific class culture may not have similar political, social, or religious views. Instead, Rose argues that class "delineates the form that movements take rather than any particular political content."[47] As noted in chapter 1, Rose suggests that working-class movements tend to have more marked insider/outsider boundaries than middle-class groups. Similarly, in chapter 1 I also cited Swidler's discussion of Basil Bernstein, who found that working-class schoolchildren spoke in less elaborated codes than middle-class children.

Given these suggestions, two things to compare in the assemblies are the different levels of boundary marking between insiders and outsiders and the extent of elaborated language in public speech. I suggest that the differences between the Brown Hill Church of God and the Holiness Road Pentecostal Church may be partly interpreted as an instance of two diverging class cultures. In brief, the oral histories transmitted among members suggest that both churches began among Jefferson's working-class Appalachian migrants. Over time, Brown Hill mirrored its national denomination and became more culturally and economically diverse. Holiness Road, on the other hand, remained relatively more homogeneous socioeconomically. Accompanying the demographic change at Brown Hill are (1) less restrictive holiness codes, (2) loosened community boundaries, (3) more elaborated worship and sermon language, and (4) fewer ecstatic religious practices.

First, the Brown Hill Church of God mirrored the changes of its denomination, the Church of God (Cleveland, TN), in having looser and more ambiguously drawn holiness codes concerning dress and appearance. The denominational statement that it is not displeasing to God that someone is

more acceptable to people from non-Pentecostal and more "middle-class" so-cial locations. Holiness Road, remaining more working-class and homoge-neous, engaged in more demonstrative worship activities.

Conclusion

In this chapter I contested deprivation explanations of Brown Hill and Holi-ness Road assemblies by suggesting three factors that could account for their differences. The historical connection between the material conditions of class and deprivation theories is so strong that any critique of deprivation models appears to negate the influence of class. But I suggested that class was still im-portant. I argued that the two assemblies may be viewed as having once had similar, but currently diverging, class cultures. I hope to have opened a con-versation about how class may work through social networks, family cultures, and congregational traditions. Rather than asserting the attractiveness of cer-tain theologies and rituals to deprived people, one might instead find class influence in religious group boundaries and the restricted-versus-elaborated languages of faith and worship.

Conclusion

The end is important in all things.[1]

Whether or not we like the idea, all academic humanities research in some way relates to the author's biography. The religion scholar Thomas Tweed has recently reminded us that "theories are positioned sightings."[2] This is because academics—like all humans—are socially located. The spot where they "stand" and the places in which they have previously sat enable and constrain their perceptions. Social class has always played a significant role in my life's trajectory. It has constricted my perceptions and prospects in ways that I will only ever be partly aware of. But it has also provided me a vista from which to examine the world. It is from that place that I conceived this book and argued that class is a neglected yet important variable in religious studies. I am certain that readers socially positioned both far and near to me will see things I have neglected. If this work stimulates some discussion about class in the academic study of religion, I will consider it successful.

To conclude, I briefly do two things. First, I address a vexing unanswered question. Specifically, how does one understand, weigh, and discuss social class in relation to other variables such as race, place, and gender? Second, what are the implications for our research and teaching if we put class back into the study of religion?

Duct-Taping a Loose End

In the first chapter, I argued that class matters in the study of religion, and I hope this book has offered evidence to support that broad thesis. But I also noted that other things such as race, gender, place, and age also mattered. How does one weigh, or even discuss, how these things affect one's religious preferences? As someone trained in the humanities, I will leave the weighing and measuring to others more qualified. But I do want to suggest an idiom. One's physical location (rural versus urban, for example), racial identification, gender, and age can influence one's social networks and opportunities in a manner similar to social class. We need an idiom with which to discuss their interplay, a term to mark how these components combine and conflict in peoples' life trajectories and thus enable and constrain them in their religious affiliations and preferences. In chapter 1, I noted that my notion of class as availability and constraint closely mirrored the social theorist Pierre Bourdieu's "habitus" concept. At the same time, the ambiguities, silences, and scholarly debates that surround the concept of habitus weigh down its usage. Because of this I suggest an alternative that mines from Bourdieu's term but also elaborates and discards aspects of it. The term I propose is "socially habituated subjectivities."

I define socially habituated subjectivities as the repertoire of beliefs, practices, attitudes, assumptions, and gestures that have been inculcated by our social locations. The term refers to our enabling and constraining habits of mind and body. Breaking it down, "subjectivity" refers to our sense of being, identity, and embodied knowledge. That these things are "socially habituated" alludes to the process by which our social locations inscribe particular—and often corporately shared—conventions of being and acting. By "social location" I mean the demographical positions of social class (income, occupation, education, wealth), race, gender, age, place, and region.

I see the influence of socially habituated subjectivities—similar to Bourdieu's habitus—as mostly unacknowledged (i.e., semidoxic). But the term I proffer differs from habitus in at least three ways. First, I acknowledge the possibility of conscious habituation. In other words, individuals may deliberately and actively engage in various disciplinary routines in order to cultivate particular habits or extinguish existing ones.[3] Second, I view socially habituated subjectivities as multiple and at times conflicted within a single individual. This means that the different social locations that individuals exist within may influence them in contradictory ways.[4] Third, and related closely to the first two, socially habituated subjectivities are not necessarily static throughout one's lifespan. People may move in and out of various material and social circumstances throughout their lives. Like bell hooks—whose location shifted from rural working-class to best-selling author and academic—or like workers who are impelled to migrate and look for new types of employment because of deteriorating economic conditions in their locality, people sometimes experience situations (personal and societal) that transplant them into social locations with which they were previously unfamiliar. When such changes occur, socially habituated subjectivities and the doxic assumptions they inculcate may be called into question. In such circumstances, one may find oneself "betwixt and between" social locations, existing in a state of "liminal subjectivity."[5] Though outside the scope of this conclusion, I have argued elsewhere that the concept of "liminal subjectivities" offers an alternative to deprivation and cultural crisis theories.[6] In general, I think that the concepts of socially habituated and liminal subjectivities provide an emergent, interpretive language for numerous religious studies subjects, including spiritual disciplines, combinative religious practices, and conversion.

Class in the Academic Field and the Classroom

What are the implications of studying religion and class for our research? I argued in the first chapter that the study of religion and class must be interdisciplinary, and thus it should mirror what the field of religious studies ideally is. There are many ways to study religion. But religious studies is foremost the study of humans, in groups and as individuals, and what they believe and do that they—or we—call "religion." A focus on religion and class (and, for that matter, other social locations) involves researching and teaching not just *what* people do, but also *why* they believe and do what they do. Such a question is too broad and complex to answer tersely, and most likely it could never be answered completely. But it is a crucial question because it forces us out of our comfortable habits of scholarship and into an encounter with the field's historical tangle of boldness, folly, and social power. As I suggested in part 1, past scholars often interpreted other people's religions in ways that accorded well with their own social locations but did little to recognize the complexity of their subjects. Because I don't think we should replicate the symbolic violence committed in past scholarship, a resurrected study of religion and class demands that we front our biases and reflect upon our potential blind spots. At the same time, this does not mean we discard the questions of why religion is important for most people and how it might function in their lives. Such issues highlight the interdisciplinary strength of our field. It may be impossible for all of us to become experts in history, anthropology, sociology, folklore, theory, philosophy, and other approaches that religious studies utilizes. But in seeking to understand how and why people live their religions, we have a plethora of useful methods at hand, yet are constrained by none of them.

Finally, teaching about religion and class fronts a subject that is often absent. Class has recently been missing from the ways we teach religious studies, but it has also frequently been invisible in the classroom itself. Scholars and their students are socially located. Both are "classed" in ways that enable and constrain them in the desks and at the chalkboard. While we may notice that our students differ in terms of race, gender, age, or dialect, social class— despite its tremendous importance in predicting student success—often remains invisible and unacknowledged. And despite the stereotype, academics do not live in ivory towers that stand immune to material conditions. They reside in a range of dwellings, including Victorian mansions, one-room apartments, ranch-style houses, and double-wide trailers. Salaries and benefits, access to research tools, and teaching loads differ dramatically in the United States. In effect, colleges and universities have their own class system, one that marks faculty, staff, and students for present and future prospects. Teachers, along with their students, bring assumptions and habits into the classroom inculcated by their socially habituated subjectivities. While subjects and approaches vary, the most general goal of any humanities course is to ultimately "break" habits of mind so that we can see the world from multiple perspectives and thus better perceive its socially constructed nature. This applies to teachers as much as it does to students. By putting some class back into the study of religion, we have the opportunity as researchers and teachers to open new discussions, make our classrooms more inclusive, and fracture habituated ways of understanding.

Notes

Introduction

1. See, for example, Seeyle, "Moral Values Cited."

2. See Langer and Cohen, "Voters and Values."

3. See Connelly, "How Americans Voted."

4. See Hout and Greeley, "Hidden Swing Vote." It must be noted that level of income also positively correlates with likelihood of voting. In other words, while poor, white, southern Evangelicals would be more likely to vote Democratic than Republican, they would also be less likely to vote than more affluent Evangelicals.

5. Congressional Budget Office statistics from the period 1979–2002 show the gap between the richest and poorest Americans widening. See Francis, "How Social Security Could." For other articles noting the growing class divide in the United States, see Leonhardt, "More Americans Were Uninsured"; and "Defining the Rich."

6. Skeggs, *Class, Self, Culture*, 44.

7. A discussion of social class, bread, and other food preferences occurs in the film *People like Us*.

8. For the plastic flowers example, see Mitchell, *Dropping Ashes on the Buddha*, 121–23. For a discussion of rapture and end-time beliefs, see Paul Boyer, *When Time Shall Be No More*. For an examina-

tion of the *Left Behind* book series readers, see Frykholm, *Rapture Culture*.

9. See Tyson, Peacock, and Patterson, "Method and Spirit," 4.

10. I am not asserting here that it is the only field for such a study. For a similar argument about the discourse on magic, see Styers, *Making Magic*.

11. For discussion of "sites" for narrating the history of American religion, see Tweed, "Narrating U.S. Religious History."

12. Orsi, *Between Heaven and Earth*, 188.

13. See Gould, *Mismeasure of Man*.

Chapter 1

1. See Goldthorpe and Marshall, "Promising Future of Class Analysis"; and Pakulski and Waters, "Reshaping and Dissolution of Social Class."

2. See Milner, *Class*.

3. Christiano, Swatos, and Kivisto, *Sociology of Religion*, 123. There has, however, also been some recent scholarship urging the reconsideration of class in the study of American religion. See, for example, Hackett, Maffly-Kipp, Moore, and Tentler, "Forum"; and Smith and Faris, "Socioeconomic Inequality." For an argument to include religion in the study of the American working

resentation and verbal expression. More like a class unconscious than a 'class consciousness' in the Marxist sense" (Bourdieu, "Social Space and Genesis," 728).

32. Savage, *Class Analysis and Social Transformation*, xiii.

33. Ibid., 102.

34. Skeggs, *Class, Self, Culture*, 117.

35. Stuart Hall, introduction, 3.

36. Skeggs, *Class, Self, Culture*, 1.

37. Bourdieu, "Symbolic Power," 115.

38. Ortner, *New Jersey Dreaming*, 13.

39. Savage, *Class Analysis and Social Transformation*, 40.

40. Goldthorpe and Marshall, "Promising Future of Class Analysis," 384.

41. Park and Reimer, "Revisiting the Social Sources," 742.

42. Bourdieu, "Social Space and Genesis," 725.

43. For a useful discussion about this, see Christian Smith, *American Evangelicalism*, 90–95.

44. Ibid., 105.

45. Skeggs, *Class, Self, Culture*, 99–100.

46. See Fussell, *Class*, 35.

47. Ibid., 29, 52, 57, 63, 71, 79, 99, 110, 124.

48. See Bourdieu, *Distinction*, 2.

49. See Harding, "Representing Fundamentalism"; and Marsden, *Fundamentalism and American Culture*, 184–90. Also see Smout, "Attacking (Southern) Creationists."

50. H. L. Mencken, "Fundamentalism: Divine and Secular," in Joshi, *H. L. Mencken on Religion*, 12.

51. H. L. Mencken, "Homo Neandertalensis," in ibid., 167.

52. Ibid.

53. Ibid.

54. Hutchinson, "Have We a 'New' Re-

ligion?," 138. For an extended discussion of the article, see McCloud, *Making the American Religious Fringe*, 39–41.

55. McCloud, *Making the American Religious Fringe*, 169.

56. See Alexander, *Televangelism Reconsidered*. For a critique of media portrayals of the larger Evangelical movement, of which Pentecostals and Fundamentalists are a part, see Christian Smith, *Christian America?*, esp. 4–9, 92–93.

57. See the *Oxford English Dictionary Online*, <http://www.oed.com>, s.v. "subculture."

58. Christian Smith, *American Evangelicalism*, 93. He views Evangelicals in the United States as a subculture.

59. Hebdige, *Subculture*, 62–70. Also see Hall and Jefferson, *Resistance through Rituals*.

60. Lydon and Zimmerman, *Rotten*, 49.

61. hooks, *Where We Stand*, 25, 26. The name of the chapter I refer to here is "Coming to Class Consciousness."

62. Ibid., 27.

63. Ibid., 36.

64. Ibid., 37.

65. For several useful works on the Peoples Temple, see John Hall, *Gone from the Promised Land*; Chidester, *Salvation and Suicide*; and Maaga, *Hearing the Voices of Jonestown*. For a collection of primary sources, see Stephenson, *Dear People*.

66. Chidester, *Salvation and Suicide*, 66–72. For Jones's specific claim that he was black, see 71.

67. Ibid., 63.

68. Applegate, "Henry Ward Beecher," 111. See also Applegate, *Most Famous Man in America*.

69. Beecher quoted in Applegate, "Henry Ward Becher," 118.

70. Kilsdonk, "Scientific Church Music," 126.

71. For an examination of representations of blacks and "Blackness," see Stuart Hall, "Spectacle of the 'Other,'" 223–77.

72. Skeggs, *Class, Self, Culture*, 98.

73. Perry, *Shades of White*, 110.

74. Ibid., 48–49.

75. "Heaven Can Wait," 62.

76. Quoted in Hendershot, *Shaking the World for Jesus*, 32.

77. McCloud, *Making the American Religious Fringe*, 74–75.

78. Marcus, *Lipstick Traces*, 168. For two examples of Situationist writing, see Debord, *Society of the Spectacle*; and Vaneigem, *Revolution of Everyday Life*.

79. Harding writes, "Fundamentalists create themselves through their own cultural practices, but not exactly as they please. They are also constituted by modern discursive practices, an apparatus of thought that presents itself in the form of popular 'stereotypes,' media 'images,' and academic 'knowledge'" ("Representing Fundamentalism," 373–74).

80. Machalek and Snow, "Conversion to New Religious Movements," 61.

81. Ibid.

82. Ibid.

83. Ibid., 63. See also Lofland and Stark, "Becoming a World Saver"; Stark and Bainbridge, "Networks of Faith"; and Bainbridge and Stark, "Friendship, Religion, and the Occult."

84. Erickson, "Culture, Class, and Connections," 219.

85. Ibid.

86. Ibid., 249.

87. Ibid.

88. Ibid., 236.

89. Ibid., 236, 237.

90. Ibid., 240–41.

91. Swidler, *Talk of Love*, 25.

92. Ibid., 52. Also see Bernstein, *Class, Codes, and Control*.

93. Swidler, *Talk of Love*, 52.

94. See Lareau, *Unequal Childhoods*. Lareau found that class trumped race in parenting styles. Middle- and upper-middle-class parents engaged in "concerted cultivation," which fostered a "robust sense of entitlement" that "plays an especially important role in institutional settings, where middle-class children learn to question adults and address them as relative equals" (ibid., 2). She dubbed the parenting style of poor and working-class parents "accomplishment of natural growth," a "cultural logic of child rearing" that is "out of synch with the standards of institutions" and leads to "an emerging sense of distance, distrust, and constraint in their institutional experiences" (ibid., 3).

95. Swidler, *Talk of Love*, 7.

96. Ibid., 25.

97. Ibid., 89.

98. Ibid., 93.

99. Ibid., 99.

100. In addition to the sources cited in note 83 above, see Stark and Finke, *Acts of Faith*, 116–19.

101. Verter writes, "spiritual omnivorosity—the sort witnessed in individuals who combine multiple religious traditions (imagine someone who considers herself Buddhist but attends seders, practices Yoga, consults an astrologer, wears a crystal, and professes an interest in American Indian spirituality)—may be the most exclusive form of spiritual capital" ("Spiritual Capital," 167–68).

Both Verter and Erickson utilize emerging scholarship on cultural "omnivores" and "univores." See, for example, Peterson, "Understanding Audience Segmentation"; Peterson and Kearn, "Changing Highbrow Tastes"; Bryson, "What about Univores?"; and Relish, "It's Not All Education."

102. See Wuthnow, *After Heaven*. Also see Roof, *Spiritual Marketplace*, and *Generation of Seekers*. For another study, see Reimer, "Look at Cultural Effects."

103. Harris poll, "The Religious and Other Beliefs of Americans 2003," *Harris Interactive*, 26 February 2003, <http://www.harrisinteractive.com/harris_poll/index.asp?PID=359>.

104. For statistics on Neopagan belief in reincarnation, see Berger, Leach, and Shaffer, *Voices from the Pagan Census*, 47.

105. Smith and Denton, *Soul Searching*, 85.

106. Verter, "Spiritual Capital," 168.

107. Ibid.

108. See, for example, Bill Ellis, *Lucifer Ascending*, and *Raising the Devil*; Kerr and Crow, *Occult in America*; and Long, *Spiritual Merchants*. For a journalistic account of popular 1960s and early 1970s occultism, see Godwin, *Occult America*.

109. Bourdieu, *Outline of a Theory*, 82–83.

110. Ibid., 72.

111. See Fred Rose, "Toward a Class-Cultural Theory."

112. See Coreno, "Fundamentalism as a Class Culture."

113. See Smith and Faris, "Socioeconomic Inequality."

114. Emerson and Smith, *Divided by Faith*, 76.

115. Ibid., 75.

116. Ibid., 107.

117. Oberdeck, *Evangelist and Impresario*, 29.

118. Coreno, "Fundamentalism as a Class Culture." One wonders, in fact, how much region shapes the class aspect of Coreno's analysis, given that the American South is poorer than the rest of the United States.

119. See Billings, "Religion as Opposition."

120. Soltero and Saravia, "Dimensions of Social Stratification," 15.

121. Ibid., 17.

Chapter 2

1. Ward, "Social Classes," 620. For a brief discussion of Ward, see Hofstadter, *Social Darwinism in American Thought*, 67–73.

2. Ward, "Social Classes," 624.

3. See Zenderland, "Biblical Biology"; Durst, "Evangelical Engagements with Eugenics"; and Haslan, *Rhetoric of Eugenics*, 89–111. Also see Rosen, *Preaching Eugenics*.

4. Probably the best-known history of eugenics is Kevles, *In the Name of Eugenics*. See also Carlsen, *Unfit*; English, *Unnatural Selections*; Kline, *Building a Better Race*; Larson, *Sex, Race, and Science*; Sheldon, *Inheriting Shame*; and Rafter, *White Trash*.

5. Taves, "From Religious History," 892.

6. Popenoe and Johnson, *Applied Eugenics*, 214. Popenoe served on the board of the American Eugenics Society and was an early proponent of both marriage counseling and sterilization of the eugenically unfit. Johnson was the one-time president of the American Eugenics Society and a University of Pittsburgh

professor. For a selection of book reviews demonstrating the mostly positive reception various editions of *Applied Eugenics* received, see Gillin, review of *Applied Eugenics*; Woobury, review of *Applied Eugenics*; Ogburn, review of *Applied Eugenics*; Himes, review of *Applied Eugenics*; and Reuter, review of *Applied Eugenics*. While it should not be surprising that the negative review is found in 1935, it remains striking that even as late as 1934 a reviewer suggested that using the textbook "would add a much needed touch of realism to introductory courses. It would also act as a corrective against overemphasis on social genesis and social conditioning" (Himes, review of *Applied Eugenics*, 715).

7. The date 1905 marks the publication of Davenport's *Primitive Traits in Religious Revivals*, while 1934 is the year that Simon Stone's "Miller Delusion" appeared in *American Journal of Psychiatry*.

8. English, *Unnatural Selections*, 1.

9. Anne Rose, "'Race' Speech," 84.

10. See Bourdieu, "On Symbolic Power," and *Outline of a Theory*. For more on the concept of spiritual capital and its usefulness in religious studies, see Verter, "Spiritual Capital."

11. Stocking, *Race, Culture, and Evolution*, 237.

12. Anne Rose, "'Race' Speech," 101.

13. See Taves, *Fits, Trances, and Visions*, 278–79, 294.

14. I have two other considerations: First, there are many useful ways to examine any subject, and here I have chosen to do a thematic, as opposed to chronological, study. I take a time period, bounded by a selection of works on religious affiliation that share certain characteristics, and elaborate on the common elements in the literature. Because my analysis does not move chronologically, it does not address all the subtle changes that take place over time. My hope is that method will enable me to recognize many such changes but also aid in focusing attention on the more striking continuities over time. Second, I hope that this chapter might spur additional research, particularly something focusing on minority and religious community responses to these writings. How, for example, did an African American scholar such as W. E. B. Du Bois (himself a proponent of eugenics) respond to Davenport's argument about black religion? How did Catholics respond to being labeled "cacogenic"? What about Pentecostals and Cutten's book on speaking in tongues? These are important questions, some of which have been addressed by other writers, but they are beyond the scope of this work.

15. See Galton, *Inquiries into the Human Faculty*. Though coined in 1883, Galton's idea of eugenics was present in his 1869 work, *Hereditary Genius*, described by Nancy Leys Stepan as the "founding text of eugenics" (*"Hour of Eugenics,"* 22).

16. Gould, *Mismeasure of Man*, 20.

17. Stepan, *"Hour of Eugenics,"* 28.

18. Kevles, *In the Name of Eugenics*, 85.

19. Carlsen, *Unfit*, 12.

20. Stepan, *"Hour of Eugenics,"* 27.

21. Rafter, *White Trash*, 1.

22. See Strong, *Our Country*; and McDougall, *Is America Safe?*

23. For an overview of American nativism, see Higham, *Strangers in the Land*.

24. Huntington and Whitney, *Builders of America*, 197.

25. Ibid.

26. Ibid., 196.

27. Ibid., 198.

28. Ibid.

29. Ibid., 199.

30. Ibid.

31. McDougall was not the first to suggest this tripartite division of Europeans. European ethnologists developed this system of classification in the late nineteenth century, and the American economist and geographer William Ripley brought the idea to a wider American audience with his 1899 work, *The Races of Europe*. Note that Ripley's category of "Teutonic" was replaced by "Nordic" in McDougall. Also note that Madison Grant's 1916 work, *The Passing of the Great Race*, used the three-part division as well. See Higham, *Strangers in the Land*, 154–57.

32. McDougall, *Is America Safe?*, 100.

33. Ibid., 114.

34. Ibid., 102.

35. Huntington and Whitney, *Builders of America*, 193. See table, 195.

36. Ibid., 194.

37. Ibid., 203.

38. Ibid.

39. Ibid.

40. Binder, *Modern Religious Cults*, 57. One scholar has dubbed insanity the "official" nineteenth-century theory of religion. See Bainbridge, "Religious Insanity in America." Also see Rubin, *Religious Melancholy*.

41. See Simon Stone, "Miller Delusion."

42. Ibid., 596.

43. Brunner, *Village Communities*, 76.

44. Wilson, *Farmer's Church*, 58.

45. Ibid., 148.

46. Ibid., 159.

47. Finke and Stark, *Churching of America*, 209. For historical studies of the rural church and country life movement, see Madison, "Reformers and the Rural Church"; and Swanson, "'Country Life Movement.'"

48. Stark and Finke, *Acts of Faith*, 44.

49. McDougall, *Is America Safe?*, 42; Binder, *Modern Religious Cults*, 145.

50. See Frazier, *Golden Bough*; and Tylor, *Primitive Culture*.

51. Burris, *Exhibiting Religion*, 64.

52. Binder, *Modern Religious Cults*, 145.

53. Ibid.

54. Ibid., 57.

55. Cutten, *Speaking with Tongues*, 2.

56. Ibid., 4.

57. Ibid., 6.

58. Ibid., 10.

59. Ibid.

60. Greene, "Frederick Morgan Davenport," 12.

61. Ibid.,

62. Ibid., 13.

63. Taves, *Fits, Trances, and Visions*, 294.

64. Davenport, *Primitive Traits*, 323.

65. Ibid., 259.

66. Ibid., 323.

67. Ibid., 259.

68. Ibid., 260.

69. Ibid., 2–3.

70. Ibid., 3, 217.

71. Ibid., 235–36.

72. Ibid., 236.

73. Ibid., 235.

74. Ibid., 259.

75. Ibid., 45–58.

76. Ibid., 45.
77. Ibid.
78. Ibid.
79. Ibid., 58.
80. Ibid., 47.
81. Ibid.
82. Ibid., 48, 49, 16.
83. Ibid., 48–49.
84. Ibid., 230.
85. Ibid., 44.
86. Ibid., 230.
87. Ibid.
88. Stocking, *Race, Culture, and Evolution*, 242.
89. Davenport, *Primitive Traits*, 30.
90. Ibid.
91. Ibid., 60.
92. Ibid., 61.
93. Ibid., 63.
94. Ibid.
95. Ibid., 65.
96. Ibid., 8.
97. Ibid., 45.
98. Ibid., 63.
99. Ibid., 64.
100. Ibid., 9.
101. Ibid.
102. Ibid., 62.
103. Kippenberg, *Discovering Religious History*, 56–58. See also, as cited by Kippenberg, Burrow, *Evolution and Society*.
104. Davenport, *Primitive Traits*, 299.
105. Ibid., 298.
106. Ibid., 299.
107. Orsi, "Crossing the City Line," 5.
108. Ibid., 18. See also Rafter, *White Trash*, 7.
109. Galton, *Inquiries into the Human Faculty*, 241.
110. McDougall, *Is America Safe?*, 156.
111. Binder, *Modern Religious Cults*, 145.

112. Boisen, *Religion in Crisis*, 33.
113. Wilson, "Church and Rural Community," 677.
114. Wilson, *Farmer's Church*, 145.
115. Ibid.
116. See Hooker, "Leaders in Village Communities"; and Gist and Clark, "Intelligence as a Selective Factor."
117. Gist and Clark, "Intelligence as a Selective Factor," 57.
118. Ibid., 58.
119. Anne Rose, "'Race' Speech," 101.
120. The disappearance of biological explanations of religion has never been complete. The cognitive science of religion is the most recent subfield of religious studies to incorporate biological models. See Barrett, *Why Would Anyone Believe in God?*; Pascal Boyer, *Naturalness of Religious Ideas*; Guthrie, *Faces in the Clouds*; Luther Martin, "Cognition, Society, and Religion"; and Whitehouse, *Arguments and Icons*, and *Modes of Religiosity*. For a newspaper article that suggests the genetic influence on culture, see Wade, "Twists and Turns of History."
121. For a critical overview of deprivation theories, see Hine, "Deprivation and Disorganization"; and Cook, *Prophecy and Apocalypticism*, 12–17.
122. See Niebuhr, *Social Sources*; Weber, *Sociology of Religion*, esp. 80–117; and Troeltsch, *Social Teaching*. And for a selection of readings from Marx on religion, see Raines, *Marx on Religion*. One could argue—correctly, I think—that social scientific classifications of churches, sects, denominations, and cults frequently categorized certain religions as "bad" and "good" in less explicit, but just as powerful and effective, ways as eugenicist classifications of cacogenic and

eugenic religions. In other words, social scientific typologies of religion tended to replicate the same hierarchies as the eugenics writings.

Chapter 3

1. See "In the White Man's Image."
2. Ibid.
3. Ibid.
4. See Herberg, *Protestant Catholic Jew.*
5. These scholars will be addressed in the next chapter. See La Barre, *Ghost Dance*; Wallace, "Revitalization Movements"; and Glock, "Role of Deprivation."
6. See, for example, Benedict, *Patterns of Culture.*
7. Anne Rose, "'Race' Speech," 101.
8. Stocking, *Race, Culture, and Evolution*, 267.
9. Hinkle, *Developments in American Sociological Theory*, 116.
10. Friedel and Brinkley, *America in the Twentieth Century*, 27.
11. Ibid., 24.
12. Cited in ibid., 180.
13. Ibid., 186.
14. See Lears, "From Salvation to Self-Realization."
15. For a historical overview of religion in the period, see Marty, *Modern American Religion*, vol. 2.
16. An additional trend from the period entailed the growing utilization of the "frontier" as a theme in American church history. Works by early church historians such as Peter Mode and William Warren Sweet focused on, in the scholar Thomas Tweed's words, "not just the gaining and losing of land and re-

sources but also the attitudes and behaviors associated with that environment, including the influence of individualist and democratic impulses on the fate of American denominations" ("Narrating U.S. Religious History," 14). Also see Mode, *Frontier Spirit in American Christianity*; and Sweet, *Story of Religion in America.*

17. Holt, "Holiness Religion," 740.
18. Ibid., 741.
19. Ibid.
20. Ibid.
21. Ibid.
22. Ibid.
23. Ibid.
24. Ibid., 744.
25. Ibid., 745.
26. Ibid., 746.
27. Ibid.
28. Marx and Engels, *On Religion*, 74–75.
29. Ibid., 74.
30. This, of course, refers to what is likely Marx's most quoted statement on religion: "Religious distress is at the same time the expression of real distress and the protest against real distress. Religion is the sigh of the oppressed creature, the heart of a heartless world, just as it is the spirit of a spiritless situation. It is the opium of the people" (ibid., 42).
31. See Weber, *Sociology of Religion*, esp. chapters 6, 7, 9, 10, 11, 12, 15, 16.
32. Ibid., 101, 107.
33. Weber, "Social Psychology of the World Religions," 280.
34. See, for example, Ward, "Social Classes in the Light."
35. Niebuhr, *Social Sources*, 6.
36. Ibid., 27.
37. *Social Teaching* originally appeared

in German in 1911. It was published in English, with an introduction by Niebuhr, in 1931.

38. Niebuhr, *Social Sources*, 29.

39. Ibid., 28.

40. Ibid., 21.

41. Ibid., 31.

42. Ibid., 76.

43. Ibid.

44. Ibid., 264.

45. See Eister, "H. Richard Niebuhr."

46. See, for example, Christiano, Swatos, and Kivisto, *Sociology of Religion*, 136; and Park and Reimer, "Revisiting the Social Sources."

47. Niebuhr, *Social Sources*, 82.

48. Ibid.

49. Ibid., 30.

50. Ibid., 79.

51. Sombart, *Quintessence of Capitalism*, 205. For a useful examination of Sombart's work, see Grundman and Stehr, "Why Werner Sombart?"

52. Sombart, *Quintessence of Capitalism*, 210.

53. Ibid., 212.

54. Ibid., 251.

55. Ibid., 256.

56. Ibid., 265.

57. Ibid., 217, 272.

58. Ibid., 265.

59. Niebuhr, *Social Sources*, 79.

60. Ibid., 96.

61. Ibid., 203.

62. Ibid.

63. Ibid.

64. Davenport, *Primitive Traits*, 45.

65. Ibid.

66. Krueger, "Negro Religious Expression," 25.

67. Ibid.

68. Ibid.

69. Ibid., 26.

70. Ibid.

71. Ibid., 27.

72. Ibid.

73. Ibid., 28.

74. Ibid.

75. Ibid.

76. Ibid.

77. Ibid., 29.

78. Ibid.

79. Ibid.

80. Ibid., 29–30.

81. Ibid., 30.

82. Ibid., 31.

83. Ibid.

84. See Bruce and Wallis, "Rescuing Motives"; and Wallis and Bruce, "Accounting for Action."

85. Boisen, *Religion in Crisis*, xiv. Historian E. Brooks Holifield notes that Boisen hospitalized himself ("Pastoral Care and Counseling," in *Encyclopedia of American Religious Experience*, 1590).

86. Cutten, *Speaking with Tongues*, 168.

87. Ibid., 2.

88. Ibid., 10.

89. Boisen, "Economic Distress," 185, 186.

90. Ibid., 192.

91. Ibid., 192–93.

92. Ibid., 193.

93. Ibid.

94. Ibid.

95. Ibid., 194.

96. Ibid.

97. Ibid., 193.

98. Ibid.

99. Ibid., 193–94.

100. Ibid., 194.

101. Ibid.

102. Ibid.

103. Ibid.

104. Ibid.

105. Fletcher, "Indian Messiah," 58.

106. Ibid., 59.

107. Ibid.

108. Ibid., 60.

109. Ibid., 59–60.

110. Ibid., 60.

111. Joel W. Martin, "Before and Beyond," 680.

112. Ibid.

113. Ibid., 682.

114. For excerpts from the court case, see Alley, *Constitution and Religion*, 483–501. For a journalist's narrative of the case, see Epps, *To an Unknown God*.

115. See *Oxford English Dictionary Online*, <http://dictionary.oed.com>, s.v. "autistic."

116. Lasswell, "Collective Autism," 232.

117. Ibid.

118. Ibid.

119. Ibid., 237.

120. Ibid., 245.

121. Ibid., 244–45.

122. Ibid., 246.

123. For one overview, see Coleman, *American Indian Children*. For a case study of one school, see Clyde Ellis, *To Change Them Forever*.

124. See Pfister, *Individuality Incorporated*.

125. Barber, "Acculturation," 664, 665.

126. Ibid., 665. See also Nash, "Place of Religious Revivalism."

127. Barber, "Acculturation," 665.

128. Ibid., 666.

129. Ibid., 667.

130. Ibid., 668.

131. Ibid.

132. Barber, "Socio-Cultural Interpretation," 674.

133. Ibid.

134. Ibid.

135. Ibid.

136. Ibid., n6. While not named as such, the "autistic religion" concept as applied to Native Americans can be seen in another 1940s work by Ralph Linton and A. Irving Hallowell, who define "nativistic movements" as "any conscious, organized attempt on the part of a society's members to revive or perpetuate selected aspects of its culture" ("Nativistic Movements," 230). After proposing a taxonomy of such movements, Linton and Hallowell note that two of their categories—messianic and magical nativistic cults—were similar in that "they represent frankly irrational flights from reality. Their differences relate only to the ways in which such flights are implemented and are, from the point of view of their functions, matters of minor importance" (ibid., 233).

137. Barber, "Acculturation," 667.

Chapter 4

1. See *HarperCollins Dictionary of Religion*, 763.

2. Ibid.,

3. Ibid., 927.

4. Ibid., 928.

5. Ibid.

6. In arguing this, I have no desire to reproduce my sources' collective assumption that religion and class is about the study of religion and the poor. As noted in chapter 1, I explicitly argue that this is not the case. While some scholars, such as Charles Glock, utilized deprivation theories across the social class spectrum, the historiography I conduct sug-

gests that the "usual suspects" garnered the most attention. Those wanting to research how scholarly studies of religion may have been utilized by elites might consider Bradford Verter's "spiritual omnivores" concept—first mentioned in chapter 1—to examine the ways in which some people have used knowledge of diverse religions as a status marker. See Verter, "Spiritual Capital." Although it is beyond the current study's scope, one could also examine the ambivalent idealizations of indigenous and "poor" religions within the larger culture. As demonstrated by the historian Philip Jenkins, such a focus appears particularly fruitful in regard to Native American religions. See Jenkins, *Dream Catchers.*

7. Masuzawa, *In Search of Dreamtime,* 14.

8. Wallace, "Revitalization Movements," 265.

9. Ibid., 264.

10. Ibid., 265.

11. Ibid., 267.

12. Ibid.

13. Ibid., 268.

14. Wallace, "Mazeway Disintegration," 24.

15. Ibid.

16. For a brief biographical chronology, see Anna Thompson, "Register to the Papers."

17. See La Barre, *They Shall Take Up Serpents,* and *Peyote Cult.*

18. La Barre, *Ghost Dance,* 41.

19. Ibid., 41–42.

20. Ibid., 44.

21. Ibid.

22. Ibid.

23. Ibid.

24. Ibid., 46.

25. Ibid., 50.

26. Ibid., 45.

27. Ibid.

28. Wallace, *Religion,* 265.

29. La Barre, *Ghost Dance,* 610.

30. Freud, *Future of an Illusion,* 55.

31. La Barre, again mirroring Wallace, suggests that "prophetic movements seem especially common among socially, economically, politically, educationally, and otherwise deprived populations" (*Ghost Dance,* 287).

32. Glock later distanced himself from deprivation theory. See "On Nature, Sources, and Consequences."

33. Glock, "Role of Deprivation," 29.

34. Aberle, "Note on Relative Deprivation Theory," 209.

35. Glock, "Role of Deprivation," 27.

36. Ibid.

37. Ibid.

38. Ibid.

39. Ibid., 28.

40. Ibid.

41. Ibid., 29.

42. Ibid.

43. Ibid.

44. Ibid., 30.

45. Ibid., 30–31.

46. Ibid., 31–32.

47. Ibid., 32.

48. Ibid., 30.

49. Ibid., 34.

50. Ibid.

51. Ibid., 36.

52. Ibid.

53. There are, of course, exceptions. For a study by Glock and colleagues of the Episcopalian Church, see Glock, Ringer, and Babbie, *To Comfort and to Challenge.*

54. In 1965, *Current Anthropology* fea-

tured fifteen scholarly reviews of *Religions of the Oppressed*, plus a précis and response from Lanternari. Many of the reviews were critical. See Review of *Religions of the Oppressed*.

55. For a brief overview of cargo cults, see *HarperCollins Dictionary of Religion*, 180–81.

56. Worsley, *Trumpet Shall Sound*, 12.

57. Ibid., 225.

58. Ibid., 233.

59. Ibid., 232.

60. Ibid., 233.

61. Ibid.

62. Elmer Clark, *Small Sects of America*, 16.

63. Ibid.

64. Ibid., 17.

65. Ibid., 218.

66. Ibid.

67. Ibid.

68. Ibid., 219.

69. Ibid.

70. Davies, *Challenge of the Sects*, 21.

71. For discussions of Christian Science demographics, see Gottschalk, *Emergence of Christian Science*, 256–59; and Prothero, *White Buddhist*, 48–49.

72. Mathison, *Faiths, Cults, and Sects*, 34.

73. Ibid.

74. For the comment on Jehovah's Witnesses, see ibid., 64. For the Black Muslims (Nation of Islam), see ibid., 254.

75. Ibid., 36–37.

76. Hoffer, *True Believer*, 31.

77. Ibid.

78. See Pattison, "Ideological Support"; and Schwartz, *Sect Ideologies and Social Status*, 45–46.

79. "Despair Serves Purposes," 917.

80. See McCloud, *Making the American Religious Fringe*, 55–94.

81. Lincoln, *Black Muslims in America*, 252.

82. See Laue, "Contemporary Revitalization Movement."

83. Ibid., 323.

84. Wilson, *Farmer's Church*, 58, 148.

85. Weller, *Yesterday's People*, 29.

86. Weller, "How Religion Mirrors," 124.

87. Ibid., 124–25.

88. Ibid., 124.

89. Ibid.

90. McCauley, *Appalachian Mountain Religion*, 7–8. While McCauley's focus is on Protestant missionaries and progressives, one must immediately note that such explanations often came in the form of academic scholarship on the region and its religions. See, for example, Photiadis, *Religion in Appalachia*.

91. Weller, *Yesterday's People*, 126. For a discussion of the characteristics of mountaineer religion, see ibid., 121–33.

92. Ibid., 130.

93. Ibid.

94. Ibid., 130–31.

95. Ibid., 131.

96. For the suggestion that it was otherworldly and socially passive, see ibid.

97. See Victor, *Satanic Panic*.

98. For other studies, see Bill Ellis, *Raising the Devil*; Hicks, *In Pursuit of Satan*; and Richardson, Best, and Bromley, *Satanism Scare*.

99. Victor, *Satanic Panic*, 55.

100. Ibid., 248. Also see Gusfield, *Symbolic Crusade*.

101. Victor, *Satanic Panic*, 248.

102. See Holt, "Holiness Religion."

103. See Alma White, *Demons and Tongues*, 9. In the 1920s, White's church, The Pillar of Fire, publicly endorsed the Ku Klux Klan. In addition to speaking at

Klan rallies, White wrote three books on the Klan's role in biblical prophecy and the end-times. In brief, she viewed the Klan as God's army that would fight the battle of Armageddon against a Satanic minion of Roman Catholics, Jews, and African Americans. See her *Ku Klux Klan in Prophecy*; *Klansmen*; and *Heroes of the Fiery Cross*. For a biography, see Stanley, *Feminist Pillar of Fire*.

104. Wacker, "Taking Another Look," 19.

105. The brief overview here comes from several sources. See Anderson, *Vision of the Disinherited*; Synan, *Holiness-Pentecostal Movement*; and Wacker, *Heaven Below*. For useful denominational studies, see Blumhofer, *Restoring the Faith*; Crews, *Church of God*; and Poloma, *Assemblies of God*.

106. Blumhofer, *Restoring the Faith*, 5–6.

107. For a useful discussion of Holiness Second Blessing theology and early Pentecostalism, see Wacker, "Pentecostalism."

108. Wacker, *Heaven Below*, 35–57.

109. Ibid., 7. Wacker also suggests that Pentecostals, when combined with Charismatics, are currently second only to Roman Catholics as the largest aggregate of Christians in the world (ibid., 8).

110. For scholarly attention to snake-handling Holiness Pentecostals, see Burton, *Serpent-Handling Believers*. Burton includes a lengthy bibliography of press coverage. Also see Kimbrough, *Taking Up Serpents*; and La Barre, *They Shall Take Up Serpents*. For a journalist's account, see Covington, *Salvation on Sand Mountain*.

111. See McGuire, *Pentecostal Catholics*; Neitz, *Charisma and Community*;

and Poloma, *Charismatic Movement*. For a popular examination of the Charismatic movement, see Quebedeaux, *New Charismatics*.

112. I. M. Lewis, *Ecstatic Religion*, 28.

113. Wacker, *Heaven Below*, 186.

114. Ibid., 198.

115. Ibid.

116. Ibid., 205.

117. Benton Johnson, "Do Holiness Sects Socialize?," 309.

118. Ibid.

119. Ibid., 311.

120. In addition to Holt, Johnson cites Liston Pope and Walter Goldschmidt, ibid., 312.

121. Anderson, *Vision of the Disinherited*, 223.

122. Ibid., 239.

123. Ibid., 231.

124. Ibid.

125. Ibid., 240.

126. Ibid.

127. La Barre, *They Shall Take Up Serpents*, 167.

128. Ibid., 175.

129. See William Wood, *Culture and Personality Aspects*, 103.

130. Ibid., 98.

131. Ibid.

132. Ibid., 109.

133. See Castelein, "Glossolalia and Psychology," 47.

134. Ibid.

135. Ibid., 48.

136. Ibid.

137. De Artega, *Quenching the Spirit*, 16.

138. Ibid.

139. See Goodman, *Speaking in Tongues*. For the varieties of approaches to glossolalia, see Maloney and Lovekin, *Glossolalia*; Mills, *Speaking in Tongues*;

Samarin, *Tongues of Men and Angels*; and Cyril Williams, *Tongues of the Spirit*.

140. One exception to this is the religious marketplace/rational choice theories proposed by certain scholars, such as Stark and Finke; see *Acts of Faith*.

141. Gerlach, "Pentecostalism," 671.

142. Ibid.

143. Ibid.

144. Ibid., 672.

145. Ibid., 698.

146. Hine, "Deprivation and Disorganization," 660.

147. Ibid.

148. Ibid.,

149. Hine had also earlier published an article suggesting that glossolalia should not be considered a pathological behavior but rather an act of commitment to one's religious community. See "Pentecostal Glossolalia."

150. Cone, *Black Theology of Liberation*, 5.

151. Cook, *Prophecy and Apocalypticism*, esp. 16, 41, 42.

152. See Castelein, "Glossolalia and Psychology." Also see Albert Miller, "Pentecostalism as a Social Movement."

153. Joel Martin, *Sacred Revolt*, 3.

154. Ibid.

155. Ibid., 175.

156. Ibid., 179.

157. Ibid.

158. Ibid., 178.

159. Ibid., 179.

Chapter 5

1. Griffith, *Born Again Bodies*, 7.

2. E. P. Thompson, *Making of the English Working Class*, 42.

3. Paul Johnson, *Shopkeeper's Millennium*, 138.

4. Ibid.

5. Gutman, "Protestantism and American Labor Movement," 80.

6. See Fones-Wolf, *Trade Union Gospel*; Sutton, *Journeymen for Jesus*, 20.

7. See Sterne, *Ballots and Bibles*.

8. See Lazerow, *Religion and the Working Class*.

9. Murphy, *Ten Hours' Labor*, 3.

10. Schantz, *Piety in Providence*, 2.

11. For a discussion suggesting a lack of "class consciousness" in the Jacksonian United States, see Gienapp, "Myth of Class."

12. Burke, *Conundrum of Class*, 2.

13. Gary Day notes that the first time "class" appeared in an English-language dictionary was 1656, and its definition was "a ship, or Navy, an 'order' or distribution of people according to their several Degrees" (*Class*, 5–6).

14. I examined eight textbooks and one "textbooklike" monograph on American religious history. Five included reference to the sermon. See Ahlstrom, *Religious History of the American People*, 146–47; Corrigan and Hudson, *Religion in America*, 53–54; Chidester, *Patterns of Power*, 30; Gaustad and Noll, *Documentary History*, 67–69; and Peter Williams, *America's Religions*, 97–98. The four that do not mention the sermon are Albanese, *America*; Bednarowski, *American Religion*; and Hemeyer, *Religion in America*. For the monograph, see Mead, *Lively Experiment*.

15. Gaustad and Noll, *Documentary History*, 67.

16. Winthrop quoted in Perry Miller, *American Puritans*, 79.

17. Ibid.

18. Ibid.

19. Ibid.

20. Chidester, *Patterns of Power*, 30–31.

21. Perry Miller, *American Puritans*, 79–80.

22. Ibid., 80.

23. Chidester, *Patterns of Power*, 31.

24. Ibid.

25. Day, *Class*, 4.

26. For Puritans such as Winthrop, democracy was dangerous—if not literally demonic—because it usurped God's divinely ordained hierarchy. Winthrop referred to it as "the meanest and worst of all forms of government" (Corrigan and Hudson, *Religion in America*, 107–8).

27. For an examination of the antinomian trials of Anne Hutchison and Roger Williams, as well as persecution of Quakers, see Erikson, *Wayward Puritans*. For a study that discusses the clergy concerns with lay folk practices, see Godbeer, *Devil's Dominion*.

28. The essay was reprinted in Andrew Carnegie, *Gospel of Wealth*.

29. Rockefeller quoted in Christiano, Swatos, and Kivisto, *Sociology of Religion*, 135. They cite the quote as being from Josephson, *Robber Barons*, 318.

30. Andrew Carnegie, *Gospel of Wealth*, 1.

31. Ibid.

32. Ibid., 3–4.

33. Perry Miller, *American Puritans*, 79–80.

34. Andrew Carnegie, *Gospel of Wealth*, 14.

35. Ibid., 5.

36. Ibid., 15.

37. Ibid.

38. See Hatch, *Democratization*.

39. Thomas, *Revivalism and Cultural Change*, 22.

40. See Beecher, *Plymouth Pulpit*.

41. See, for example, McLoughlin, *Meaning of Henry Ward Beecher*; Clifford Clark, *Henry Ward Beecher*; and Applegate, "Henry Ward Beecher."

42. Beecher, *Plymouth Pulpit*, 353.

43. Ibid.

44. Ibid., 359.

45. Ibid., 358–60.

46. Ibid., 360.

47. Ibid., 357.

48. Mead, *Lively Experiment*, 160.

49. See Conwell, *Acres of Diamonds*. There are many published versions of Conwell's speech. For an Internet version, see *American Rhetoric*, <http://www.americanrhetoric.com/speeches/rconwellacresofdiamonds.htm>. (All citations are to the online version.)

50. Ibid.

51. Ibid.

52. Ibid.

53. Ibid.

54. Ibid.

55. Lienesch, *Redeeming America*, 118.

56. Ibid., 132.

57. Ibid., 134.

58. Ibid., 111–20.

59. Definitional problems ensue when discussing the New Age movement. Religion scholar Steven Sutcliffe has suggested that the term itself is misleading, as neither "new" nor "movement" really seem to fit much of what is termed "New Age." He argues that New Age is "best understood as a very diffuse milieu of popular practices and beliefs with unstable boundaries, goals, and personnel," suggesting that it is not so much a movement as "a diffuse collectivity: a cluster of seekers affiliated by choice—if at all—to a particular term in a wider culture of alternative spiritual practice" ("Dynam-

ics of Alternative Spirituality," 467). Also see Sutcliffe, *Children of the New Age*.

60. See "Ramtha's School of Enlightenment," <http://ramtha.com/html/aboutus.stm>.

61. *Ramtha's School of Enlightenment: An Introduction* (n.p.: n.d.), 2.

62. Ibid.

63. Michael Brown, *Channeling Zone*, 65.

64. Ibid.

65. Ibid.

66. My attempt in this chapter is to sketch several theologies of class and illustrate them with selected examples. In a more comprehensive survey, one could examine forms of economic Arminianism present in "world religions" in the United States. I am immediately reminded of the Arizona Sikh leader who, in the 1995 documentary *Road Scholar*, tells writer Andrei Codrescu that God meant for his followers to be well off, adding, "if you are poor, you are stupid."

67. Harrison, *Righteous Riches*, 6.

68. Ibid., 8.

69. Ibid., 150, 136.

70. Ibid., 60.

71. See Lee, *T. D. Jakes*; Pappu, "Preacher," 92.

72. Jakes, *Great Investment*, 29.

73. Ibid., 25.

74. Ibid., 37.

75. Ibid., 39.

76. Ibid., 57, 40–41.

77. Ibid., 44.

78. Ibid., 22.

79. Ibid., 27.

80. Ibid.

81. Ibid., 13, 11.

82. Ibid., 57.

83. Ibid., 21.

84. Ibid.

85. Ibid.

86. Ibid., 62.

87. Rice, *Minding the Machine*, 4.

88. Ibid.

89. Burke, *Conundrum of Class*, 108.

90. Ibid. For a discussion of Wayland, see 109.

91. Handy, introduction to *Social Gospel*, 5–6.

92. Ibid.

93. Gladden quoted in Handy, *Social Gospel*, 27.

94. Gladden, *Applied Christianity*, 14.

95. Ibid., 176.

96. Ibid., 33.

97. Ibid., 8.

98. Ibid.

99. Ibid., 16.

100. Gladden quoted in Handy, *Social Gospel*, 28.

101. Gladden, *Applied Christianity*, 20.

102. Ibid., 224.

103. Ibid., 25.

104. Ibid., 224.

105. Ibid.

106. White and Hopkins, *Social Gospel*, 206.

107. Ibid., 366.

108. See Pope Leo XIII, *Rerum Novarum* (1891), <http://www.osjspm.org/cst/rn.htm> (English translation). Each paragraph on the website is numbered. The phrase "capital evil" appears in paragraph 28.

109. Ibid.

110. Ibid.

111. Ibid., paragraph 26.

112. Ibid.

113. Ibid.

114. Ibid., paragraph 36.

115. Ibid., paragraph 65.

116. Ibid., paragraph 9.

117. Ibid., paragraph 36.

118. Ibid., paragraph 44.

119. Ibid., paragraph 45.

120. Dolan, *American Catholic Experience*, 334, 335.

121. Ibid., 336.

122. Ibid.

123. Sheedy, "Encyclical," 851.

124. Ibid., 851–52.

125. Ibid., 852.

126. Ibid., 861.

127. Ibid.

128. Spalding, "Socialism and Labor," 798.

129. Ibid., 799.

130. Ibid.

131. Ibid., 800.

132. Ibid., 802.

133. Ibid., 800.

134. Ibid., 803.

135. Ibid., 807.

136. White and Hopkins, *Social Gospel*, 218–19.

137. Darren Wood, *Blue Collar Jesus*, 14.

138. Ibid., 41.

139. Ibid., 34.

140. Ibid., 28.

141. Ibid., 31.

142. Ibid., 149.

143. Ibid.

144. Halker argues that 23 percent of the melodies and 28 percent of the tunes of labor song-poems came from religious hymnody (*For Democracy, Workers, and God*, 178).

145. Ibid., 138–39.

146. Ibid., 176.

147. Ibid., 145.

148. Ibid., 147.

149. Ibid., 171, 156.

150. Ibid., 153.

151. Ibid., 150.

152. Ibid., 151.

153. See Winters, *Soul of the Wobblies*; Eugene Debs, "Jesus, the Supreme Leader," *Marxist Internet Archive*, <http://www.marxists.org/history/usa/parties/spusa/1914/0300-debs-jesussupreme.pdf>; and Woody Guthrie, "Jesus Christ," *Woody Guthrie Foundation*, <http://woodyguthrie.org/Lyrics/Jesus_Christ.htm>.

154. Bouck White, *Call of the Carpenter*, 24, 305.

155. Ibid., 40.

156. Ibid., 182.

157. Ibid., 196.

158. Ibid., 17, 46.

159. Ibid., 104.

160. Ibid., 107.

161. Ibid., 120, 326.

162. Ibid., 336.

163. Ibid., 264.

164. Ibid., 226–49.

165. Ibid., 235.

166. Ibid., 250.

167. Ibid., 334.

168. Ibid.

169. Ibid.

170. Ibid., 334–35.

171. Ibid., 20.

172. Ibid., 22.

173. Ibid., 59.

174. Ibid., 23.

175. Ibid., 22–23.

176. Ibid., 80.

177. Ibid., 81.

178. Ibid., 76, 78.

179. Ibid., 76, 73.

180. Ibid., 81. White also expressed an evangelizing hope that contemporary Jews would rediscover Jesus. He suggested Jews were currently "foremost among the agitators for a new social order" and found this understandable, "for in their veins courses the blood that

coursed in the veins of the Carpenter" (ibid., 312).

181. Ibid., 279.

182. Ibid., 280.

183. Ibid., 289.

184. Ibid., 283.

185. Ibid., 289.

186. Kilsdonk, "Scientific Church Music," 125–26.

187. See Kasson, *Rudeness and Civility*.

188. Skeggs, *Class, Self, Culture*, 99–100.

189. For a biography of Peter Cartwright, see Bray, *Peter Cartwright*.

190. Cartwright, *Autobiography*, 45–46.

191. Ibid., 48.

192. Ibid., 51.

193. Ibid., 122, 50–51. On these latter pages, Cartwright suggests that the unrepentant drunk was actually killed by the jerks.

194. Ibid., 48–49.

195. Ibid.

196. Ibid., 51.

197. Ibid.

198. Ibid., 46.

199. Ibid., 51.

200. Ibid.

201. Ibid., 51–52.

202. Ibid., 52.

203. Kilsdonk, "Scientific Church Music," 134.

204. Ibid.

205. For brief overviews of both men's lives, see *Encyclopedia of American Religious History*, 107, 235–37. For a biography of Finney, see Hardman, *Charles Grandison Finney*.

206. Finney, *Lectures on Revivals*, 13.

207. Lippy, *Being Religious*, 76.

208. Hatch, *Democratization*, 199.

209. Ibid.

210. Dayton, *Reflections on Revival*, 47.

211. Ibid.

212. Ibid., 48.

213. Ibid., 49–51.

214. Ibid., 48–49.

215. Ibid., 52.

216. Ibid.

217. Ibid., 53.

218. Ibid., 54.

Chapter 6

1. Wray, "White Trash Religion," 196.

2. Ibid.

3. Ibid., 207.

4. Ibid.

5. The material in this chapter stems from my master's thesis, "Tale of Two Churches."

6. Examples of combinative religion are numerous and stretch from pre-Puritans to the present. For a few examples, see Albanese, "Exchanging Selves"; Butler, *Awash in a Sea of Faith*; Lynn Clark, *From Angels to Aliens*; Doss, *Elvis Culture*; David Hall, *Worlds of Wonder*; and Roof, *Generation of Seekers*.

7. See, for example, Spickard, Landres, and McGuire, *Personal Knowledge and Beyond*. For examples of two ethnographies that address these questions, see Behar, *Translated Woman*; and Karen Brown, *Mama Lola*.

8. Skeggs, *Class, Self, Culture*, 128.

9. A brief note on methods: First, the initial fieldwork examined speech and ritual activity during public religious services. As is the case in much ethnography, I did not collect participants' demographic information on income, education, wealth, and occupation. Second, the focus on public speech and ritual, in turn, meant a lack of in-depth partici-

pant interviews. What people think and do in the privacy of their homes—the domestic aspect of "lived religion"—is important and in great need of attention in religious studies. But such a focus was outside the original study's scope. Instead, I collected written notes based on my observations of public services and the sermons, testimonials, and ritual activities that occurred at them. I have no illusion that such a focus tells me everything about the two churches. But I am certain that it does reveal some important things, which I detail in what follows. Finally, I have changed the names of the churches, the city, and those who spoke. Everything else is verbatim. There are no composite characters, and everything in quotations is an exact statement as I originally (and to the best of my ability) recorded it.

10. Worley, "Social Characteristics," 49.

11. For a study of African American congregations during the early years of the Great Migration, see Sernett, *Bound for the Promised Land.*

12. Wagner, "Too Few Tomorrows," 3–4. For studies that feature Appalachian migrant enclaves in two cities in the Great Lakes region, see Gitlin and Hollander, *Uptown*; Hartigan, *Racial Situation*; and Howell, *Hard Living on Clay Street.*

13. Crews, *Church of God*, 170.

14. See Wacker, "Pentecostalism."

15. Poloma, *Assemblies of God*, 204.

16. Ibid.

17. Ibid., 206.

18. Ibid.

19. Ibid.

20. See Turner, *Ritual Process*, esp. 126–28.

21. Poloma, *Assemblies of God*, 205.

22. See Lawless, *God's Peculiar People*; Abell, *Better Felt than Said*; and Goodman, *Speaking in Tongues*. In her examination of Mexican Pentecostal churches in the same volume, Goodman found that in some congregations, men spoke in tongues more often.

23. Abell, *Better Felt than Said*, 137.

24. See Lawless, "Rescripting Their Lives."

25. See Bourdieu, *Outline of a Theory.*

26. Ibid., 82–83.

27. I. M. Lewis, *Ecstatic Religion*, 28.

28. Schwartz, *Sect Ideologies and Social Status*, 33.

29. Weber, *Sociology of Religion*, 107.

30. See Goodman, *Speaking in Tongues.*

31. See ibid.; Abell, *Better Felt than Said*; and Cyril Williams, *Tongues of the Spirit.*

32. Goodman, *Speaking in Tongues*, 75.

33. Ibid., 76; Abell, *Better Felt than Said*, 137.

34. See Ostling, "Church Search."

35. Crews, *Church of God*, 56.

36. Ibid., 58.

37. Ibid.

38. Ibid., 60–61, 63.

39. In this way, the Church of God (Cleveland, TN) seems to fit sociologist Joseph Tamney's suggestion that those conservative Protestant churches remaining resilient or even growing in the contemporary era are those that are authoritative, yet allow flexibility of interpretation. See Tamney, *Resilience of Conservative Religion*. One study examining the *Yearbook of American and Canadian Churches* suggests that the Church of God grew 183 percent from 1965 to 1989 (Ostling, "Church Search," 47).

40. Church of God, *Our Statements of Faith* (Cleveland, Tenn., n.d.), 14–15.

41. *The Holy Bible, Containing the Old and New Testaments* (Nashville, Tenn.: Gideons International, n.d.).

42. See Poloma, *Assemblies of God.* Also see her study of the Toronto Blessing, *Main Street Mystics.*

43. Bourdieu, *Outline of a Theory*, 82–83.

44. Bourdieu, "Social Space and Genesis," 725. Bourdieu suggests that a class on paper "is not really a class, an actual class, in the sense of a group, a group mobilized for struggle; at most it might be called a probable class, inasmuch as it is a set of agents that will present fewer hindrances to efforts at mobilization than any other set of agents" (725). I disagree with Bourdieu, noting that this Marxian conception of class unnecessarily implies a "class-conscious" group "mobilized for struggle." As noted in chapter 1, I see no reason why class must necessarily entail class consciousness, let alone any mobilization.

45. Fred Rose, "Toward a Class-Cultural Theory," 472.

46. Ibid., 487, 475.

47. Ibid., 488.

48. Quoted in Applegate, "Henry Ward Beecher," 111.

49. Swidler, *Talk of Love*, 52.

50. Ibid.

51. Ibid.

52. Skeggs, *Class, Self, Culture*, 99–100.

53. Hatch, *Democratization*, 199.

Conclusion

1. Tsunetomo, *Hagakure*, 71.

2. Tweed, *Crossing and Dwelling*, 181.

3. While Bourdieu's use of "habitus" sees it as mostly doxa, Saba Mahmood has used the term "habitus" in its Aristotelean sense to mean the conscious inculcation of habits. See *Politics of Piety.*

4. Bourdieu tends to see societies and fields as having a single doxa, yet given his concept of habitus, it seems more accurate to argue that different groups, classes, and individuals have different doxa. While some doxic assumptions may be shared by most within the broader field, subculture, or society, other doxa may be particular to groups who share class, racial, ethnic, gender, religious, regional, and occupational locations. John Hall makes a similar argument about Bourdieu's concept of "cultural capital"; see "Capital(s) of Cultures". Here, I suggest that the case may be the same for individuals.

5. Some have criticized Bourdieu's conception of habitus as being static. For example, Deborah Reed-Danahay writes that "newer forms of hybrid identities, shifting forms of subjectivity related to either geographic mobility or rapid social change, cannot be easily accommodated with this view of habitus as something inculcated in early childhood and then providing a set of dispositions that guide a person's life trajectory" (*Locating Bourdieu*, 156).

6. See McCloud, "Prophecy."

Bibliography

Abell, Troy. *Better Felt than Said: The Holiness-Pentecostal Experience in Southern Appalachia*. Waco, Tex.: Markham, 1982.

Aberle, David. "A Note on the Relative Deprivation Theory as Applied to Millenarian and Other Cult Movements." In *Millennial Dreams in Action: Studies in Revolutionary Religious Movements*, edited by Sylvia L. Thrupp, 209–14. New York: Schocken, 1970. First published 1962 by Mouton.

Agee, James, and Walker Evans. *Let Us Now Praise Famous Men*. Boston: Houghton Mifflin, 1941.

Ahlstrom, Sydney E. *A Religious History of the American People*. New Haven, Conn.: Yale University Press, 1972.

Albanese, Catherine L. *America: Religions and Religion*. 3rd ed. Belmont, Calif.: Wadsworth, 1999.

———. "Exchanging Selves, Exchanging Souls: Contact, Combination, and American Religious History." In *Retelling U.S. Religious History*, edited by Thomas A. Tweed, 200–226. Berkeley: University of California Press, 1997.

Alexander, Bobby. *Televangelism Reconsidered: Ritual in the Search for Human Community*. Atlanta: Scholars' Press, 1994.

Algeo, Katie. "Locals in Local Color: Imagining Identity in Appalachia." *Southern Cultures* 9, no. 4 (Winter 2003): 27–54.

Allan, Graham. "A Theory of Millennialism: The Irvingite Movement as an Illustration." *British Journal of Sociology* 25 (1974): 296–311.

Alley, Robert S., ed. *The Constitution and Religion: Leading Supreme Court Cases on Church and State*. Amherst, N.Y.: Prometheus, 1999.

Anderson, Robert Mapes. *Vision of the Disinherited: The Making of American Pentecostalism*. Peabody, Mass.: Hendrickson, 1979.

Applegate, Debby. "Henry Ward Beecher and the 'Great Middle Class': Mass-Marketed Intimacy and Middle-Class Identity." In *The Middling Sorts: Explorations in the History of the American Middle Class*, edited by Burton J. Bledstein and Robert D. Johnston, 107–24. New York: Routledge, 2001.

———. *The Most Famous Man in America: The Biography of Henry Ward Beecher*. New York: Doubleday, 2006.

Aronowitz, Stanley. *How Class Works: Power and Social Movements*. New Haven, Conn.: Yale University Press, 2003.

Brunner, Edmund deS. *Village Communities*. New York: George H. Doran, 1927.

Bryson, Bethany. "What about Univores?: Musical Dislikes and Group-Based Identity Construction among Americans with Low Levels of Education." *Poetics* 25 (1997): 141–56.

Burchinal, Lee. "Some Social Status Criteria and Church Membership and Church Attendance." *Journal of Social Psychology* 49 (1959): 53–64.

Burke, Martin J. *The Conundrum of Class: Public Discourse on the Social Order in America*. Chicago: University of Chicago Press, 1995.

Burris, John. *Exhibiting Religion: Colonialism and Spectacle at International Expositions, 1851–1893*. Charlottesville: University of Virginia Press, 2001.

Burrow, J. W. *Evolution and Society: A Study in Victorian Social Theory*. Cambridge: Cambridge University Press, 1966.

Burton, Thomas. *Serpent-Handling Believers: And These Signs Shall Follow*. Knoxville: University of Tennessee Press, 1993.

Butler, Jon. *Awash in a Sea of Faith: Christianizing the American People*. Cambridge, Mass.: Harvard University Press, 1990.

Calvert, Peter. *The Concept of Class: An Historical Introduction*. New York: St. Martin's Press, 1982.

Cantril, Hadley. "Educational and Economic Composition of Religious Groups." *American Journal of Sociology* 48 (1943): 574–79.

Carlsen, Elof Axel. *The Unfit: A History of a Bad Idea*. Cold Harbor Spring, N.Y.: Cold Harbor Spring Laboratory, 2001.

Carnegie, Andrew. *The Gospel of Wealth and Other Timely Essays*. Garden City, N.J.: Doubleday, 1933.

Carnegie, Dale. *How to Win Friends and Influence People*. New York: Pocket Books, 1982.

Carroll, Michael P. "Revitalization Movements and Social Structure: Some Quantitative Tests." *American Sociological Review* 40 (1975): 389–401.

———. "Stark Realities and Eurocentric/Androcentric Bias in the Sociology of Religion." *Sociology of Religion* 57:3 (1996): 225–39.

Carter, Paul. *The Spiritual Crisis of the Gilded Age*. DeKalb: Northern Illinois University Press, 1971.

Carter, Richard. "That Old-Time Religion Comes Back." *Coronet*, February 1958, 125–30.

Cartwright, Peter. *The Autobiography of Peter Cartwright: The Backwoods Preacher*. Edited by W. P. Strickland. New York: Carlton and Porter, 1856.

Castelein, John Donald. "Glossolalia and the Psychology of the Self and Narcissism." *Journal of Religion and Health* 23 (1984): 47–62.

Centers, Richard. *The Psychology of Classes: A Study of Class Consciousness*. New York: Russell and Russell, 1949.

Chamberlain, J. Edward, and Sander Gilman, eds. *Degeneration: The Dark Side of Progress*. New York: Columbia University Press, 1985.

Chesnut, R. Andrew. *Born Again in Brazil: The Pentecostal Boom and the Pathogens of Poverty*. New Brunswick, N.J.: Rutgers University Press, 1997.

Chevreau, Guy. *Catch the Fire: The Toronto Blessing, an Experience of Renewal and Revival*. Toronto: HarperCollins, 1994.

Chidester, David. *Patterns of Power: Religion and Politics in American Culture*. Englewood Cliffs, N.J.: Prentice Hall, 1988.

———. *Salvation and Suicide: An Interpretation of Jim Jones, the Peoples Temple, and Jonestown*. Bloomington: Indiana University Press, 1988.

Christiano, Kevin. "Religion and Radical Labor Unionism: American States in the 1920s." *Journal for the Scientific Study of Religion* 27 (1988): 378–88.

Christiano, Kevin, William H. Swatos Jr., and Peter Kivisto. *Sociology of Religion: Contemporary Developments*. Walnut Creek, Calif.: Altamira, 2002.

Clark, Clifford E., Jr. *Henry Ward Beecher: Spokesman for a Middle-Class America*. Urbana: University of Illinois Press, 1978.

Clark, Elmer T. *The Small Sects of America*. Rev. ed. Nashville: Abingdon, 1965.

Clark, Lynn Schofield. *From Angels to Aliens: Teenagers, the Media, and the Supernatural*. New York: Oxford University Press, 2003.

Coleman, Michael C. *American Indian Children at School, 1850–1930*. Jackson: University of Mississippi Press, 1993.

Cone, James H. *A Black Theology of Liberation*. Twentieth anniversary ed. Maryknoll, N.Y.: Orbis, 1990.

Connelly, Marjorie. "How Americans Voted: A Political Portrait." *New York Times*, 7 November 2004, 4.

Conwell, Russell. *Acres of Diamonds*. New York: Harper, 1915.

Cook, Stephen. *Prophecy and Apocalypticism: The Postexilic Social Setting*. Minneapolis: Fortress, 1995.

Coreno, Thaddeus. "Fundamentalism as a Class Culture." *Sociology of Religion* 63 (2002): 335–60.

Correspondents of the *New York Times*. *Class Matters*. New York: Times Books and Henry Holt, 2005.

Corrigan, John, and Winthrop S. Hudson. *Religion in America*. 7th ed. Upper Saddle River, N.J.: Prentice Hall, 2004.

Covington, Dennis. *Salvation on Sand Mountain: Snake Handling and Redemption in Southern Appalachia*. New York: Penguin, 1995.

Cox, Harvey. *Fire from Heaven: The Rise of Pentecostal Spirituality and the Reshaping of Religion in the Twenty-first Century*. Reading, Mass.: Addison-Wesley, 1995.

Crane, Diana. *Fashion and Its Social Agendas: Class, Gender, and Identity in Clothing*. Chicago: University of Chicago Press, 2000.

Crews, Mickey. *The Church of God: A Social History*. Knoxville: University of Tennessee Press, 1989.

Cutten, George Barton. *Speaking with Tongues, Historically and Psychologically Considered*. New York: Yale University Press, 1927.

Daugherty, Mary Lee. "The Sacrament of Serpent Handling." In *Beyond Androcen-*

trism: New Essays on Women and Religion, edited by Rita M. Gross, 139–59. Missoula, Mont.: Scholars' Press, 1977.

Davenport, Frederick Morgan. *Primitive Traits in Religious Revivals: A Study in Mental and Social Evolution*. New York: Macmillan, 1905.

Davidson, James. *Religion among America's Elite: Persistence and Change in the Protestant Establishment*. Notre Dame, Ind.: Cushwa Center for the Study of American Catholicism, 1991.

———. "Socio-Economic Status and Ten Dimensions of Religious Commitment." *Sociology and Social Research* 61 (1977): 462–85.

Davies, Horton. *Challenge of the Sects*. Philadelphia: Westminster, 1961.

Day, Gary. *Class*. New York: Routledge, 2001.

Dayton, Donald, ed. *Reflections on Revival by Charles Grandison Finney*. Minneapolis: Bethany Fellowship, 1979.

De Artega, William. *Quenching the Spirit: Examining Centuries of Opposition to the Moving of the Holy Spirit*. Altamonte Springs, Fla.: Creation House, 1992.

Debord, Guy. *The Society of the Spectacle*. Detroit: Black and Red, 1983.

"Defining the Rich in the World's Wealthiest Nation." *New York Times*, 12 January 2003, K1, K16.

Demerath, N. J., III. *Social Class in American Protestantism*. Chicago: Rand McNally, 1965.

"Despair Serves Purposes of Bizarre Cults." *Christian Century*, 10 August 1960, 917.

Dolan, Jay P. *The American Catholic Experience: A History from Colonial Times to Present*. Notre Dame, Ind.: University of Notre Dame Press, 1992.

Doss, Erika. *Elvis Culture: Fans, Faith, and Image*. Lawrence: University Press of Kansas, 1999.

Douglass, H. Paul, and Edmund Brunner. *The Protestant Church as a Social Institution*. New York: Russell and Russell, 1935.

Du Bois, W. E. B. *The Souls of Black Folk*. New York: Signet Classic, 1982.

Durst, Dennis. "Evangelical Engagements with Eugenics, 1900–1940." *Ethics and Medicine* 18, no. 2 (2002): 45–53.

Earle, John, Dean Knudson, and Donald Shriver. *Spindles and Spires: A Re-Study of Religion and Social Change in Gastonia*. Atlanta: John Know, 1976.

Eder, Klaus. *The New Politics of Class: Social Movements and Cultural Dynamics in Advanced Societies*. London: Sage, 1993.

Eister, Alan W. "H. Richard Niebuhr and the Paradox of Religious Organization: A Radical Critique." In *Beyond the Classics? Essays in the Scientific Study of Religion*, edited by Charles Y. Glock and Phillip E. Hammond, 358–98. New York: Harper and Row, 1973.

Ellis, Bill. *Lucifer Ascending: The Occult in Folklore and Popular Culture*. Lexington: University Press of Kentucky, 2004.

———. *Raising the Devil: Satanism, New Religions, and the Media*. Lexington: University Press of Kentucky, 2000.

Ellis, Clyde. *To Change Them Forever: Indian Education at the Rainy Mountain Boarding School, 1893–1920*. Norman: University of Oklahoma Press, 1996.

Emerson, Michael, and Christian Smith. *Divided by Faith: Evangelical Religion and the Problem of Race in America*. New York: Oxford University Press, 2000.

Encyclopedia of American Religious History. Edited by Edward L. Queen II, Stephen R. Prothero, and Gardiner H. Shattuck Jr. New York: Facts on File, 1996.

Encyclopedia of the American Religious Experience. Edited by Charles H. Lippy and Peter W. Williams. New York: Scribner, 1988.

English, Daylanne. *Unnatural Selections: Eugenics in American Modernism and the Harlem Renaissance*. Chapel Hill: University of North Carolina Press, 2004.

Epps, Garrett. *To an Unknown God: Religious Freedom on Trial*. New York: St. Martin's Press, 2001.

Erickson, Bonnie. "Culture, Class, and Connections." *American Journal of Sociology* 102, no. 1 (1996): 217–51.

Erikson, Kai. *Wayward Puritans: A Study in the Sociology of Deviance*. New York: Wiley, 1966.

Evans-Pritchard, E. E. *Theories of Primitive Religion*. London: Oxford University Press, 1965.

Fantasia, Rick. "From Class to Culture, Action, and Social Organization." *Annual Review of Sociology* 21 (1995): 269–87.

Festinger, Leon, Henry Riecken, and Stanley Schachter. *When Prophecy Fails: A Social and Psychological Study of a Modern Group That Predicted the Destruction of the World*. New York: Harper Torchbooks, 1956.

Finke, Roger, and Rodney Stark. *The Churching of America, 1776–1990: Winners and Losers in Our Religious Economy*. New Brunswick, N.J.: Rutgers University Press, 1992.

Finney, Charles Grandison. *Lectures on Revivals of Religion by Charles Grandison Finney*. 1835. Edited by William G. McLoughlin. Cambridge, Mass.: Harvard University Press, 1960.

Fletcher, Alice C. "The Indian Messiah." *Journal of American Folklore* 4 (January–March 1891): 57–60.

Fones-Wolf, Ken. *Trade Union Gospel: Christianity and Labor in Industrial Philadelphia, 1865–1915*. Philadelphia: Temple University Press, 1989.

Fowler, Newton. "Religion beyond the Churches: The Appeal of Sect and Non-Traditional Religions." *Lexington Theological Quarterly* 16 (1981): 78–84.

Fox, Richard Wightman. *Jesus in America: Personal Savior, Cultural Hero, National Obsession*. San Francisco: Harper, 2004.

Fox, Richard Wightman, and T. Jackson Lears, eds. *The Culture of Consumption: Critical Essays in American History, 1880–1980*. New York: Pantheon, 1982.

Francis, David. "How Social Security Could Narrow Rich-Poor Gap." *Christian Science Monitor*, 28 March 2005, <www.csmonitor.com/2005/0328/p17s01-cogn.html>.

Frazier, James. *The Golden Bough: A Study in Magic and Religion*. New York: Macmillan, 1950.

Freud, Sigmund. *The Future of an Illusion*. Translated and edited by James Strachey. With an introduction by Peter Gay. New York: W. W. Norton, 1989.

Friedel, Frank, and Alan Brinkley. *America in the Twentieth Century*. 5th ed. New York: Alfred A. Knopf, 1982.

Frykholm, Amy Johnson. *Rapture Culture: Left Behind in Evangelical America*. New York: Oxford University Press, 2004.

Fussell, Paul. *Class: A Guide through the American Status System*. New York: Summit, 1983.

Galton, Francis. *Inquiries into the Human Faculty and Its Development*. New York: Macmillan, 1883.

Gans, Herbert. *Popular Culture and High Culture: An Analysis and Evaluation of Taste*. New York: Basic Books, 1974.

Gaustad, Edwin S., and Mark A. Noll, eds. *A Documentary History of Religion in America to 1877*. 3rd ed. Grand Rapids, Mich.: William B. Eerdmans, 2003.

Gerlach, Luther P. "Pentecostalism: Revolution or Counter-Revolution?" In *Religious Movements in Contemporary America*, edited by Irving I. Zaretsky and Mark P. Leone, 669–99. Princeton, N.J.: Princeton University Press, 1974.

Gerlach, Luther P., and Virginia H. Hine. *People, Power, Change: Movements of Social Transformation*. Indianapolis: Bobbs-Merrill, 1970.

Gerrard, Nathan. "The Serpent Handling Religion of West Virginia." *Transaction* 5 (1968): 22–28.

Gerth, H. H., and C. Wright Mills, eds. *From Max Weber: Essays in Sociology*. New York: Oxford University Press, 1946.

Giddens, Anthony. *Modernity and Self-Identity: Self and Society in the Late Modern Age*. Stanford, Calif.: Stanford University Press, 1991.

Gienapp, William E. "The Myth of Class in Jacksonian America." *Journal of Policy History* 6, no. 2 (1994): 232–59.

Gilbert, Dennis, and Joseph Kahl. *The American Class Structure: A New Synthesis*. Homewood, Ill.: Dorsey, 1982.

Gillin, J. L. Review of *Applied Eugenics*, by Paul Popenoe and Roswell Hill Johnson. *American Journal of Sociology* 25, no. 1 (July 1919): 104–5.

Gist, Noel, and Carroll Clark. "Intelligence as a Selective Factor in Rural-Urban Migrations." *American Journal of Sociology* 44 (July 1938): 36–58.

Gitlin, Todd, and Nanci Hollander. *Uptown: Poor Whites in Chicago*. New York: Harper and Row, 1970.

Gladden, Washington. *Applied Christianity: Moral Aspects of Social Questions*. New York: Arno, 1976.

Glenn, Max, ed. *Appalachia in Transition*. St. Louis: Bethany, 1970.

Glock, Charles Y. "On Nature, Sources, and Consequences." *Religious Studies Review* 11, no. 1 (1985): 20–23.

———. "The Role of Deprivation in the Origin and Evolution of Religious Groups."

In *Religion and Social Conflict*, edited by Robert Lee and Martin Marty, 24–36. New York: Oxford University Press, 1964.

Glock, Charles Y., Benjamin B. Ringer, and Earl R. Babbie. *To Comfort and to Challenge: A Dilemma of the Contemporary Church*. Berkeley: University of California Press, 1967.

Godbeer, Richard. *The Devil's Dominion: Magic and Religion in Early New England*. New York: Cambridge University Press, 1992.

Godwin, John. *Occult America*. Garden City, N.Y.: Doubleday, 1972.

Goldthorpe, John, and Gordon Marshall. "The Promising Future of Class Analysis: A Response to Recent Critiques." *Sociology* 26 (1992): 381–400.

Goodman, Felicitas. *Speaking in Tongues: A Cross-Cultural Study of Glossolalia*. Chicago: University of Chicago Press, 1972.

Gottschalk, Stephen. *The Emergence of Christian Science in American Religious Life*. Berkeley: University of California Press, 1973.

Gould, Stephen Jay. *The Mismeasure of Man*. New York: W. W. Norton, 1981.

Greene, John Robert. "Frederick Morgan Davenport: Portrait of a Progressive." *Theodore Roosevelt Association Journal* 12 (Spring–Summer 1986): 12–21.

Griffith, R. Marie. *Born Again Bodies: Flesh and Spirit in American Christianity*. Berkeley: University of California Press, 2004.

Grundmann, Reiner, and Nico Stehr. "Why Is Werner Sombart Not Part of the Core of Classical Sociology?" *Journal of Classical Sociology* 1 (2001): 257–87.

Gusfield, Joseph R. *Symbolic Crusade: Status Politics and the American Temperance Movement*. Urbana: University of Illinois Press, 1963.

Guthrie, Stewart. *Faces in the Clouds: A New Theory of Religion*. New York: Oxford University Press, 1993.

Gutman, Herbert. "Protestantism and the American Labor Movement: The Christian Spirit in the Gilded Age." *American Historical Review* 72 (October 1966): 74–101.

Hackett, David, Laurie Maffly-Kipp, R. Laurence Moore, and Leslie Woodcock Tentler. "Forum: American Religion and Class." *Religion and American Culture* 15 (2005): 1–29.

Halker, Clark D. *For Democracy, Workers, and God: Labor Song-Poems and Labor Protest, 1865–95*. Urbana: University of Illinois Press, 1991.

Hall, David D. *Worlds of Wonder, Days of Judgment: Popular Religious Beliefs in Early New England*. Cambridge, Mass.: Harvard University Press, 1990.

Hall, John R. "The Capital(s) of Cultures: A Nonholistic Approach to Status Situations, Class, Gender, and Ethnicity." In *Cultivating Differences: Symbolic Boundaries and the Making of Inequality*, edited by Michele Lamont and Marcel Fournier, 257–85. Chicago: University of Chicago Press, 1992.

———. *Gone from the Promised Land: Jonestown in American Cultural History*. New Brunswick, N.J.: Transaction, 1987.

———, ed. *Reworking Class*. Ithaca, N.Y.: Cornell University Press, 1997.

Hall, Peter Dobkin. "The Problem of Class." *History of Education Quarterly* 26, no. 4 (1986): 569–79.

Hall, Stuart. Introduction to *Representation: Cultural Representations and Signifying Practices*, edited by Stuart Hall, 1–11. London: Sage, 1997.

———. "The Spectacle of the 'Other.'" In *Representation: Cultural Representations and Signifying Practices*, edited by Stuart Hall, 223–90. London: Sage, 1997.

Hall, Stuart, and Tony Jefferson, eds. *Resistance through Rituals: Youth Subcultures in Postwar Britain*. London: Routledge, 1993.

Handy, Robert, ed. *The Social Gospel in America, 1870–1920*. New York: Oxford University Press, 1966.

Harding, Susan. "Representing Fundamentalism: The Problem of the Repugnant Cultural Other." *Social Research* 58 (1991): 373–93.

Hardman, Keith J. *Charles Grandison Finney, 1792–1875: Revivalist and Reformer*. Syracuse, N.Y.: Syracuse University Press, 1987.

HarperCollins Dictionary of Religion. Edited by Jonathan Z. Smith. New York: HarperCollins, 1995.

Harrison, Milmon F. *Righteous Riches: The Word of Faith Movement in Contemporary African American Religion*. New York: Oxford University Press, 2005.

Hartigan, John, Jr. *Racial Situations: Class Predicaments of Whiteness in Detroit*. Princeton, N.J.: Princeton University Press, 1999.

Haslan, Marouf Arif, Jr. *The Rhetoric of Eugenics in Anglo-American Thought*. Athens: University of Georgia Press, 1996.

Hatch, Nathan. *The Democratization of American Christianity*. New Haven, Conn.: Yale University Press, 1989.

Heathorn, Stephen. "Review Essay: E. P. Thompson, Methodism, and the 'Culturalist' Approach to the Historical Study of Religion." *Method and Theory in the Study of Religion* 10 (1998): 210–26.

Heaton, Tim. "Socio-Demographic Characteristics of Religious Groups in Canada." *Sociological Analysis* 47 (1986): 54–65.

"Heaven Can Wait." *Newsweek*, 8 June 1987, 58–65.

Hebdige, Dick. *Subculture: The Meaning of Style*. London: Routledge, 1979.

Hemeyer, Julia Corbett. *Religion in America*. 5th ed. Upper Saddle River, N.J.: Prentice Hall, 2006.

Hendershot, Heather. *Shaking the World for Jesus: Media and Conservative Evangelical Culture*. Chicago: University of Chicago Press, 2004.

Herberg, Will. *Protestant Catholic Jew*. 2nd ed. Garden City, N.Y.: Anchor, 1960.

Hickman, Frank. *Introduction to the Psychology of Religion*. New York: Abingdon, 1926.

Hicks, Robert. *In Pursuit of Satan: The Police and the Occult*. Buffalo, N.Y.: Prometheus, 1991.

Higginbotham, Evelyn Brooks. *Righteous Discontent: The Women's Movement in the Black Baptist Church, 1880–1920*. Cambridge, Mass.: Harvard University Press, 1993.

Higham, John. *Strangers in the Land: Patterns of American Nativism, 1860–1925*. New York: Atheneum, 1966.

Himes, Norman E. Review of *Applied Eugenics*, by Paul Popenoe and Roswell Hill Johnson. *American Journal of Sociology* 39 (March 1934): 714–15.

Hine, Virginia. "The Deprivation and Disorganization Theories of Social Movements." In *Religious Movements in Contemporary America*, edited by Irving I. Zaretsky and Mark P. Leone, 646–61. Princeton, N.J.: Princeton University Press, 1974.

———. "Pentecostal Glossolalia: Toward a Functional Interpretation." *Journal for the Scientific Study of Religion* 8 (1969): 211–26.

Hinkle, Roscoe C. *Developments in American Sociological Theory, 1915–1950*. Albany: SUNY Press, 1994.

Hodgen, Margaret. "The Doctrine of Survivals: The History of an Idea." *American Anthropologist* 33 (1931): 307–24.

———. "Survivals and Social Origins: The Pioneers." *American Journal of Sociology* 38 (1933): 583–94.

Hoffer, Eric. *The True Believer*. New York: Harper and Row, 1966. First published 1951.

Hofstadter, Richard. *Social Darwinism in American Thought*, rev. ed. Boston: Beacon, 1955.

Holt, John. "Holiness Religion: Cultural Shock and Social Reorganization." *American Sociological Review* 5 (October 1940): 740–47.

Hooker, Elizabeth. "Leaders in Village Communities." *Social Forces* 6 (June 1928): 605–14.

hooks, bell. *Where We Stand: Class Matters*. New York: Routledge, 2000.

Hostetler, John, and William Mather. "The Rural Church: Is It Free of Class Distinction?" *Scientific Farmer*, Summer 1953, 5–6.

Hout, Michael, and Andrew Greeley. "A Hidden Swing Vote: Evangelicals." *New York Times*, 4 September 2004, A27.

Howell, Joseph T. *Hard Living on Clay Street: Portraits of Blue Collar Families*. Garden City, N.Y.: Anchor, 1973.

Hunt, Stephen. "The 'Toronto Blessing': A Rumor of Angels?" *Journal of Contemporary Religion* 10 (1995): 257–71.

Huntington, Ellsworth, and Leon Whitney. *The Builders of America*. London: Chapman and Hall, 1928.

Hutchinson, Paul. "Have We a 'New' Religion?" *Life*, 11 April 1955.

"In the White Man's Image." Produced by Christine Lesiak and Matthew Jones. *American Experience*. Alexandria, Va.: PBS Video, 1991.

Jakes, T. D. *The Great Investment: Faith, Family, and Finance*. New York: G. P. Putnam's Sons, 2000.

Jarvie, I. C. *The Revolution in Anthropology*. Chicago: Henry Regnery, 1967.

Jenkins, Philip. *Dream Catchers: How Mainstream America Discovered Native Spirituality*. New York: Oxford University Press, 2004.

———. *Mystics and Messiahs: Cults and New Religions in American History*. New York: Oxford University Press, 2000.

Lienesch, Michael. *Redeeming America: Piety and Politics in the New Christian Right.* Chapel Hill: University of North Carolina Press, 1993.

Lincoln, C. Eric. *Black Muslims in America.* 3rd ed. Grand Rapids, Mich.: William B. Eerdmans, 1994. Originally published 1951.

Linton, Ralph, and A. Irving Howell. "Nativistic Movements." *American Anthropologist* 45 (April–June 1943): 230–40.

Lippy, Charles H. *Being Religious, American Style: A History of Popular Religiosity in the United States.* Westport, Conn.: Praeger, 1994.

Lofland, John, and Rodney Stark. "Becoming a World Saver: A Theory of Conversion to a Deviant Perspective." *American Sociological Review* 30 (December 1965): 862–75.

Long, Carolyn Morrow. *Spiritual Merchants: Religion, Magic, and Commerce.* Knoxville: University of Tennessee Press, 2001.

Lydon, John, and Keith Zimmerman. *Rotten: No Irish, No Blacks, No Jews.* New York: St. Martin's Press, 1994.

Lynd, Robert S., and Helen Merrell Lynd. *Middletown: A Study in American Culture.* New York: Harcourt Brace, 1929.

Maaga, Mary McCormick. *Hearing the Voices of Jonestown: Putting a Human Face on an American Tragedy.* Syracuse, N.Y.: Syracuse University Press, 1998.

Machalek, Richard, and David Snow. "Conversion to New Religious Movements." In *The Handbook of Sects and Cults in America*, edited by David Bromley and Jeffrey Hadden, pt. B, 53–74. Greenwich, Conn.: Jai, 1993.

MacLeod, Jay. *Ain't No Making It: Aspirations and Attainment in a Low-Income Neighborhood.* Boulder, Colo.: Westview, 1995.

Madison, James H. "Reformers and the Rural Church, 1900–1950." *Journal of American History* 73 (December 1986): 645–68.

Mahmood, Saba. *Politics of Piety: The Islamic Revival and the Feminist Subject.* Princeton, N.J.: Princeton University Press, 2005.

Maloney, H. Newton, and A. Adams Lovekin. *Glossolalia: Behavioral Science Perspectives on Speaking in Tongues.* New York: Oxford University Press, 1985.

Marcus, Greil. *Lipstick Traces: A Secret History of the Twentieth Century.* Cambridge, Mass.: Harvard University Press, 1989.

Marsden, George. *Fundamentalism and American Culture: The Shaping of Twentieth-Century Evangelicalism, 1870–1925.* New York: Oxford University Press, 1980.

Marshall, Gordon. *Repositioning Class: Social Inequality in Industrial Societies.* London: Sage, 1997.

Martin, David. *Pentecostalism: The World Their Parish.* Oxford: Blackwell, 2002.

Martin, Everett. *The Behavior of Crowds.* New York: Harper, 1920.

Martin, Joel W. "Before and Beyond the Sioux Ghost Dance: Native and Prophetic Movements and the Study of Religion." *Journal of the American Academy of Religion* 59, no. 4 (1991): 677–701.

———. *Sacred Revolt: The Muskogees' Struggle for a New World.* Boston: Beacon, 1991.

Martin, Luther. "Cognition, Society, and Religion: A New Approach to the Study of Culture." *Culture and Religion: An Interdisciplinary Journal* 4 (2003): 207–32.

Marty, Martin. *Modern American Religion*. Vol. 2, *The Noise of Conflict, 1919–1941*. Chicago: University of Chicago Press, 1991.

———, ed. *Protestantism and Social Christianity*. New York: K. G. Saur, 1992.

Marx, Karl, and Friedrich Engels. *The German Ideology: Including Thesis on Feuerbach*. Amherst, N.Y.: Prometheus, 1998.

———. *On Religion*. Introduction by Reinhold Niebuhr. New York: Schocken, 1964.

Masuzawa, Tomoko. *In Search of Dreamtime: The Quest for the Origin of Religion*. Chicago: University of Chicago Press, 1993.

Mathison, Richard R. *Faiths, Cults, and Sects of America: From Atheism to Zen*. Indianapolis: Bobbs-Merrill, 1960.

Mayer, Albert, and Harry Sharp. "Religious Preference and Worldly Success." *American Sociological Review* 27 (1962): 218–27.

McCauley, Deborah Vansau. *Appalachian Mountain Religion: A History*. Urbana: University of Illinois Press, 1995.

McCloud, Sean. *Making the American Religious Fringe: Exotics, Subversives, and Journalists, 1955–1993*. Chapel Hill: University of North Carolina Press, 2004.

———. "Prophecy, American New Religions, and Liminality: Toward a Non-Deprivationist Approach to Prophetic Movements." In *"I Am No Prophet": Functions of Prophecy in Holy Books and Beyond*, edited by Armin Lange et al. Boston: Brill, forthcoming.

———. "A Tale of Two Churches: Similarity and Difference in Two Holiness Pentecostal Assemblies." Master's thesis, Miami University of Ohio, 1994.

McCracken, Grant. *Culture and Consumption: New Approaches to the Symbolic Character of Consumer Goods and Activities*. Bloomington: Indiana University Press, 1990.

McDannell, Colleen. *Picturing Faith: Photography and the Great Depression*. New Haven, Conn.: Yale University Press, 2004.

McDougall, William. *Is America Safe for Democracy?* New York: Arno, 1977. Originally published 1921.

McGuire, Meredith B. *Pentecostal Catholics: Power, Charisma, and Order in a Religious Movement*. Philadelphia: Temple University Press, 1982.

McLoughlin, William G. *The Meaning of Henry Ward Beecher: An Essay on the Shifting Values of Mid-Victorian America, 1840–1870*. New York: Alfred A. Knopf, 1970.

Mead, Sidney. *The Lively Experiment: The Shaping of Christianity in America*. New York: Harper and Row, 1963.

Miller, Albert G. "Pentecostalism as a Social Movement: Beyond the Theory of Deprivation." *Journal of Pentecostal Theology* 9 (1996): 97–114.

Miller, Perry, ed. *The American Puritans: Their Prose and Poetry*. Garden City, N.Y.: Doubleday, 1956.

Mills, Watson E., ed. *Speaking in Tongues: A Guide to Research on Glossolalia*. Grand Rapids, Mich.: William B. Eerdmans, 1986.

Milner, Andrew. *Class*. London: Sage, 1999.

Mirola, William. "Asking for Bread, Receiving a Stone: The Rise and Fall of Religious Ideologies in Chicago's Eight-Hour Movement." *Social Problems* 50 (2003): 273–93.

———. "Religious Protest and Economic Conflict: Possibilities and Constraints on Religious Resource Mobilization and Coalitions in Detroit's Newspaper Strike." *Sociology of Religion* 64 (2003): 443–61.

Mitchell, Stephen, ed. *Dropping Ashes on the Buddha: The Teaching of Zen Master Seung Sahn*. New York: Grove, 1976.

Mode, Peter G. *The Frontier Spirit in American Christianity*. New York: Macmillan, 1923.

Murphy, Teresa Anne. *Ten Hours' Labor: Religion, Reform, and Gender in Early New England*. Ithaca, N.Y.: Cornell University Press, 1992.

Nash, Phileo. "The Place of Religious Revivalism in the Formation of the Intercultural Community on Klamath Reservation." In *Social Anthropology of North American Tribes*, by Fred Eggan, William Gilbert Jr., Gilbert McAllister, Phileo Nash, Morris Opler, John Provinse, and Sol Tax, 377–442. Chicago: University of Chicago Press, 1937.

Neitz, Mary Jo. *Charisma and Community: A Study of Commitment within the Charismatic Renewal*. New Brunswick, N.J.: Transaction, 1987.

Niebuhr, H. Richard. *The Social Sources of Denominationalism*. Cleveland: Meridian, 1968. Originally published 1929 by Henry Holt.

Oberdeck, Kathryn. *The Evangelist and the Impresario: Religion, Entertainment, and Cultural Politics in America, 1884–1914*. Baltimore: Johns Hopkins University Press, 1999.

Obermiller, Phillip, and William Philliber, eds. *Too Few Tomorrows: Urban Appalachians in the 1980s*. Boone, N.C.: Appalachian Consortium, 1987.

Ogburn, William F. Review of *Applied Eugenics*, by Paul Popenoe and Roswell Hill Johnson. *Political Science Quarterly* 36 (September 1921): 533–35.

Orsi, Robert A. *Between Heaven and Earth: The Religious Worlds People Make and the Scholars Who Study Them*. Princeton, N.J.: Princeton University Press, 2005.

———. "Crossing the City Line." Introduction to *Gods of the City*, edited by Robert Orsi, 1–78. Bloomington: Indiana University Press, 1999.

Ortner, Sherry. *New Jersey Dreaming: Capital, Culture, and the Class of '58*. Durham, N.C.: Duke University Press, 2003.

Ostling, Richard N. "The Church Search." *Time*, 5 April 1993, 45–49.

Pakulski, Jan, and Malcolm Waters. *The Death of Class*. London: Sage, 1996.

———. "Misreading Status as Class: A Reply to Our Critics." *Theory and Society* 25 (1996): 731–36.

———. "The Reshaping and Dissolution of Social Class in Advanced Society." *Theory and Society* 25 (1996): 667–91.

Pappu, Sridhar. "The Preacher." *Atlantic Monthly*, March 2006, 92–103.

Park, Jerry, and Samuel Reimer. "Revisiting the Social Sources of American Christianity 1972–1998." *Journal for the Scientific Study of Religion* 41 (2002): 733–46.

Pattison, E. "Ideological Support for the Marginal Middle Class: Faith Healing and Glossolalia." In *Religious Movements in Contemporary America*, edited by Irving I. Zaretsky and Mark P. Leone, 418–55. Princeton, N.J.: Princeton University Press, 1974.

People like Us: Social Class in America. Directed by Louis Alvarez and Andrew Kolker. New York: CNAM Film Library, 2001.

Perry, Pamela. *Shades of White: White Kids and Racial Identities in High School*. Durham, N.C.: Duke University Press, 2002.

Peterson, Richard A. "Understanding Audience Segmentation: From Elite and Mass to Omnivore and Univore." *Poetics* 21 (1992): 243–58.

Peterson, Richard A., and Roger M. Kearn. "Changing Highbrow Tastes: From Snob to Omnivore." *American Sociological Review* 61, no. 5 (October 1996): 900–907.

Pfister, Joel. *Individuality Incorporated: Indians and the Multicultural Modern*. Durham, N.C.: Duke University Press, 2004.

Photiadis, John, ed. *Religion in Appalachia: Theological, Social, and Psychological Dimensions and Correlates*. Morgantown: West Virginia University Press, 1978.

Poloma, Margaret. *The Assemblies of God at the Crossroads: Charisma and Institutional Dilemma*. Knoxville: University of Tennessee Press, 1989.

———. *The Charismatic Movement: Is There a New Pentecost?* Boston: Twayne, 1982.

———. *Main Street Mystics: The Toronto Blessing and Reviving Pentecostalism*. Walnut Creek, Calif.: Altamira, 2003.

Pope, Liston. *Millhands and Preachers: A Study of Gastonia*. New Haven, Conn.: Yale University Press, 1942.

Pope Leo XIII. *Rerum Novarum* (1891), <http://www.osjspm.org/cst/rn.htm>.

Popenoe, Paul, and Roswell Hill Johnson. *Applied Eugenics*. Rev. ed. New York: Macmillan, 1933.

Prothero, Stephen. *The White Buddhist: The Asian Odyssey of Henry Steele Olcott*. Bloomington: Indiana University Press, 1996.

Pyle, Ralph. "Faith and Commitment to the Poor: Theological Orientation and Support for Government Assistance Measures." *Sociology of Religion* 54 (1993): 385–401.

———. *Persistence and Change in the Protestant Establishment*. Westport, Conn.: Praeger, 1996.

———. "Trends in Religious Stratification: Have Religious Group Socioeconomic Distinctions Declined in Recent Decades?" *Sociology of Religion* 67, no. 1 (2006): 61–79.

Quebedeaux, Richard. *The New Charismatics: The Origins, Development, and Significance of Neo-Pentecostalism*. New York: Doubleday, 1976.

Rafter, Nicole Hahn, ed. *White Trash: The Eugenic Family Studies, 1877–1919*. Boston: Northeastern University Press, 1988.

Raines, John, ed. *Marx on Religion*. Philadelphia: Temple University Press, 2002.

Rauschenbusch, Walter. *Christianity and the Social Crisis*. New York: Macmillan, 1907.

Reed-Danahay, Deborah. *Locating Bourdieu*. Bloomington: Indiana University Press, 2005.

Reimer, Samuel H. "A Look at Cultural Effects on Religiosity: A Comparison between the United States and Canada." *Journal for the Scientific Study of Religion* 34 (December 1995): 445–57.

Relish, Michael. "It's Not All Education: Network Measures as Sources of Cultural Competency." *Poetics* 25 (1997): 121–39.

Reuter, E. B. Review of *Applied Eugenics*, by Paul Popenoe and Roswell Hill Johnson. *American Journal of Sociology* 40 (January 1935): 549.

Review of *Religions of the Oppressed: A Study of Modern Messianic Cults*, by Vittorio Lanternari. *Current Anthropology* 6, no. 4 (1965): 447–65.

Rey, Terry. "Marketing the Goods of Salvation: Bourdieu on Religion." *Religion* 34 (2004): 331–43.

Rice, Stephen P. *Minding the Machine: Languages of Class in Early Industrial America*. Berkeley: University of California Press, 2004.

Richardson, James T., Joel Best, and David G. Bromley, eds. *The Satanism Scare*. New York: Aldine De Gruyter, 1991.

Road Scholar. Directed by Roger Weisberg. Los Angeles: Hallmark Entertainment, 1995.

Roof, Wade Clark. *A Generation of Seekers: The Spiritual Journeys of the Baby Boom Generation*. New York: Harper, 1993.

———. *Spiritual Marketplace: Baby Boomers and the Remaking of American Religion*. Princeton, N.J.: Princeton University Press, 1999.

Roof, Wade Clark, and William McKinney. *American Mainline Religion: Its Changing Shape and Future*. New Brunswick, N.J.: Rutgers University Press, 1987.

Rose, Anne. "'Race' Speech—'Culture' Speech—'Soul' Speech: The Brief Career of Social Science Language in American Religion during the Fascist Era." *Religion and American Culture: A Journal of Interpretation* 14 (Winter 2004): 83–108.

Rose, Fred. "Toward a Class-Cultural Theory of Social Movements: Reinterpreting New Social Movements." *Sociological Forum* 12 (1997): 461–94.

Roseberry, William. "The Rise of Yuppie Coffees and the Reimagination of Class in the United States." *American Anthropologist* 98 (1996): 762–75.

Rosen, Christine. *Preaching Eugenics: Religious Leaders and the American Eugenics Movement*. New York: Oxford University Press, 2004.

Rubin, Julius H. *Religious Melancholy and Protestant Experience in America*. New York: Oxford University Press, 1994.

Samarin, William J. *Tongues of Men and Angels: The Religious Language of Pentecostalism*. New York: Macmillan, 1972.

Savage, Mike. *Class Analysis and Social Transformation*. Philadelphia: Open University Press, 2000.

Schantz, Mark. *Piety in Providence: Class Dimensions of Religious Experience in Antebellum Rhode Island*. Ithaca, N.Y.: Cornell University Press, 2000.

Schwartz, Gary. *Sect Ideologies and Social Status*. Chicago: University of Chicago Press, 1970.

Scott, Joan Wallach. "Gender: A Useful Category of Historical Analysis." *American Historical Review* 91 (1986): 1053–75.

Seeyle, Katherine Q. "Moral Values Cited as a Defining Issue of the Election." *New York Times*, 4 November 2004, P4.

Sernett, Milton C. *Bound for the Promised Land: African American Religion and the Great Migration*. Durham, N.C.: Duke University Press, 1997.

Sharot, Stephen. "Beyond Christianity: A Critique of the Rational Choice Theory of Religion from a Weberian and Comparative Religions Perspective." *Sociology of Religion* 63, no. 4 (2002): 427–54.

Sheedy, Morgan M. "The Encyclical and American Iron-Workers and Coal-Miners." *Catholic World* 53 (September 1891): 850–61.

Sheldon, Steve. *Inheriting Shame: The Story of Eugenics and Racism in America*. New York: Teacher's College, 1999.

Skeggs, Beverley. *Class, Self, Culture*. New York: Routledge, 2004.

Smith, Barbara Ellen. "Legends of the Fall: Contesting Economic History." In *Christianity in Appalachia*, edited by Bill J. Leonard. Knoxville: University of Tennessee Press, 1999.

Smith, Christian. *American Evangelicalism: Embattled and Thriving*. Chicago: University of Chicago Press, 1998.

———. *Christian America? What Evangelicals Really Want*. Berkeley: University of California Press, 2000.

Smith, Christian, and Melinda Lundquist Denton. *Soul Searching: The Religious and Spiritual Lives of American Teenagers*. New York: Oxford University Press, 2005.

Smith, Christian, and Robert Faris. "Socioeconomic Inequality in the American Religious System: An Update and Assessment." *Journal for the Scientific Study of Religion* 44 (2005): 95–104.

Smout, Kary. "Attacking (Southern) Creationists." In *Religion in the Contemporary South: Diversity, Identity, and Community*, edited by O. Kendall White Jr. and Daryl White, 59–66. Athens: University of Georgia Press, 1995.

Soltero, José, and Romeo Saravia. "Dimensions of Social Stratification and Anomie as Factors of Religious Affiliation in El Salvador." *Sociology of Religion* 64 (2003): 1–19.

Sombart, Werner. *The Quintessence of Capitalism: A Study of the History and Psychology of the Modern Business Man*. Translated and edited by M. Epstein. New York: Howard Fertig, 1967. Originally published 1915.

Spalding, J. L. "Socialism and Labor." *Catholic World* 53 (September 1891): 791–807.

Spickard, James V., J. Shawn Landres, and Meredith B. McGuire, eds. *Personal Knowledge and Beyond: Reshaping the Ethnography of Religion*. New York: New York University Press, 2002.

Stanley, Susie Cunningham. *Feminist Pillar of Fire: The Life of Alma White*. Cleveland: Pilgrim, 1993.

Stark, Rodney. "Class, Radicalism, and Religious Involvement in Great Britain." *American Sociological Review* 29 (1964): 698–706.

———. "The Economics of Piety: Religion and Social Class." In *Issues in Social Inequality*, edited by Gerald Theilbar and Saul Feldman, 483–503. New York: Little, Brown, 1971.

———. "Upper Class Asceticism: Social Origins of Ascetic Movements and Medieval Saints." *Review of Religious Research* 45 (2003): 5–19.

Stark, Rodney, and William Sims Bainbridge. "Networks of Faith: Interpersonal Bonds and Recruitment to Cults and Sects." *American Journal of Sociology* 85 (May 1980): 1376–95.

Stark, Rodney, and Roger Finke. *Acts of Faith: Explaining the Human Side of Religion*. Berkeley: University of California Press, 2000.

Stepan, Nancy Leys. *"The Hour of Eugenics": Race, Gender, and Nation in Latin America*. Ithaca, N.Y.: Cornell University Press, 1991.

Stephenson, Denice, ed. *Dear People: Remembering Jonestown*. San Francisco: California Historical Society, 2005.

Sterne, Evelyn Savidge. *Ballots and Bibles: Ethnic Politics and the Catholic Church in Providence*. Ithaca, N.Y.: Cornell University Press, 2003.

———. "Bringing Religion into Working-Class History." *Social Science History* 24, no. 1 (2000): 149–82.

Stocking, George W., Jr. *Race, Culture, and Evolution: Essays in the History of Anthropology*. New York: Free Press, 1968.

Stone, Jon R., ed. *Expecting Armageddon: Essential Readings in Failed Prophecy*. New York: Routledge, 2000.

Stone, Simon. "The Miller Delusion: A Comparative Study in Mass Psychology." *American Journal of Psychiatry* 91 (1934): 593–623.

Strong, Josiah. *Our Country: Its Possible Future and Its Present Crisis*. New York: American Home Missionary Society, 1885.

Styers, Randall. *Making Magic: Religion, Magic, and Science in the Modern World*. New York: Oxford University Press, 2004.

Sutcliffe, Steven. *Children of the New Age: A History of Spiritual Practices*. New York: Routledge, 2003.

———. "The Dynamics of Alternative Spirituality: Seekers, Networks, and 'New Age.'" In *The Oxford Handbook of New Religious Movements*, edited by James Lewis, 466–90. New York: Oxford University Press, 2004.

Sutton, William R. *Journeymen for Jesus: Evangelical Artisans Confront Capitalism in Jacksonian Baltimore*. University Park: Pennsylvania State University Press, 1998.

Swanson, Merwin. "The 'Country Life Movement' and the American Churches." *Church History* 46 (1977): 358–73.

Sweet, William Warren. *The Story of Religion in America*. New York: Harper and Brothers, 1939.

Swidler, Ann. "Culture in Action: Symbols and Strategies." *American Sociological Review* 51 (1986): 273–86.

———. *Talk of Love: How Culture Matters*. Chicago: University of Chicago Press, 2001.

Synan, Vinson. *The Holiness-Pentecostal Movement in the United States*. Grand Rapids, Mich.: William B. Eerdmans, 1971.

Tamney, Joseph. *The Resilience of Conservative Religion: The Case of Popular Conservative Protestant Congregations*. New York: Cambridge University Press, 2002.

Tamney, Joseph, Ronald Burton, and Stephen Johnson. "Christianity, Social Class, and the Catholic Bishops' Economic Policy." *Sociological Analysis* 49 (1988): 79–96.

Taves, Ann. *Fits, Trances, and Visions: Experiencing Religion and Explaining Experience from Wesley to James*. Princeton, N.J.: Princeton University Press, 1999.

———. "From Religious History to the Cultural History of Religion." *Journal of the American Academy of Religion* 71 (December 2003): 885–93.

Thomas, George M. *Revivalism and Cultural Change: Christianity, Nation Building, and the Market in the Nineteenth-Century United States*. Chicago: University of Chicago Press, 1989.

Thompson, Anna Z. "Register to the Papers of Raoul Weston La Barre." Washington, D.C.: National Anthropological Archives at the Smithsonian Institution, 1998.

Thompson, E. P. *The Making of the English Working Class*. New York: Vintage, 1966.

Thrupp, Sylvia L., ed. *Millennial Dreams in Action: Essays in Comparative Study*. The Hague: Mouton, 1962. Reprinted as *Millennial Dreams in Action: Studies in Revolutionary Religious Movements*. New York: Schocken, 1970.

Troeltsch, Ernst. *The Social Teaching of the Christian Churches*. 2 vols. New York: Harper Torchbooks, 1960. Originally published 1931 by Macmillan.

Trompf, G. W., ed. *Cargo Cults and Millennial Movements*. New York: Mouton De Gruyter, 1990.

Tsunetomo, Yamamoto. *Hagakure: The Book of the Samurai*. Translated by William Scott Wilson. Tokyo: Kodansha International, 1979.

Turner, Victor. *The Ritual Process: Structure and Anti-Structure*. Chicago: University of Chicago Press, 1969.

Tweed, Thomas. *Crossing and Dwelling: A Theory of Religion*. Cambridge, Mass.: Harvard University Press, 2006.

———. "Narrating U.S. Religious History." Introduction to *Retelling U.S. Religious History*, edited by Thomas Tweed, 1–23. Berkeley: University of California Press, 1997.

Tylor, Edward Burnett. *Primitive Culture*. 2 vols. New York: Harper, 1958.

Tyson, Ruel W., Jr., James L. Peacock, and Daniel W. Patterson. "Method and Spirit: Studying the Diversity of Gestures in Religion." Introduction to *Diversities of Gifts: Field Studies in Southern Religion*, edited by Ruel Tyson Jr., James Peacock, and Daniel Patterson, 1–21. Urbana: University of Illinois Press, 1988.

Vaneigem, Raoul. *The Revolution of Everyday Life*. London: Aldgate, 1983.

Verter, Bradford. "Response: Bourdieu and the Bauls Reconsidered." *Method and Theory in the Study of Religion* 16 (2004): 182–92.

————. "Spiritual Capital: Theorizing Religion with Bourdieu against Bourdieu." *Sociological Theory* 21 (June 2003): 150–74.

Victor, Jeffrey. *Satanic Panic: The Creation of a Contemporary Legend*. Chicago: Open Court, 1993.

Vidich, Arthur, and Joseph Bensman. *Small Town in Mass Society: Class, Power, and Religion in a Rural Community*. Rev. ed. Urbana: University of Illinois Press, 2000.

Wacker, Grant. *Heaven Below: Early Pentecostals and American Culture*. Cambridge, Mass.: Harvard University Press, 2001.

————. "Pentecostalism." In *The Encyclopedia of the American Religious Experience*, edited by Charles H. Lippy and Peter W. Williams, 933–45. New York: Scribners, 1988.

————. "Taking Another Look at the *Vision of the Disinherited*." *Religious Studies Review* 8, no. 1 (1982): 15–22.

Wade, Nicholas. "The Twists and Turns of History, and of DNA." *New York Times Week in Review*, 12 March 2006, 14.

Wagner, Thomas. "Too Few Tomorrows." In *Too Few Tomorrows: Urban Appalachians in the 1980s*, edited by Phillip Obermiller and William Philliber, 3–12. Boone, N.C.: Appalachian Consortium, 1987.

Wallace, Anthony F. C. "Mazeway Disintegration: The Individual's Perception of Socio-Cultural Disorganization." *Human Organization* 16 (1957): 23–27.

————. *Religion: An Anthropological View*. New York: Random House, 1966.

————. "Revitalization Movements." *American Anthropologist* 58 (1956): 264–81.

Wallis, Roy, and Steve Bruce. "Accounting for Action: Defending the Common Sense Heresy." *Sociology* (U.K.) 17 (1983): 97–100.

Ward, Lester F. "Social Classes in the Light of Modern Sociological Theory." *American Journal of Sociology* 13 (March 1908): 617–27.

Watt, David Harrington. *Bible-Carrying Protestants: Conservative Protestants and Social Power*. New York: Oxford University Press, 2002.

Weber, Max. *The Protestant Ethic and the Spirit of Capitalism*. London: Unwin Hyman, 1989. Originally published 1930 by Unwin Hyman.

————. "The Social Psychology of the World Religions." In *From Max Weber: Essays in Sociology*, edited by H. H. Gerth and C. Wright Mills, 267–301. New York: Oxford University Press, 1946.

————. *Sociology of Religion*. Boston: Beacon, 1963.

Weller, Jack. "How Religion Mirrors and Meets Appalachian Culture." In *Appalachia in Transition*, edited by Max Glenn, 122–39. St. Louis: Bethany, 1970.

————. *Yesterday's People: Life in Contemporary Appalachia*. Lexington: University of Kentucky Press, 1965.

White, Alma. *Demons and Tongues*. Zarephath, N.J.: Pillar of Fire, 1949.

————. *Heroes of the Fiery Cross*. Zarephath, N.J.: Pillar of Fire, 1928.

————. *Klansmen: Guardians of Liberty*. Zarephath, N.J.: Pillar of Fire, 1926.

————. *The Ku Klux Klan in Prophecy*. Zarephath, N.J.: Pillar of Fire, 1925.

White, Bouck. *The Call of the Carpenter*. Garden City, N.Y.: Doubleday, Page, 1912.

White, Harvey W. "Deprivation." In *Guide to the Study of Religion*, edited by Willi Braun and Russell T. McCutcheon, 85–95. New York: Cassell, 2000.

White, Ronald C., Jr., and C. Howard Hopkins, eds. *The Social Gospel: Religion and Reform in Changing America*. Philadelphia: Temple University Press, 1976.

Whitehouse, Harvey. *Arguments and Icons: Divergent Modes of Religiosity*. New York: Oxford University Press, 2000.

———. *Modes of Religiosity: A Cognitive Theory of Religious Transmission*. Lanham, Md.: Altamira, 2004.

Wilentz, Sean. *Chants Democratic: New York City and the Rise of the American Working Class, 1788–1850*. New York: Oxford University Press, 1984.

Williams, Cyril. *Tongues of the Spirit: A Study of Pentecostal Glossolalia and Related Phenomena*. Cardiff: University of Wales Press, 1981.

Williams, Peter W. *America's Religions: Traditions and Cultures*. New York: Macmillan, 1990.

Wilson, Warren. "The Church and the Rural Community." *American Journal of Sociology* 16 (1911): 668–702.

———. *The Farmer's Church*. New York: Century, 1925.

Winters, Donald, Jr. *The Soul of the Wobblies: The I.W.W., Religion, and American Culture in the Progressive Era, 1905–1917*. Westport, Conn.: Greenwood, 1985.

Woobury, Robert M. Review of *Applied Eugenics*, by Paul Popenoe and Roswell Hill Johnson. *Quarterly Publication of the American Statistical Association* 17 (March 1920): 125–26.

Wood, Darren Cushman. *Blue Collar Jesus: How Christianity Supports Workers' Rights*. Santa Ana, Calif.: Seven Locks, 2004.

Wood, William. *Culture and Personality Aspects of the Pentecostal Holiness Religion*. The Hague: Mouton, 1965.

Worley, William. "Social Characteristics and Participation Patterns of Rural Migrants in an Industrial Community." Master's thesis, Miami University of Ohio, 1961.

Worsley, Peter. *The Trumpet Shall Sound: A Study of "Cargo" Cults in Melanesia*. 2nd ed. New York: Schocken, 1968. Originally published 1957.

Wray, Matt. "White Trash Religion." In *White Trash: Race and Class in America*, edited by Matt Wray and Annalee Newitz, 193–210. New York: Routledge, 1997.

Wright, Erik Olin. *Class Counts*. New York: Cambridge University Press, 1997.

Wuthnow, Robert. *After Heaven: Spirituality in America since the 1950s*. Berkeley: University of California Press, 1998.

Zaretsky, Irving I., and Mark P. Leone, eds. *Religious Movements in Contemporary America*. Princeton, N.J.: Princeton University Press, 1974.

Zenderland, Leila. "Biblical Biology: American Protestant Social Reformers and the Early Eugenics Movement." *Science in Context* 11 (1998): 511–25.

Index